BUCKINGHAM PALACE

26th May, 2004

Dear Mr. Hardcastle

The Queen has asked me to thank you for your letter of 6th May asking Her Majesty to contribute an essay for a book called *Monty Python and Philosophy* which will be edited by you and Mr. George Reisch.

Although it was kind of you to invite The Queen to participate in your project, I am afraid that your offer must be declined.

Yours sincerely,

MRS. GILL MIDDLEBURGH
Chief Clerk

Mr. Gary Hardcastle

Bloomsburg
UNIVERSITY

May 6, 2004

The Queen
Buckingham Palace
London SW1A 1AA.

Your Majesty,

It is with great pleasure that I invite you to contribute an essay to a volume entitled *Monty Python and Philosophy*. I will edit the book with George A. Reisch and it will be published by Open Court Publishing Company.

As you are no doubt aware, Monty Python's humour has touched on fascinating and important philosophical themes. Our volume will contain essays that take up this intersection of Monty Python and philosophy. Eminent philosophers and public intellectuals have signed on, and I can assure you that your contribution will be in fine intellectual company.

Perhaps you are stymied for ideas. Recall that Python humor as often been at the expense of your own Royal Family, and of institutions dear to England. This could be your chance to even the score or, if that is not to your liking (I tend to just ignore criticism, myself, and maybe this is how you handle it), you may find this just the chance to comment on the place the Pythons have in the hearts of the Royal family. Your call entirely.

Of course, you must have a very busy schedule. But I hope you will find time to contribute an essay—even just a few words—to our volume. Space *is* limited, though, so please do not delay in your response. On the other hand, we could bump an assistant professor from the volume to make room for your contribution, if it came to that. But please keep that fact under your crown.

I eagerly await your response. Ever Yours,

Gary L. Hardcastle
Assistant Professor of Philosophy
Bloomsburg University

Bakeless Center for the Humanities ● Bloomsburg University ● 400 East Second Street ● Bloomsburg, PA 17815-1301
(570) 389-4246 ● Fax (570) 389-2094
A Member of Pennsylvania's State System of Higher Education

Monty Python and Philosophy

Popular Culture and Philosophy™
Series Editor: William Irwin

Popular Culture and Philosophy™

Monty Python and Philosophy

Nudge Nudge, Think Think!

Edited by
GARY L. HARDCASTLE
and
GEORGE A. REISCH

OPEN COURT
Chicago and La Salle, Illinois

Volume 19 in the series Popular Culture and Philosophy™

To order books from Open Court, call 1–800–815–2280, or visit our website at www.opencourtbooks.com.

Open Court Publishing Company is a division of Carus Publishing Company

Printed and bound in the United States of America

Library of Congress Cataloging-in-Publication Data

Monty Python and philosophy : nudge nudge, think think! / edited by Gary L. Hardcastle and George A. Reisch.
    p. cm. — (Popular culture and philosophy ; 19)
  Includes bibliographical references and index.
  ISBN-13: 978-0-8126-9593-9 (trade paper : alk. paper)
  ISBN-10: 0-8126-9593-3 (trade paper : alk. paper)
  1. Monty Python (Comedy troupe) I. Hardcastle, Gary L.
II. Reisch, George A., 1962– III. Series.
PN2599.5.T54M65 2006
791.45'028092241—dc22
                          2006003083

To Kiah, Cheshire, and Quinn,
who've never had to be told to think for themselves

—G.L.H.

And to Bruces Everywhere

—G.A.R.

Contents

Aspects of Pythonic Philosophy   123

Pythonic Aspects of Philosophy   215

1

"What's All This Then?" The Introduction

GARY L. HARDCASTLE
and GEORGE A. REISCH

> Pythonist: A person who professes to prophesy through some divine or esoteric inspiration.
>
> — *Webster's Third New International Dictionary, Unabridged*

England. Sunday evening, October 5th, 1969. A big surprise awaits those switching on their television sets and settling in for an evening of entertainment. A game show features Genghis Khan dying, his death scored by panelists. An advertisement for butter heralds its superior taste, all but indistinguishable from that of dead crab. And excited sportscasters cover Pablo Picasso painting while riding a bicycle through England ("It will be very interesting to see how he copes with the heavy traffic round Wisborough Green!"). It's . . . *Monty Python's Flying Circus*!

At the end of the 1960s—a decade of race riots, student protests, undeclared wars, political assassinations, Woodstock, the first moon landing, and the rise of the sensitive singer-songwriter—perhaps nothing could be entirely new and unexpected. Yet Graham Chapman, John Cleese, Terry Gilliam, Eric Idle, Terry Jones, and Michael Palin—collectively, Monty Python—pulled it off week after week. When a tuxedoed John Cleese intoned "And now for something completely different . . . " (mocking the BBC, naturally), he was completely right. Characters suddenly announced their desire to be not only lumberjacks, but cross-dressing lumberjacks. Sketches were interrupted by characters from *other* sketches. Viewers were taught self-defense techniques against fresh fruit. Somehow, the Pythons consistently found ways to move their audiences—within minutes, sometimes even seconds—from blunt incomprehension (the Fish Slapping Dance?) to fits of hearty, memorable laughter. Python fans vividly remember their first time.

For many of us, this kind of humor was just what we needed to survive the 1970s, not to mention the 1980s. By then, Monty Python had found its audience, wiggled into the collective consciousness, and become one of the most successful and influential comedy institutions of the twentieth century. After four seasons and forty-five episodes of *Monty Python's Flying Circus*, the Pythons did the proper British thing and established an empire of books, audio recordings, and feature films, notably *Monty Python and the Holy Grail* (1975), *Monty Python's Life of Brian* (1979), and *Monty Python's The Meaning of Life* (1983). As of this writing, the empire has conquered Broadway, where *Monty Python's Spamalot*, a musical adaptation of *Monty Python and the Holy Grail*, plays to packed houses (well, at least, *we* can't get tickets) while its creators, chief among them Eric Idle, try out various spots on the mantel for the Tony Awards© that the show has won. Indeed, much of popular culture has been Pythonized. Watch George Carlin, Richard Pryor, Steve Martin, Andy Kaufman, Mike Myers, and their comedic progeny, or *Saturday Night Live, The Simpsons, In Living Color, Kids in the Hall, Arrested Development*, and *their* comedic progeny, and you'll see Python again, echoed in dozens of ways. Read contemporary criticism of entertainment and culture, or nearly anything "postmodern," and you'll see the word 'pythonesque' or knowing references to "spam" or "nudge nudge, wink wink" that mark a common bond between author and reader—yep, Python fan.

Not everyone, of course, belongs to the club. We all know one or two who stare at a Python sketch the way a dog looks at a card trick. They just don't *get it*. That's okay, of course—just don't offer them a Whizzo Chocolate or tell them you weren't expecting the Spanish Inquisition, lest you get a blank stare in return. This book, on the other hand, is for people who *do* get it. Actually, it's a book for people who not only get it, but who have, on occasion, wondered what that "it" is exactly. You've probably noticed the book's title, so you won't be surprised that we think that Monty

Python's absurdities bear a deep and interesting connection to philosophy.

Really? What sort of "deep and interesting" connection? It's a good thing we didn't have to answer that question before we found contributors and put this book together, for back then we didn't have an answer. Fortunately, our philosophical colleagues and acquaintances (whom, naturally, we hit up for chapters) were as intrigued with that question as we were. Now that we've assembled the book, however, we still won't declare any simple, final theory about this connection. It remains somewhat mysterious. But thanks in no small part to our contributors, we understand much better why Monty Python and philosophy go together. It all starts with . . .

The Importance of Being British

Britain was a philosophical mecca for much of the twentieth century, especially the universities of Cambridge and Oxford, where the British Pythons studied in the 1960s. Here, too, philosophical superstars like Bertrand Russell, Ludwig Wittgenstein, A.J. Ayer, G.E. Moore, and Gilbert Ryle spent the first half of the twentieth century living, working, playing, and, apparently, threatening one another with pokers.[1] (Gilliam, for the record, spent the 1960s at Occidental College in Southern California, which, as they say, explains a lot.) For better or worse, what gets taught in philosophy classrooms around the world to this very day derives from what these philosophers achieved at Oxford and Cambridge.

True, none of the Pythons specialized in philosophy. Chapman studied to be a physician, Cleese a barrister, Jones an historian, and so on.[2] But they didn't have to be philosophers to get a healthy dose of Russell, Wittgenstein, and the rest. The way

---

[1] According, at least, to David Edmonds and John Eidinow, *Wittgenstein's Poker: the Story of a Ten-Minute Argument between Two Great Philosophers* (New York: Harper Collins, 2001).

[2] Though one gets the impression Cleese might well study philosophy if he had it all to do over again, given that philosophy has become one of his main post-Python interests. Concerned about the meager attention accorded philosophical questions in contemporary life, for example, in 2002 Cleese recorded a well-received set of radio "blurbs" on philosophical topics for the American

these philosophers approached philosophical issues, leaning heavily on an analysis of the language in which philosophical problems were cast, was in the air and influenced nearly every region of the intellectual landscape. And thus it seeped, much like advertising, muzak, or spilt Tate & Lyle's golden syrup, into so much of what the Pythons did.

   That's why we're calling the first part of this volume *Philosophical Aspects of Python.* These chapters look at the ways in which particular Python sketches or films illustrate some issue or idea from philosophy. They differ in a number of ways, but they all take up a particular bit of Python and wring from it the philosophical content that we suspect is, more often than not, the vestige of an Oxbridge education, *circa* 1965. These chapters show what happens when twentieth-century philosophy gets run through a filter consisting of equal parts British music-hall tradition, 1960s-style anti-authoritarianism, and straightforward intelligence.

   For Kevin Schilbrack, it's *Monty Python's Life of Brian* that serves as grist for the philosophical mill. His "'Life's a Piece of Shit': Heresy, Humanism, and Heroism in *Monty Python's Life of Brian*" (winner, incidentally, of the Award for Best Title in this Particular Volume, solely on the grounds of profanity and use of H's) argues that Brian, the film's hero, has existentialism written all over him (namely, the form of existentialism championed by Albert Camus (1913–1960)). Ten-year olds, and others similarly intrigued by the limits of the human digestive system, may want to turn immediately to Noël Carroll's sensitive and delicate treatment of the wonderfully insensitive and indelicate Mr. Creosote. In "What Mr. Creosote Knows about Laughter," Carroll finds an explanation for why we (well some of us, at least) find Mr. Creosote, from *Monty Python's Meaning of Life*, disgustingly funny rather than just plain disgusting. Enjoy the chapter with a wafer-thin after-dinner mint.

   In "The Limits of Horatio's Philosophy," Kurt Smith takes up the delightfully absurd sketch "Piston Engine (a Bargain)" from

Philosophical Association (see www.udel.apa.edu). He's also shared the stage repeatedly with Pomona University's E. Wilson Lyon Professor of Humanities Stephen Erickson in public discussions of the meaning of life (the topic, not the film) and, from 1999 to 2005, was A.D. White Professor-at-Large at Cornell University where he lectured on, among other things, philosophy and religion.

Episode 43 of *Monty Python's Flying Circus* (titled "Hamlet") and asks a simple but vexing question: What are these women, these pepperpots, saying? Smith's answer leads us through the philosophical evolution of Ludwig Wittgenstein (1889–1951), the Austrian philosophical luminary transplanted to Cambridge in the 1930s. Harry Brighouse's contribution, "Why Is An Argument Clinic Less Silly than an Abuse Clinic or a Contradiction Clinic?," makes use of the Python's famous "Argument Clinic" sketch (originally in Episode 29 of *Monty Python's Flying Circus*, "The Money Programme") to illuminate how the political philosopher John Rawls (1926–2002) analyzed our beliefs about the rightness or wrongness of social practices and institutions. Far from being a ridiculous scenario, Brighouse suggests, a real argument clinic could serve a genuine and much-needed social function.

Taking us back to Brian (Cohen, that is), Randall Auxier makes an offer that you don't see everyday, at least not in a book of relatively serious philosophy. Auxier is willing to save your soul, both mortal and immortal, by way of the heroic anti-hero of *Monty Python's Life of Brian*. Sound good? Do be warned: the salvation involves a dose of Nietzsche, a smidgen of Pascal, and a heads-on confrontation with the evidence we have, or lack, that God is British. Rebecca Housel's "*Monty Python and The Holy Grail*: Philosophy, Gender, and Society," on the other hand, invites us to view *Monty Python and the Holy Grail* from the dual perspectives of Arthurian legend and feminist ethics. Amidst the humor, Housel argues, are serious and intriguing philosophical and ethical undertones. Stephen Asma's chapter, "Against Transcendentalism: The Meaning of Life and Buddhism," explores the recurring themes of dehumanization in *Monty Python's The Meaning of Life* and links these to a deeper dualistic framework embedded in many religions. In the end, Asma argues, the film leads us to something completely different (naturally): the Buddhist value of mindfulness. Stephen Erickson's "Is There Life After *Monty Python's The Meaning of Life*?" then offers a critique of the idea that life is a journey, its meaning somehow tied up with the journey's destination. Erickson sees the Pythons unwittingly reducing that notion to absurdity as they offer a more compelling alternative, a view Erickson calls "comedic eliminativism."

What, That's Not Enough for You?

Okay. On then to the second part, *Aspects of Pythonic Philosophy*. Here the chapters focus not on a particular sketch or film but rather on a particular philosophical topic or idea—one that connects to several different Monty Python sketches or scenes. If you've come to this book looking for a particular philosophical topic (as opposed to a particular bit of Python), this is the section for you. Leading it off is Stephen Faison's chapter, "God Forgive Us." We are pleased to announce, in fact, that Faison's chapter has finally settled, once and for all, those thorny and unresolved questions of God's existence, God's nature, and God's relation to humanity. Well, not really. But Faison does argue that the Pythons, in consistently doing such a spectacular job parodying God's relation to us, have provided two invaluable services. They have *raised the question* of God's relationship to us and made immeasurably harder the jobs of well-meaning Sunday school teachers. John Huss's "Monty Python and David Hume on Religion" keeps the focus on God by drawing illuminating parallels between the treatment of theological questions by the Pythons and David Hume (1711–1776), the skeptical philosopher who contributed greatly to philosophy despite his being Scottish. Huss has convinced us, at least, that Hume, but for his dying in the eighteenth century, would plainly have become the seventh Python.

Taking us from God to madness, Michelle Spinelli makes use of "The Idiot in Society" (Episode 20 of *Monty Python's Flying Circus*, "The Attila the Hun Show"), among other classic Python skits, to get a grip on the claim, articulated by the social historian and philosopher Michel Foucault (1926–1984), that what counts as madness or insanity is something created—'constructed' is the word—by the society in question. Don't be surprised if, after reading Spinelli's "Madness in *Monty Python's Flying Circus*," you find yourself watching *Monty Python's Flying Circus*, Foucault in hand.

Moving the focus from theology to morality, Patrick Croskery's "Monty Python and the Search for the Meaning of Life" performs the remarkable feat of illustrating several notions of the ethical life, as well as its pitfalls, solely by way of Monty Python. Not unlike other authors, Croskery addresses the

Pythonic flirtation with *nihilism*, the denial of values of any sort, and offers a sensible verdict: the Pythons know nihilism well, but they are not nihilists. Nihilism is also the starting point for Edward Slowik's "Existentialism in Monty Python: Kafka, Camus, Nietzsche, and Sartre" (winner of the award for Most Names In A Single Title In This Volume. Congratulations, Ed). For Slowik, though, the Pythons's message is more existentialist and less nihilist. He notes a particular resonance between Monty Python's impatience with pretension and the philosophical message about life's meaning offered by the German philosopher and redoubtable laugh-meister Friedrich Nietzsche (1844–1900).

The ghost of Wittgenstein looms large in Monty Python and in Rosalind Carey's delightfully Gumbyish "My Brain Hurts!" Carey takes on the difficult question of what philosophy *is* exactly, a question that Wittgenstein himself answered in different ways throughout his life. Ludwig, sadly, could not avail himself of the Pythons to illustrate his ideas. But Carey has nicely filled the gap, matching bits of Python to bits of Wittgenstein in a manner that might not have pleased Wittgenstein himself (not much pleased him, to be honest) but, we think, enlightens and entertains us. Finally, anyone who has waded in philosophy's waters will have noted the far-fetched, perplexing, and often downright silly "thought-experiments" that brighten philosophers' eyes. In "Why Is a Philosopher Like a Python? How Philosophical Examples Work," James Taylor faces head-on and explains this distinctly philosophical thing called the thought experiment. By comparing such experiments to sketches that are equally far-fetched and sometimes utterly absurd (but, we grant, much more entertaining), he shows that the philosophical thought experiment is not *quite* as crazy as it may first appear.

Bloody Hell, There's More!?!

It depends how you look at it. Wittgenstein wrote that the same figure can be seen as a duck or a rabbit. So, you may see the remaining chapters as a misfit bunch of leftovers or, very differently, as a natural class defined by similarities of form and content. We see them as a school of ducks, each of which looks at philosophy (or some aspect of it) in light of the *phenomenon* of Monty

Python. It is remarkable, after all, not only that the utterly bizarre *Monty Python's Flying Circus* was sponsored by the BBC in the first place, but that Monty Python itself grew into an institution of enormous cultural influence. In light of that success and the many connections between philosophy and Monty Python explored in the earlier chapters, this section asks, What might be gleaned about the fortunes—or misfortunes—of the otherwise unworldly enterprise of philosophy? These authors (your two editors among them) think there is much to explore. Hence, our final section: *Pythonic Aspects of Philosophy*.

Alan Richardson's "Tractatus Comedio-Philosophicus" wants us to know that the only difference between Monty Python and academic philosophy is that philosophy isn't funny. Sensing philosophy's imminent disaster, Richardson conducts an intervention (of sorts) to which he has invited Wittgenstein and Nietzsche, if you can picture that. George Reisch's "Monty Python's Utterly Devastating Critique of Ordinary Language Philosophy" makes the case that the Pythons imbibed, and found unsatisfying, far more of the analytic philosophy afoot in Cambridge and Oxford than might have otherwise been thought. Reisch then calls for a Python-inspired rehabilitation of philosophy, but one quite different from Richardson's.

Yet a third style of rehabilitation is suggested—okay, demanded—by Bruce Baldwin's "Word and Objection: How Monty Python Destroyed Modern Philosophy." Though less sympathetic to the intersection of philosophy with popular culture than the other chapters, we chose to include Baldwin's chapter (in the form of a faithfully transcribed lecture) in order to promote debate about philosophy in popular culture and because Baldwin's personal investment in things Pythonic proved too ironic for us to resist.

Finally, Gary Hardcastle's "My Years With Monty Python" recounts his adventures over the past ten years lecturing about Monty Python and philosophy to non-academic audiences. Hardcastle tries to make sense of why anyone would find the combination palatable, let alone entertaining. Taking up a similar question that Hume, that almost-seventh Python, posed centuries ago, Hardcastle finds a satisfying answer (note, however, that he is easily pleased). Hardcastle's chapter makes frequent reference to his earlier essay, "Themes in Contemporary Analytic Philosophy as Reflected in the Work of Monty Python," so we've included that here, too. Call it a *Special Bonus Track*.

Okay, That's All for Now

That's how it goes. There is no *one* "deep and interesting" connection between Monty Python and philosophy, it turns out, because there are many. There are bits of Python that are better understood and appreciated by philosophical analysis; there are bits of philosophy that are well served by Python sketches and themes; and the whole, enduring empire of Monty Python has a thing or two to say about the status of philosophy and its role in the world. If you were hoping for something pithier, less obvious, or pythonesque (see?), well, we're sorry.

We know, much has been left out of this book, too. As Heather Douglas reminds one of the editors daily, there are not nearly enough mentions of the Holy Hand Grenade (even counting that one). Other colleagues, we rest assured, will complain that their personal philosophical heroes had to be left out ("What, no Bosanquet?! No Nicolas de Cusa?!?!"). Who knows—maybe there is room on the shelf for a sequel volume of *Monty Python and Philosophy* in which the Holy Hand Grenade and other topics can be philosophically analyzed. If you want to see that sequel, make sure you buy at least *two* copies of this book. Going farther still, one might consider a new academic organization, something like a society dedicated to the philosophical analysis of Monty Python. Those plans, alas, will remain exceedingly tentative so long as a suitably catchy and marketable acronym remains elusive.

And Where the @#$%^& is the Queen?

From the very start, we wanted the Queen to participate. We really did. We tried. And our correspondence with her Highness (displayed at the very start of this book, for we have nothing to hide) shows that we offered her a really sweet deal: unlimited length, no set topic, and not even a real deadline. But, alas, it was not to be, at least if this "Mrs. Gill Middleburgh" is to be believed. Where we went wrong we don't know, but we're undeterred. For this volume's sequel (and have you bought your second copy yet?), we *promise* you . . . Prince Charles.

Philosophical Aspects of Monty Python

"Welcome to a packed Olympic stadium!"

Scenes from "International Philosophy," originally produced for German TV and later included in *Monty Python Live at the Hollywood Bowl*.

2

"Life's a Piece of Shit": Heresy, Humanism, and Heroism in *Monty Python's Life of Brian*

KEVIN SCHILBRACK

rian whimpers. He is pushed around by his mother. As a revolutionary, he is incompetent and he cannot compose a proper sentence in Latin, even one composed of just three words. Nevertheless, circumstances conspire so that he is taken to be a prophet or a messiah, revered by a multitude. He nearly inaugurates a new religion.

What exactly is Brian? And what are the Pythons trying to do in telling the story of his life? Many took this movie to be an insult to God; they saw it as blasphemy. But the Pythons were famously interested in philosophical questions, especially about the meaning of life, and if one watches the movie with this in mind, one gets a very different message.

"Blessed Are the Cheese Makers": The Question of Heresy

Is *Monty Python's Life of Brian* blasphemous?

After the success of *Monty Python and the Holy Grail*, the Monty Python gang were not sure what to do for their next project. As a lark, one proposed the title: *Jesus Christ: Lust for Glory*. Apparently, the idea for a Biblical comedy was just spontaneous. Once the idea caught on, however, the troupe took their work seriously: they read the Bible and Dead Sea Scrolls, for example, trying to see where funny material might be found. After reading about Jesus, however, they came to the conclusion that they respected the things he said and that they did not want to make fun of him. So they shifted to the idea of a thirteenth apostle, perhaps one who would always be late and miss the miracle, and this idea continued to morph until they came to the idea of someone born at the same time as Jesus who is mistaken as a messiah, and this became Brian.

Even before it came out, the idea of a Biblical spoof was controversial. The project was originally financed by EMI, but they backed out of the project, fearing that the script was blasphemous. (The film was eventually financed by George Harrison, the Beatle.) Once the film was made, it was picketed by Christian groups and was banned in Ireland and Norway and in parts of the United States and Britain.

Yet the movie never suggests that God does not exist. It never suggests that God is less than what believers take God to be, or even that Jesus is not the Son of God. Jesus appears in the movie twice—once at his birth and once giving the Sermon on the Mount—and his miracles have left ex-lepers behind him. Throughout the movie, Jesus is portrayed in a respectful and even orthodox way.

The movie satirizes not what Christian believers believe, but instead the *way* that some believers believe. First, it mocks a certain religious eagerness to believe. Some philosophers of religion have also criticized this. David Hume (1711–1776) is one of the most insightful. Hume complains about "the strong propensity of mankind to [believe in] the extraordinary and the marvellous," and notes that this alone "ought reasonably to beget a suspicion against all relations of this kind."[1] To believe that one has a secret, that one knows something remarkable that others don't know, can bring a palpable sense of one's own specialness that is so agreeable that it is hard to resist. According to Hume, the desire to feel this is the primary motivation for gossip—and it is also the motivation to create and to spread stories of miracles. *Monty Python's Life of Brian* illustrates this process perfectly, when the crowd convinces itself that Brian's inability to tell others the secret of life is

[1] David Hume, "Of Miracles," in his *Writings on Religion*, edited by Antony Flew (Chicago: Open Court, 1992), p. 73.

a sign that he is hiding it; when they decide that Mandy, his mother, must be a virgin; and when losing a sandal creates a small storm of debate about whether true followers should gather sandals or cast them away. In this way *Monty Python's Life of Brian* teaches a brand of healthy skepticism toward the pontifications of the religious.

Even more sharply, the film mocks a certain religious smugness. Religious belief can feed a sense of satisfaction with oneself that can lead to carelessness, hypocrisy, and even violence. Think of those in the film who are attending the Sermon on the Mount with their parasols, congratulating themselves for attending a religious event, but unengaged with the significance of the message. As they bicker with each other about big noses, they mistake "Blessed are the peacemakers" for "Blessed are the cheesemakers," and eventually break out in a fistfight. They figure out that Jesus has said, "The meek will inherit the earth" (not, as they first thought, "the Greek"), but it does not touch them: "That's nice, I'm glad they're getting something 'cos they have a hell of a time." Monty Python's target is not the belief in a perfect being, a being that is all-loving, all-knowing, and all-powerful, what is sometimes called "the God of the philosophers." The target of the movie's ridicule is instead the popular belief in a more human-like God. David Hume targeted this idea as well; he calls it "anthropomorphism." Anthropomorphism in this sense is a belief that is focused not on a perfect being, or a benevolent creator, but on an extremely powerful being that, one hopes, is on one's side. We see this anthropomorphic belief in the prayer offered in *Monty Python's The Meaning of Life*: "O Lord, Ooh, you are so big, so absolutely huge, Gosh, we are all just absolutely impressed down here, I can tell you. Forgive us, Lord, for our dreadful toadying. And barefaced flattery. But You are so strong and, well, just so super. Amen." And the belief in a powerful being who takes sides can easily be used to justify violence. There are, after all, prayers like this one from *Monty Python and the Holy Grail*: "O Lord, bless this Thy hand grenade that, with it, Thou mayest blow Thine enemies to tiny bits in Thy mercy."

Monty Python's Life of Brian does not blaspheme against God but it does hold religious hypocrisy up for ridicule. Terry Jones calls this "heresy." He says, "The Life of Brian isn't blasphemous,

it's heretical. It's not blasphemous because it takes the Bible story
as gospel; you have to believe in the Bible, you have to understand
and know the Bible story to understand it for the film really. It's
heretical because it's making fun of the way the church represents
it. Heresy is basically talking against the church's interpretation,
not against the basic belief."[2] It's true that Monty Python's criticism is directed at religious believers, but it is not necessarily anti-
religious: in fact, one could be religious and agree with it completely.

"A New World, a Better Future": The Question of Humanism

In their eager desire to be followers, a crowd of people takes
Brian as a prophet. But does Brian actually teach anything? Does
he have a message or a philosophy of any kind?

In fact, Brian "preaches" twice in the movie: once in the marketplace when he is masquerading as a prophet to hide from the
centurions, and once to the multitude from the window of his
mother's apartment. In the market, Brian's message is a hodge-
podge of phrases and parables presumably taken from the other
apocalyptic teachers—and some clearly pilfered from Jesus. For
example, Brian says, "Don't pass judgment on other people, or you
might get judged yourself," which sounds as if Brian is parroting
what Jesus says in Matthew 7:1. And in Brian's rising panic he
blurts: "Blessed are they . . . who convert their neighbor's ox . . .
for they shall inhibit their girth . . . ." At this point, Brian's ser-
mons have no message—or, at least, he is too scared to express it.

At his mother's apartment, however, Brian speaks his own
words, and if anything can be called Brian's religious teaching, it
would be found here. To the crowd gathered outside his mother's
window, he says with real passion: "You've got it all wrong. You
don't need to follow me. You don't need to follow anybody.
You've got to think for yourselves. You're all individuals."
"You've all got to work it out for yourselves," he adds. "Don't let
anyone tell you what to do."

---

[2] Graham Chapman, John Cleese, Terry Gilliam, Eric Idle, Terry Jones, Michael
Palin, with Bob McCabe, *The Pythons' Autobiography* (New York: St Martin's
Press, 2003), p. 281.

From this one might deduce that Brian does have at least one principle, for his philosophy seems to be that one should be an *individual*. One should think for oneself. One shouldn't be a follower. Perhaps this teaching is meant only to set up the joke when Brian says, "You're all different!" and from the crowd a man named Dennis objects, "I'm not!" Dennis thereby creates a nice little paradox, since he both rejects Brian's teaching and accepts it at the same time, whereas all the rest who follow the crowd in accepting Brian's teaching actually fail to accept it. But the passion in Brian's voice when he says this, and his pained look, suggest that this is more than a joke; it suggests that here he is sincere, that this reflects his real thoughts. That this quote is in fact a message that the Pythons wanted to send comes through in this comment from Michael Palin, who says that *Monty Python's Life of Brian* reflects "the basis of what Python comedy was all about, which is really resisting people telling you how to behave and how not to behave. It was the freedom of the individual, a very Sixties thing, the independence which was part of the way Python had been formed" (*The Pythons' Autobiography*, p. 306).

Yet Brian's "sermon" reflects not only the Sixties but also a principle basic to most modern philosophy, and especially the eighteenth-century movement called the Enlightenment, namely, the principle that individuals should think for themselves. Immanuel Kant (1724–1804) is often taken to identify the motto of the Enlightenment in his slogan: "*Sapere aude*! Have courage to use your own reason!"[3] But Brian's central principle can also plausibly be seen to represent a kind of existentialism. Existentialists maintain that human beings have no intrinsic purpose or essence; there is no such thing as "human nature." Therefore it is up to each individual to determine the meaning of one's own life and to take responsibility for one's actions. In fact, every individual is "condemned" to do so. Existentialist philosophers like Søren Kierkegaard (1813–1855), Friedrich Nietzsche (1844–1900), and Jean-Paul Sartre (1905–1980) were all, in different ways, interested in seeing how individuals could live authentic lives, how one could be true to oneself. Brian's "sermon" certainly fits this tradition.

---

[3] Immanuel Kant, "What Is Enlightenment?" in Kant, *On History*, edited by Lewis White Beck (New York: Macmillan, 1963), p. 3.

And one might go even further and also see Brian's teaching, like that of many of the existentialists, as a form of humanism. This is the view that human beings are the fundamental source of value, and that improving this world should be the primary focus of human activities. Whether Brian intends this or not, this is what Judith sees in him when she tells Mandy that Brian will "lead them with hope to a new world, a better future."

Brian does not say much about the nature of God, but he is not necessarily teaching *secular* humanism. His message could be a religious or theistic humanism. Theistic humanism combines the belief in God with humanist values.[4] It is the view that meeting "this-worldly" human needs is the primary thing that God wants of his followers. On this view, God's primary interest is in feeding the hungry, healing those who are ill, caring for widows and orphans, and so on. If Brian thinks this way, then he would be teaching humanism not because he lacks faith in God but precisely because he has that faith. Perhaps he gets his humanism, as he got the idea that one should not judge lest one be judged, from Jesus. For example, in what is sometimes called "the Sermon on the Plain" (Luke 6: 17–49), Jesus is portrayed as having a profoundly humanistic regard for the poor, the hungry, and the excluded. It is possible, then, that Brian is not trying to be anti-religious but instead is trying to improve the religion of his followers. The idea that Brian's teachings are meant to agree with a specifically *Christian* humanism comes through in this comment from Graham Chapman (who played Brian): "We did want to annoy [many churches] quite frankly because we felt they'd rather got the wrong end of the stick. They seem to forget about things like loving one another—more interested in joining their own little club and then thinking of other people in terms of 'that lot won't go to heaven, just us' which is really stupid and rather un-Christian . . . . That movie, if it said anything at all, said think for yourselves, don't blindly follow, which I think isn't a bad message and I'm sure Mr. Christ would have agreed" (*The Pythons: Autobiography by the Pythons*, pp. 286–87). *Monty Python's Life of Brian*

---

[4] Similarly, if Brian is an existentialist, he might be either a religious or theistic existentialist (like Kierkegaard, Martin Buber (1878–1965), or Gabriel Marcel (1889–1973)) or an atheistic existentialist (like Friedrich Nietzsche, Jean-Paul Sartre, or Albert Camus (1913–1960)).

therefore criticizes religious belief, not when it involves belief in God, but when it is gullible and careless with the message.[5]

To the extent that one can say that Brian has any philosophy to offer, then, it seems to be an existentialist humanism, not necessarily divorced from belief in God.

"Life's a Piece of Shit": The Question of Heroism

Many Christians have been humanists; several have been existentialists. But, even if Brian's "teachings" are not incompatible with an authentic religious faith, one might have the sneaky suspicion that the movie as a whole has an anti-religious or anti-theistic or even nihilistic view. The movie as a whole seems to present life as meaningless or absurd.

As it happens, there is a philosopher, Albert Camus (1913–1960), who is famous for his embrace of both an existentialist humanism and the view that life is absurd. So now a question about this movie's philosophy can be asked clearly: Is *Monty Python's Life of Brian* teaching Camus's philosophy?

In Camus's novels and essays, the term 'absurd' does not mean silly, like a Prefect named Biggus Dickus or a food vender who sells ocelots' earlobes. To say that life is absurd means that it has no pre-given meaning—events happen that can crush the individual, events that are not part of a greater plan, that are not "meant to be." Camus does not believe that ours is a universe in which human beings have much importance; this is not a benevolent and rational universe. As Bob Lane has eloquently put it, Camus

> sees human beings as small and mortal specks on a minor planet, in an ordinary solar system, located no place in particular, in infinite space, and subject to all sorts of dark irrational forces, over which we have little control. Human beings must

---

[5] Theistic humanism rather than secular humanism is a common theme in *Monty Python and the Holy Grail*. Here God is portrayed as criticizing religious believers who devalue their humanity, as in this dialogue:

> **GOD**: What are you doing now?
> **KING ARTHUR**: Averting our eyes, oh Lord.
> **GOD**: Well, don't. It's just like those miserable psalms, always so depressing. . . . Every time I try to talk to someone it's "sorry this" and "forgive me that" and "I'm not worthy". . . .

therefore live and die with the fear and anxiety, the frustration
and futility that people today know. One must live in the present moment and attempt to find out the actual, bare, given
facts of human existence; to find them out, to face them and
to live with them.[6]

People long for life to make sense, and they long for happiness, but the universe fails to add up. In response to human longing, the universe is silent.

I think it's fair to say that this *is* the vision of *Monty Python's Life
of Brian*. Brian lives and moves in a world in which, as Camus says,
life is absurd. One sees Camus's influence in the film whenever
events seem meaningless or suffering calls out for remedy, but one
sees it above all in the ending of the movie. Brian and the rest are
being crucified, but they are not really criminals; their executions
are pointless. There is no sign that their deaths play a role in a
larger struggle or that they are going to a better place. The words
of their song present Camus's perspective explicitly:

> For life is quite absurd.
> And death's the final word.
> You must always face the curtain with a bow.
> Forget about your sin—give the audiences a grin.
> Enjoy it—it is your last chance anyhow.

Brian lives—and then dies—in an absurd world.

What should one do about the absurdity of life? What *can* one
do? This is a crucial question. Camus argues that in the face of
the absurd, the best that one can do—the noble life—is to rebel
against the absurdity of life. To do this, one would have to be able
to act without hope of reward, conscious that in the long run it
makes no difference how one acts. One would refuse to believe in
or hope for God-given purpose and instead fight for one's goals,
creating a meaningful life in the very choices one makes.

Several of Camus's writings illustrate what it would mean to
live one's life in this way, as an "absurd hero." Three examples of
the absurd hero are the characters of Meursault in Camus's novel

---

[6] Bob Lane, "The Absurd Hero," *Humanist in Canada* 17:4 (Winter, 1984–85).

The Stranger, Dr. Rieux in *The Plague*, and Sisyphus in *The Myth of Sisyphus*. Meursault lives unreflectively. Because he lives unreflectively he lives spontaneously, until he kills someone he does not know and is tried and executed for this murder. It is not easy to see Meursault as a hero, but Camus insists that he is. Let me come back to this. The character of Dr. Rieux is easier to like: he cares for those afflicted by a plague even though they cannot be cured and even though by doing so he may catch the disease. And Sisyphus, the character from the Greek myth, is punished by the Gods by being forced to pointlessly and eternally roll a rock up a hill just to watch it roll back down. According to Camus, however, Sisyphus would not surrender his happiness to the fact that his achievements do not last, and for this reason he would be able to find a grim satisfaction in the task. From a cosmic perspective, the actions of these three characters are insignificant, but they are heroes because they live honestly and authentically.

So the question arises: Is Brian too an absurd hero?

It seems clear that Camus himself would say "No." Speaking of the meaningless labors of Sisyphus, for example, Camus says, "There is no fate that cannot be surmounted by scorn."[7] Camus apparently means that no matter how difficult one's life becomes, one is a free being and so one can always rise above one's circumstances. But Brian is not haughty enough to scorn. He does not look down on his fate. On the contrary, he is constantly irritated and frustrated. *The Myth of Sisyphus* also says that "[t]he struggle itself towards the heights is enough to fill a man's heart" (p. 91). It is true that Brian is involved in the struggle for liberation from the Romans. But the movie makes it clear, first, that the struggle is a farce and, second, that Brian is more interested in the homier benefits of Judith. Brian may be placed in an absurd situation, but no one would think he triumphs over it by concentrating on his freedom, by refusing to hope, or by realizing the absurdity of his situation. On the contrary, Brian whines about his lack of freedom, constantly hopes that things will work out, and does not ever become conscious of the absurdity of his situation. Brian lacks a rebellious or defiant recognition of the meaningless of human life. He is not heroic in Camus's sense.

---

[7] Albert Camus, *The Myth of Sisyphus and Other Essays* (New York: Vintage, 1955), p. 90.

If Camus has the final say about heroes, then one might conclude that *Monty Python's Life of Brian* is pretty cynical. It presents
an absurd universe that does not even have a hero in it. But there
may be another way to think about the meaningfulness of life and
how one should live in a world in which death is the final word.
On this scale, Brian fares better.

One thing to note is the centrality of lying to Camus (and to
all of the French existentialists). The greatest failure of a person,
they say, is when one lives a lie, when one deceives oneself and
lives in "bad faith." Camus has said that Meursault is an absurd
hero because he does not lie and that *The Stranger* is "the story of
a man who, without any heroics, accepts death for the sake of
truth." This, Camus adds, is a portrayal of "the only Christ we
deserved."[8]   But despite what Camus says, it's not clear that
Meursault really is an ideal person. Robert C. Solomon argues persuasively that far from being a completely honest hero, Meursault
never reaches the level of consciousness where one can choose to
tell the truth or to lie. There is nothing in Meursault to which he
can be true.[9]

One thing that we can say in Brian's favor, however, is that he
does not live a lie. Brian is bluntly, almost childishly forthright. At
the beginning of the movie he caves in to the pressure of his
sharp-tongued mother, but as he comes into his own, he eventually is able to throw this off. *Monty Python's Life of Brian* is in part
the story of growing up and becoming—not becoming a hero, but
an adult. Perhaps this explains why the song at the beginning of
the movie says that there was a baby named Brian who grew up to
be . . . a teenager named Brian, who then grew and grew until he
who grew up to be . . . a man named Brian. He is not an absurd
hero, but he is also not a liar. From this perspective, *Monty Python's
Life of Brian* rejects Camus's austere idea of what human beings
should aspire to and reflects instead an appreciation for more
mundane satisfactions. Brian does live in Camus's absurd universe.
He does so, however, not as a rebellious hero but as an adult: he
does not wait for a miracle. Instead, he hates the Roman occu-

---

[8] Albert Camus, Preface to *L'Étranger*, edited by Germaine Brée (New York:
Appleton-Century-Crofts, 1955).
[9] Robert C. Solomon, "Camus' *L'Étranger*, and the Truth," in his *From Hegel to
Existentialism* (Oxford: Oxford University Press, 1987), pp. 246–260.

piers, he loves Judith, and he in general does his best. Brian is buffeted by forces that he cannot defeat, but he nevertheless tries to do good, he is sincere, and he makes for himself a life that gains meaning through his own decisions. Perhaps those of us who admire Brian should invent a term: "absurd decent guy." If this is plausible, then *Monty Python's Life of Brian* exemplifies another form—a new form—of existentialist humanism. On this perspective, what *Monty Python's Life of Brian* offers as a counterweight to nihilism is *humor*. One cannot rebel against the absurd, but one can laugh at it. Here Brian represents a different understanding of what a hero really is. It is an understanding that rivals that of Camus. If this is plausible, then one can reject the idea that the almost completely unreflective killer Meursault is a hero. From this perspective, one can find heroes closer to home.

3
What Mr. Creosote Knows About Laughter

NOËL CARROLL

And by his side rode loathsome Gluttony,
Deformed creature, on a filthie swyne:
His belly was up-blown with luxury,
And eke with fatnesse swollen were his eyne,
And like a Crane his necke was long and fyne,
With which he swallowed up excessive feast,
For want whereof poore people oft did pyne;
And all the way, most like a brutish bear,
He spued up his gorge, that all did him deteast.
. . .
In shape and life more like a monster, than a man.

—Edmund Spenser, *The Faerie Queene*

Part VI: "The Autumn Years" of *Monty Python's The Meaning of Life* begins with a song about the glories of having a penis which is appreciated by all the audience in the cabaret, including the talking fish in an aquarium in the vicinity of the piano. The fish have the human faces of the Monty Python crew superimposed over their bodies and they call to mind something of the unsettling hybrid creatures found on hellish landscapes by Hieronymus Bosch, the fifteenth- and sixteenth-century Dutch artist. Their enjoyment of the ditty, however, quickly vanishes when they catch sight of the entrance of Mr. Creosote into the restaurant. "Oh shit!" cries one of them as they whiz off-screen.

Mr. Creosote, a gargantuan figure, lumbers into the dining room. The music that accompanies his entry recalls the giant shark's in *Jaws*, and his belly is so ponderous it nearly scrapes the floor. His face, framed by muttonchops, is swollen to the point of swinishness. He is dressed in a tuxedo but his body is mis-shapen, more like a pyramid of wobbling flesh than a human form. As Creosote ambles to his table, he commands a flurry of attention from the sycophantic maitre d'. This is obviously a very, very good customer, one who could eat whole families under the exceedingly expensive tables of this lavish eatery.

Creosote is also a very churlish customer. He is consistently curt to the point of rudeness. When asked how he is faring, he says "Better" and pauses before completing his thought—"Better get a bucket." In other words, he never responds civilly, but only commands imperiously. When the aforesaid bucket is brought to him, he proceeds to vomit into it with the force of a fire hose in complete obliviousness to his surroundings and to the sensibilities of his fellow diners. He doesn't do this once but several times and then repeats the spectacle on the back of the cleaning woman who is trying to clean up the mess he is making. He shows no concern for anyone else; his inclinations are the only lights by which he steers. In every way, Creosote is crude, gruff, and utterly selfish.

Thus, his vomiting elicits no sympathy. He treats it as his privilege; he's paying for it; so he'll do whatever he wants. Creosote clearly, as a matter of course, stuffs himself to the point that his body cannot absorb the mass he ingests. He retches in order to gorge himself again. He is gluttony personified.

The maitre d' hands him a menu; he disgorges himself all over it. The servant has to wipe it off so that he can read it. Moreover, it should be added, this vomit looks pretty convincing. Even the most ardent Python fan is apt to feel a twinge of nausea coming on.

Hearing the specials, all delicacies of a diversity befitting the original Gargantua, Creosote orders the lot, mixed into a bucket with eggs on top, along with a double portion of *pâté*, six bottles of wine, two magnums of champagne and perhaps some ale. Pope Gregory the Great defined gluttony as eating too soon, too delicately, too expensively, too greedily, and too much. Creosote's nausea indicates he is not ready for his next meal; it is too soon. He eats expensive delicacies as if they were potato chips. And he eats too much; he eats the entire menu. It is no wonder that Michael Palin called this routine a "Gothic Extravaganza."[1] It is like an illustration of one of the Deadly Sins.

Creosote, reminding one of an image out of James Ensor, the nineteenth–twentieth-century Belgian expressionist, continues to vomit as he eats. Other customers are disgusted and start leaving to the visible chagrin of the maitre d'; some are heaving themselves. The maitre d' accidentally steps into Creosote's pail of vomit and Creosote erupts upon his leg, to the evident great annoyance of the maitre d'. The maitre d' is reaching the end of his tether. Finally, Creosote is finished, but the maitre d' willfully tempts him, even prods him, to take one more bite, just a bit of a thin wafer of mint, despite the fact that Creosote protests that he is absolutely full.

Almost immediately, that slice of mint does its vengeful work. Creosote literally explodes, issuing forth a tidal wave of vomit that splashes every corner of the dining room. In the center of this dripping mess, then, sits Creosote, his belly blown open so that one can see his rib cage; but his red, fist-like heart relentlessly continues pumping as it dangles under his chin. His eyes are open, his face still carrying that mask of impassive brutishness he has worn throughout the scene. The maitre d', overjoyed and very self-satisfied by the success of his revenge plot, gives Creosote the check.

To Laugh, or To Scream?

This scene, involving non-stop nausea and a graphically exploded body, sounds more horrific than comic. It, like so much of the humor of Monty Python, is on the dark side. The scene has few peers in the annals of motion picture comedy, save perhaps the pie-eating sequence in *Stand By Me*. But even that seems tame next to the spectacle of Mr. Creosote's extravasation. The philosophical question it raises is: how is it possible to laugh at humor as

---

[1] The Pythons with Bob McCabe, *The Pythons: Autobiography by the Pythons* (New York: St. Martin's Press, 2003), p. 326.

black as this? Though it may seem paradoxical that mirth could issue from depicting a situation so gruesome and disgusting, perhaps this will not strike us as so strange when we recall how much humor—such as bathroom humor—revels in the repulsive. And yet there is nevertheless something perplexing about this scene. How can the gag function as a source of comic amusement for so many, rather than leaving them trembling in horror? Why is the sequence comic rather than horrific? This seems paradoxical. Since negotiating paradoxes is one of the charges of philosophy, answering that question is the aim of this chapter. And in the process, we wish to learn what Mr. Creosote can teach us about laughter.

Let us agree from the outset that many people laugh at this scene; they find it comically amusing. This is not to deny that some also find it disgusting, and even unwatchable. And even those who enjoy the routine may experience moments during it when their stomach feels on the verge of revolting. Nevertheless, there are a significant number of people who find the scene on balance risible, and even continuously so—that is, they laugh all the way through. Our question is, How can they do so? How can anyone find the explosion of a human body to be comically amusing? If anything, the prospect is horrifying.

One way to make some headway with this problem is to think about what makes for horror, especially in mass culture.[2] In popular fictions, including literature and motion pictures, horror is typically focused upon a particular sort of object, namely, a monster—that is, a creature whose existence is unacknowledged by science and who, in addition, is dangerous and disgusting. For example, the Frankenstein monster is a scientific impossibility—electrifying dead flesh will fry it, not animate it—and the monster is disgusting, an impure being constructed of rotting, dismembered body parts. And perhaps most obviously, the monster is dangerous: it kidnaps, maims, and kills people.

---

[2] The ensuing account of horror derives from Noël Carroll, *The Philosophy of Horror* (New York: Routledge, 1990), especially the first chapter. For further background on comic amusement, see my article, "Humour," in *The Oxford Handbook of Aesthetics*, edited by Jerrold Levinson (Oxford: Oxford University Press, 2003), pp. 344–365.

Maybe we are tempted to think of the restaurant vomiting scene as horror rather than comedy because Creosote, it would appear, shares many of the attributes that characterize horror. For example, I expect that he is a physiological impossibility; even supposing that someone could reach his girth, it is unlikely that he would be able to move on his own power. Creosote is of a scale of obesity where the patient usually has to be moved by handlers. But Creosote is also beyond the ken of science, both in the manner of his explosion and, then, of his survival. People don't burst like that, balloons do; and if they did, they would not live to tell the tale. But one suspects that Creosote will have himself sewn up again in order to eat another day.

Moreover, Creosote, like Frankenstein's monster, is certainly disgusting. In the first instance, his behavior is disgusting. His constant vomiting presents a challenge to the strongest stomach. I think that were it not the case that film is odorless—that, thankfully, smell-o-rama has not yet been perfected—many viewers would be unable to hold onto their own dinners throughout this episode. Indeed, Creosote's name suggests a foul odor, inasmuch as it labels a colorless liquid, a pungent burning agent, that smells of smoked meat and tar. Creosote's incontinence, furthermore, functions metonymically in the same way in which the rats, spiders, and other vermin that inhabit the vampire's lair function— namely, as disgusting things designed to accentuate the abominableness of the thing to which they are attached or which they surround.

But it is not only what is connected to Creosote that is disgusting. Creosote himself is loathsome, an abomination. Undoubtedly, he is the sort of thing we call monstrous in ordinary language. Like the Frankenstein monster or the creatures in the *Alien* and *Predator* series, Creosote is physically repulsive. The thought of being hugged by Creosote is probably enough to make most of us squirm; and imagine what visualizing a kiss on the lips from him might do to your digestion. Once again, like the Frank-enstein monster, the Alien, and the Predator, there is something viscerally revolting, unclean, and impure about Creosote.

It's the impurity of the monster in horror fictions that elicits the response of disgust from audiences. This impurity, in turn, is rooted in the ontology, or being, of horrific creatures. Such creatures are violations or problematizations of our standing cultural categories. For that reason they are abominations possessing a combination or collection of properties that our culture trains us to revile on contact. For instance, the Frankenstein monster violates the categorical distinction between life and death. It is both. It is a walking contradiction, as is Chucky, the puppet that kills, from the film *Child's Play.* The Predator, a category violation if there ever was one, is part crab and part primate. The Blob defies our categories by not fitting into any of them; it is stuff out of control. The Amazing Colossal Man is horrifically repulsive because he is too colossal; he violates the criteria of what it is to be human in virtue of his scale. Creosote likewise is monstrous just because his figure seems to go beyond not only what is normal but even beyond what is humanly possible. He is a travesty of the human form; he is an affront to our norms of the human form. He strikes us as inhuman or nonhuman. But as a result of effectively claiming membership in that category—that is, in our species—he triggers an aversive response on our part.

Who's Afraid of Mr. Creosote?

Creosote is a monster and he incurs our disgust. So far the horror formula is realized. But two points need to be made. First, disgust, including disgust elicited by the violation of our standing norms and categories, does not belong solely to the domain of the genre of horror. It is, as noted earlier, also a natural ingredient of comedy. This, of course, should be extremely evident. Think of how much humor, especially juvenile humor, hinges on celebrating disgusting things—farts, feces, and slime. Insofar as mention of these things, which are themselves categorically interstitial (ambiguously both part of me and outside of me), is also a violation of the norms of propriety, they are staples of humor. Disgust, that is, belongs as much to comedy as to horror. But in order for a categorical violation to turn into an occasion for horror, something else must be added, namely, fear. So the second point to be addressed is whether the fear-condition for the elicitation of horror has been met in the Creosote sequence. For if it has not been, then we can start to explain why the Creosote scene is comic rather than horrific.

   In horror fictions, the monster is fearsome and disgusting because it is dangerous and impure. Standardly, the monster in a horror fiction is not threatening to the audience. They know that they are encountering a fiction and that they can suffer no harm from the creatures that rule the page and the screen. Rather they feel fear for the humans in the fiction who are being stalked or otherwise imperiled by the monsters. Insofar as we feel concern for the plight of those fictional characters—that is, insofar as we anticipate that harm will befall them at the hands, talons, or other instruments of the monsters—the fear condition of the horror formula is activated.

However, when we turn to the scene with Mr. Creosote, there is no fear factor. We do not fear for the other customers in the restaurant. They are in no great danger from Mr. Creosote. They are unquestionably offended by him. This may garner some sympathy for them (or, it may not, if you regard them as insufferable swells deserving of being taken down a peg). But it will not elicit fear in their behalf, since they are in no grievous danger, bodily or otherwise.

But perhaps Creosote is the human who should elicit our concern. After all, he's a person (ain't he got some rights?), and he does explode. And he is harmed by the machinations of the maitre d'. However, here Creosote shows us something about how comedy works. Creosote is not quite human. Not only is he too outsized. But he is utterly impervious to his repeated bouts of nausea—what human can take fits of retching in his stride the way Creosote does?—and he, of course, survives the massive explosion of his belly. In this, Creosote not only resembles the monster of horror fictions. He also resembles that staple of slapstick comedy, the clown.

The clown is not exactly human. With respect of our norms for the average human, the clown is either too fat or too tall, too thin or too short. His mouth is painted to appear exaggeratedly large and his eyes and head are often too small. He is a misproportioned human. Nor are his cognitive skills near the norm; generally he is too stupid. And his body can also take abuse that no actual person could. He can be hit on the head with a sledge hammer and suffer no more than a dizzy swoon where the rest of us would be hospitalized with a concussion. He takes falls with abandon and always pops up for another slam. It is as if his bones were made of rubber. Instead of breaking, they snap back into place.

It's because the clown is marked as so ontologically different from us—especially in terms of his imperviousness to bodily harm—that we have no fear for his life and limb. We can laugh at the way in which his body with its incongruities taunts our concept of the human, because the mayhem the clown engages is nonthreatening. We need not fear for the clown; nor, in the standard case, need we fear clowns. They are, for the most part, benign. Thus, though monstrous, clowns and the other denizens of slapstick incur no horror, since no genuine harm will result in or from their shenanigans.

Mr. Creosote belongs to the same fantastic species as the clown. He is not precisely human, so we do not fear for him as we do for the characters in horror fictions. He is able to suffer through things that would incapacitate or destroy ordinary mortals, because he is marked as of a different ontological order. Because Creosote can neither harm nor can he be harmed, his monstrosity becomes an occasion for comic amusement rather than horror. This is one thing that Mr. Creosote shows us about laughter.

It has been established experimentally that children will laugh when confronted with something incongruous—like a "funny face"—if the face is offered by someone with whom they are familiar, but they will cringe if it is presented by a stranger. This suggests that our responses to incongruities, anomalies, unexpected deviations from norms and standing categories will vary in terms of certain conditions. If the incongruity occurs in a context where it is threatening, it will dispose us toward a fearful response. This is perhaps the origin of the horror genre. On the other hand, if the context is one that is marked as non-threatening—where the prospect of harm and danger has been subtracted—the circumstances are ripe for comedy. The Mr. Creosote scene illustrates this principle dramatically by getting as perilously close to the conditions that satisfy the horrific, but remaining on the side of amusement. In this it exemplifies a principle that makes much cruel humor possible: we need not fear for the victims of all the violence and malevolence done in darker shades of comedy, including slapstick, because they are not completely human. Punch and Judy can be beaten mercilessly but they will never come within an inch of their lives. Mr. Creosote never suffers or dies. He is not precisely our kind of creature. Thus, we may laugh at him.

Just Desserts

But this is not all that Mr. Creosote tells us about laughter. It's true that in order to find a routine like his comically amusing we must not fear for him. And we do not, since he is not subject to human vulnerability. Instead we focus on his monstrous incongruity, his absurdity. But it's not just that we do not feel concern about Creosote because we know he cannot be harmed. We also are encouraged to form a positive animus against Creosote. We do not just laugh at the ontological incongruity of Creosote and what befalls him. Part of our laughter, even if it is not pure comic laughter, originates in our sense that Creosote gets what he deserves. Part of our laughter is vindictive or, at least, retributive. What has happened to Creosote, or so we are invited to suppose, is just. Though Creosote is not completely human, he is human enough to engender our scorn morally and to merit punishment. Moreover, we cannot help but think that his punishment fits his crime ever so appropriately. Think of how often we describe the aftermath of our own gluttonous escapades in terms of a feeling that we are about to explode. Creosote gets his just desserts, one might say. On the one hand, Creosote is a despicable character. He treats others with contempt, presumably because he thinks his evident wealth entitles him to do so. He spits up on servants with no sense of shame; they are beneath his selfish concern. He has no inkling of decorum and is insensitive to the existence of other people and their rightful claims. He is an egoist of stupendous proportions. And, of course, he has abused himself immensely. His vast bulk appears to be his own fault. It is the height of self-indulgence to eat so far past the point of satiation that one continues to press on while one is still egesting the surplus of one's last meal. Creosote has sown what he reaps. He has asked for what he has gotten. His own greedy appetite has backfired, so to speak. His explosion is poetic justice. The maitre d's retribution was warranted. To repeat, Creosote's predicament almost literally amounts to nothing more or less than his just desserts. The pun is intended by me, as it was also probably intended by the Pythons.

We laugh, but it is not precisely the laughter of comic amusement. It is the laughter that accompanies the apprehension that
someone has "gotten what's coming to them." Thus, there should
be no surprise that people laugh at the scene instead of being horrified by it. We are not repelled by the violence Creosote under-
goes, in part because we believe that he has brought it upon himself; he invited it. Ours is the laughter of justice—the laughter
that obtains when we perceive that the punishment suits the crime
ever so neatly.

As already suggested, there is something medieval about the
Creosote episode; indeed, a medieval theme runs throughout the
film, including dungeons and the Grim Reaper (perhaps this is a
result of taking up, and then dismissing, Roman Catholicism as a
source of the meaning of life). In many ways, the scene is the
modern equivalent of a morality play, an allegory of gluttony and
its consequences. If you eat to the point where you feel like
exploding, you will. The scene culminates in a visual pun or verbal image—that is, it literalizes the way we describe ourselves
when we've overindulged at the table gluttonously. Creosote's *sentence* is the sentence "I've eaten so much that I'd burst if took
another morsel." He does and he does. It is a punishment befitting Dante's *Inferno* or Kafka's "The Penal Colony" in its diabolical ingenuity and appropriateness. Indeed, it provokes laughter for
being *so* appropriate, so well-deserved.

The laughter engendered by Creosote's predicament is, then,
over-determined. Part of it is rooted in incongruity—the absurdities of the scene presented in a context bereft of any perceived
danger to human life and limb. But there is also another route to
laughter here: the sense that justice is served, that the punishment
matches the crime perfectly. Moreover, with respect to this second source of joy, Mr. Creosote, I think, gives us additional insight
into the springs of laughter. Much comedy, especially satire and
even much of what is called black comedy, induces laughter
because we feel that the objects of the indignities and violence
suffered by its objects is deserved.[3] It is a different kind of laugh-

---

[3] It may seem that this does not apply to a great deal of black comedy. In many
instances the cruelties dealt in black humor do not appear to be directed at
objects that morally deserve such punishment. Think of such genres of dark
humor as dead baby jokes. However, in cases like this, the cruel humorist is

ter than the laughter prompted by an innocent pun. And it is our sense of justice that makes such comic genres possible. This too is something that Mr. Creosote shows us about laughter.

Perhaps one thing that is so artistically effective about the Creosote episode is that it is able to weld these two sources of laughter so exquisitely. I suspect that it achieves this by the way in which the visual pun it articulates both comically amuses us with its absurdity—its violation of biological norms—while simultaneously satisfying our sense of justice in the most devilish manner. Like many medieval visions of hell, such as the punishments meted out in Dante's *Inferno*, the travails of Creosote mix horror and humor in a way that seems natural. Whether the scene has the same pedagogical intent is doubtful. But it is not a parody of such extravaganzas. Rather it taps into the same emotional well by being an updated version of them. Horrific imagery and humor are often interlaced. Mr. Creosote shows us how these two ostensibly opposed elements can co-exist. They belong together because they both specialize in the incongruous and the impure—in violations of our standing cultural categories and norms. But the overall effect of these subversions of our cultural categories will not dispose us toward horror, unless they occur in the context of some clear and present danger. Where there is no danger to anything we would call human, there is no cause for horror, and there is an opening for laughter. That is Creosote. Moreover, Creosote is not just comically amusing for being a biological absurdity. He is also worthy of our derision for his sins (in his case, perhaps he is the sin itself personified). And this helps us to see that underlying the vitriol of humor is often a perception of justice.

---

encouraging us to direct our moral rancor not at the babies in the jokes, but at sentimental attitudes that usually accompany discourse about infants. It is that complacent sentimentality that the dark humorist thinks deserves a moral whack.

Similarly, the recurring mentally-challenged "Gumby" characters in *Monty Python's Flying Circus* (see, for example, "Gumby Crooner" in Episode 9, "The Ant: An Introduction") seem to be basically an assault , by his own hand, on excessive sentimentality. It is not that Gumby deserves to be hit on the head with a brick, as he is; rather, the ethical energy underwriting the harsh laughter here is aimed at the sentimentalization of the mentally ill. The butt of the laughter lives off-screen, in a manner of speaking. It resides wherever pompous types congratulate themselves for caring for their "inferiors."

4
The Limits of Horatio's Philosophy

KURT SMITH

What I Think My Chapter May Be About

A working-class woman (Eric Idle) sits on a bench in the park. She is approached by another woman (Michael Palin), also working-class, who pushes a dolly on which sits a brand new automobile engine, wrapped in a red bow. "Morning Mrs. Gorilla," says the woman sitting on the bench. "Morning Mrs. Non-Gorilla," replies the woman with the dolly. She sits down on the bench. "You been shopping?" asks Mrs. Non-Gorilla. "No . . . been shopping," replies Mrs. Gorilla. "Did you buy anything?" asks Mrs. Non-Gorilla, her eyes fixed on the dolly. "A piston engine," says Mrs. Gorilla with some excitement. "What did you buy *that* for?" "Oohh," Mrs. Gorilla sings with confidence, ". . . it was a bargain!" "Oohh," sings Mrs. Non-Gorilla. "Oohh" Mrs. Gorilla adds, as the camera pans right.

We see another working-class woman (Terry Jones) sitting on a bench. She is luring birds towards her, "Chirp, chirp, chirp . . . come on little birdies; come and see what mommy's got for you . . . tweetie, tweetie. Come on little birdies . . . ." She reaches into a grocery bag, takes out a pork roast, and heaves it violently at the birds. The satisfaction on her face reveals that she has pegged one of the buggers. She again calls nicely to the birds, "Come on little birdies . . . ," reaches into the bag, this time pulling out a large can of (diced?) pineapples, and heaves it at the birds. Again, her face reveals success. We are shown the scene from her point of view: dead birds and groceries are scattered about the pond's bank.

A woman (Graham Chapman) approaches, also working-class, who pushes a dolly on which sits a brand new automobile engine (also wrapped in a red bow). "Hello Mrs. Smoker," says the woman with the groceries. "Hello Mrs. Non-Smoker," replies the woman with the dolly. She sits. "What . . . you been shopping then?" asks Mrs. Non-Smoker. "No," replies Mrs. Smoker, "I've been shopping." "Oh, what'd you buy?" asks Mrs. Non-Smoker, her eyes fixed on the dolly. "A piston engine," says Mrs. Smoker with excitement. "What'd you buy *that* for?" asks Mrs. Non-Smoker. "It was a bargain!" replies Mrs. Smoker. "How much you want for it?" asks Mrs. Non-Smoker. "Three quid," says Mrs. Smoker without hesitation. "Done," replies Mrs. Non-Smoker. "Right," replies Mrs. Smoker. Mrs. Non-Smoker counts an imaginary three quid and gives it to Mrs. Smoker. She looks at her newly purchased piston engine with delight. A subtle wave of confusion washes over her face. "How do you cook it?" she asks. "You can't cook it," replies Mrs. Smoker sternly. "You can't eat that *raw*," replies Mrs. Non-Smoker, even more sternly. "Oohh, . . ." ponders Mrs. Smoker, "I never thought of *that*."

Both sit thinking about the present problem, when all of a sudden Mrs. Smoker matter-of-factly blurts out: "O day and night, but this is wondrous strange!" Without skipping a beat Mrs. Non-Smoker replies, "And therefore as a stranger welcome it. There are more things in heaven and earth, Horatio, than are dreamt of in your philosophy." Her face reveals that she is experiencing a profound state of confusion, for she does not know the origin of her words. Yet, she continues, "The time is out of joint: O cursed spite, that ever I was born to set it right! Nay, come, let's go together." The two women rise, looking about dazed and confused, and walk away—leaving the dolly and piston engine behind.

The above skit, "Piston Engine (a Bargain)," comes from Episode 43 ("Hamlet") of *Monty Python's Flying Circus*. Its absurdity makes it one of my favorites. "Been shopping?" asks one woman. "No, been shopping," answers the other. A natural reaction to hearing this is to ask: Are they not listening to what the other is saying? Are they just going through the motions of a polite greeting? Perhaps. But what Mrs. Non-Gorilla says, namely, "It is not the case that I've been shopping and I've being shopping" is a logical contradiction. This aside, what we really want to know is why these women are lugging around piston engines (gift-wrapped no less). They bought them? Why? As Mrs. Non-Gorilla says, "It was a bargain!" To be sure, this could be counted as a reason for buying the engine, but if this is the only reason it is certainly the wrong one. What's with the one woman who kills birds? Has she gone insane? What are we to make of their sudden recital of *Hamlet*, Act I, Scene V? What are *they* to make of it? (That these women recite the play is surely connected to the fact that the episode is centered around *Hamlet*. Even so, knowing this will not answer the questions that I want to raise below.)

One wonders whether in the end it is best to accept the absurdity, as Mrs. Smoker and Mrs. Non-Smoker seem to do when they walk away, and laugh. For my part, I like this option. But, the editors of this book tell me that I had better opt for making something else of such skits. To clinch the deal, they recently sent out email letting contributors know that if the book were to sell, and I mean sell big, each author of a chapter would receive a couple of hundred bucks. That was certainly enough to motivate me to make something of the piston engine skit. What I am to make of it exactly, of course, is the rub.

I am a scholar of early modern philosophy by trade, or at least this is what I tell family, friends, students, and of late, police officers. Originally for this book I had worked up a scholarly piece on an eighteenth-century theory of humor, wit, raillery, satire, and ridicule, written by the British economist Corbyn Morris.[1] The idea behind the essay was to take a bunch of Monty Python skits set in the eighteenth century and apply Morris's theory. The theory, of course, would tell us whether Monty Python was funny— at least, whether the skits would have been considered funny by eighteenth-century standards. I was secretly hoping that the theory would not find the skits to be funny, in which case I would be able to spin the piece as a study of comical irony. But, alas, an application of the theory showed that the goddamned pieces would have been a smashing success, as the Brits would put it. So, there went the irony angle.

---

[1] Corbyn Morris, *An Essay towards Fixing the True Standards of Wit, Humour, Raillery, Satire, and Ridicule* (1744) (New York: Garland, 1970).

As I worked more on Morris's little essay in which he expounds his theory, I began to wonder why he ever found it necessary to write and publish it. After all, it isn't an obvious thing for an economist to be publishing. I was also interested in finding out more about this guy to whom Morris dedicates the essay—one Robert Earl of Orford. "Who the hell was this guy?" I wondered. As it turns out, Robert Earl of Orford is Sir Robert Walpole, who was none other than the very first British Prime Minister (well, not in the contemporary sense of Prime Minister). He's sort of like the British counterpart to the United States's George Washington. At first I was a bit embarrassed to discover this because it revealed how little I know about British history. But, the embarrassment quickly faded, for what the hell do I care about that? But, I digress.

According to Morris, Walpole's mastery of wit was known worldwide. He apparently used his wit and debating skills to pull some sort of Jedi mind trick on Parliament to pass the infamous Licensing Act of 1737, which served to censor the content of plays performed in London's theaters. As S.H. Wood puts it:

> Annoyed by the rude and abusive language of *The Vision of the Golden Rump* . . . Walpole was able to persuade them to pass the 1737 Licensing Act. In future all new plays and any alteration to old ones had to be sent to the Lord Chamberlain for approval, and playhouses were restricted to the City of Westminster. Other theatres needed parliamentary sanction, which enabled Walpole to shut down the most troublesome.[2]

Golden Rump? What the . . . ? "This could be good," I thought to myself. But as it turns out, the term 'Rump' refers to some group of old-school loyalists who constituted the "tail end" of the old something or other and made some political hay in Parliament—or some such. The play was apparently a satire about that. Boring. Prior to my discovering this, I thought for about five minutes or so that the play was about a golden ass whose *thing* was the having of visions. This, of course—*not* so boring!

---

[2] S.H. Wood, *Walpole and Early Eighteenth-Century England* (London: Methuen, 1973), p. 61.

I was convinced now more than ever that the British colonies living in North America were justified in their revolt against British rule, until I recalled that not twenty-two years after the birth of the United States, John Adams, then U.S. President, signed into law The Sedition Act of 1798, which did pretty much the same thing as the British Licensing Act of 1737. It made it illegal to say or write anything that insulted or made fun of the President. One difference, however, was that the *truth* could be used in one's defense. And so, if the President really was a cross-dresser or was too fat to ride a horse, one might be able to side-step trouble (when depicting him as a fat-non-horse-riding-cross-dresser). Strangely enough, The Sedition Act did not say anything about insulting the Vice President, which at the time was Adams's nemesis, Thomas Jefferson. Apparently one could have a field day with him.

Like Adams, Walpole was uptight or something, and many of England's playwrights of the time included Walpole-like characters in their plays. Henry Fielding's plays in particular satirized Walpole. Fielding's work suffered so greatly as a result of the Licensing Act that he turned from writing plays to writing novels. But as Morris suggests, the sort of shock felt by the entertainment business was well-deserved. He writes:

> The infamous insults there [in the theaters] offered upon all Decency, cried aloud for a Remedy.—For these profligate Attacks made Impressions more deep and venomous than Writings; As they were not fairly addressed to the Judgment, but immediately to the Sight and the Passions; for were they capable of being answered again, but by erecting an opposite Stage of Scurrility. (Morris, p. x)

The power of the stage was so great that it threatened Walpole's tenure as Britain's Minister. In light of the Licensing Act, Morris seemed to have thought that a line needed to be drawn between political satire on the one hand, and malice, libel, and treason on the other. Fixing the standards of humor, wit, raillery, satire, and ridicule—that is, fixing them as *political*, *legal*, and even *moral* concepts—appears to be Morris's real motive for publishing the essay. Even so, in a careful read of the essay, one gets the feeling that Morris was more interested in setting standards of humor that were *compatible* with the Licensing Act than he was in setting out a defense of humor.

Understanding the larger picture now, and coming to grips with the fact that the *Golden Rump* wasn't about a golden rump, I decided to abandon the historico-philosophical angle all together. At least, I decided to abandon the focus on the eighteenth century. I was a fish out of water—a fish nevertheless looking to make a quick couple of hundred bucks.

Freed from my scholarly chains, I began to consider possible 'artistic' ways by which I might approach a study of Monty Python. I had an idea! Following a paper writing strategy that I had learned from my students, I quickly got online and visited a site that sports a well-known essay generator. It immediately generated for me an essay titled, "Realities of Fatal Flaw: Capitalist Discourse and Textual Theory," the first section of which was titled, "Neotextual Narrative and Sartreist Existentialism." This was like stealing postmodern candy from a computational-based-essay-writing baby. It was a bit of work, but I read the thing in one sitting. The second section titled "Realities of Collapse" was especially difficult. I got to the end of the essay only to find an important notice, which read: "The essay you have just seen is completely meaningless and was randomly generated by the Postmodernism Generator." This was difficult to believe, for I swear that I almost understood what A. David Cameron, University of Illinois (who was listed as the essay's author), was getting at. Be that as it may, my artistic vision was almost complete! My hope was to use the postmodern generator's essay and act postmodernly, giving it the title: "This is Not an Essay, It Just Looks Like One." But, I was immediately reminded of the 1926 surrealist painting *Ceci n'est pas une Pipe*, painted by some guy from Belgium. So, the idea of a joke essay was quickly coming to an end. As much as it grieved me, I would have to say something interesting about Monty Python. Perhaps I would return to those women with their piston engines.

Wittgenstein and Meaning: The Absurd and The Funny

It's well known that Ludwig Wittgenstein (1889–1951) had once forwarded a theory of meaning that took hold of Moritz Schlick and the philosophers of the Vienna Circle. It has come to be called the "Verification Principle," which says: The meaning of a sentence is determined by its method of verification. And though Wittgenstein repeatedly denied ever having said anything like this to Schlick or to members of the Vienna Circle, this apparently has not changed the fact that it is well known that he did say it.[3] The idea of the Verification Principle is that the meaning of a sentence is determined by the various ways one could take to determine the truth of the sentence. Of course, there are some snags here. For instance, the principle itself is not subject to verification. And so, as some have argued, if we are to believe what the principle tells us, we must conclude that it is meaningless, in which case we should *un*believe it, to use a phrase from some unknown philosopher whose name I am forgetting at the moment. Be that as it may, let's look at the piston engine skit in light of this principle.

Mrs. Non-Gorilla asks, "Been shopping?" Mrs. Gorilla answers, "No . . . been shopping." As I suggested earlier, I take it that the latter amounts to saying: "It is not the case that I've been shopping *and* I've been shopping." This is a logical contradiction; and so, it is false. It *cannot* be true. Verification here is a moot point. Now, if there is no way by which one *could* verify the sentence uttered by Mrs. Gorilla, then according to the principle, it seems to follow that the sentence is not false after all, but meaningless. At least, according to at least one biographer, this is one gloss of what Wittgenstein might say (Wittgenstein says about the proposition "This circle is 3 cm long and 2 cm wide" that it is not false, but nonsensical (Monk, p. 286).) Even so, Wittgenstein states in the *Tractatus*: "The proposition shows what it says, the tautology and the contradiction [on the other hand] that they say nothing. . . . Tautology and contradiction are, however, not nonsensical; they are part of the symbolism. . . ."[4] Their meaning, if we want to call it that, is merely formal. And so, we might say that even though the sentence that Mrs. Gorilla utters has meaning (though only formally), it is for all that empirically empty. In other words, she cannot be taken to be saying anything about the world.

---

[3] Ray Monk, *Ludwig Wittgenstein: The Duty of Genius* (New York: Penguin, 1990), p. 287.

[4] Ludwig Wittgenstein. *Tractatus Logico-Philosophicus* (New York: Routledge, 1990), pp. 97–98. I quote from propositions 4.461 and 4.4611.

I think that we could take this a step further and claim that although the sentence she utters has meaning, Mrs. Gorilla isn't *saying* anything at all! Admittedly, this on its surface seems a bit odd, and I will return to it shortly. Before I do, it is worth noting that the same sort of oddity can be found in what Mrs. Smoker utters in reply to Mrs. Non-Smoker. This second exchange has an additional twist. For example, in answer to Mrs. Non-Smoker's question about how one cooks the piston engine, Mrs. Smoker says, "You can't *cook* that!" This, it seems to me, is true and can be verified. Mrs. Non-Smoker replies, "You can't eat that *raw*!" This, too, is true and can be verified. So, now we have a couple of sentences that can be verified—or, at least there is a sense in which they can. Even so, is their meaning *really* determined by the ways that we would go about verifying them? For instance, is the meaning of Mrs. Non-Smoker's reply simply our being able to verify that one cannot eat a piston engine raw? Perhaps. But, this seems so only if she is simply asserting a fact. Of course, the joke is made in her *appearing* to do just this!

With the exception of the contradictions already considered, we can easily agree that every statement made in the dialogue is true, or at least verifiably true. Even so, the conditions that underwrite their truth, and the ways by which we would verify their truth, do not appear to account for why what the women are saying is absurd (or funny). For, the joke of the skit is that even though we completely understand the *meanings* of their sentences, we cannot make heads or tails of what they are *saying*. As I mentioned above, the difference being drawn here is admittedly odd. Although I'll not be able to make it look less odd, I think that I can make it a bit clearer.

For starters, then, imagine that we meet for coffee and you say, "Hello, good to see you," and I extend out my hand, my eyes sort of wide open as I stare at it, and utter, "This is my hand." Although you clearly understand the *meaning* of the sentence I just uttered (it isn't as though I uttered, "Gobily gook muk not me fancy cakes"), my guess is that for all that you would nevertheless find my uttering "This is my hand" here a bit creepy. Rush Rhees has an answer as to why you would:

But "what it makes sense to say" is not "the sense these expressions have." It has more to do with what it makes sense

to answer or what it makes sense to ask, or what sense one
remark may have in connexion with another.[5]

The distinction that Rhees is making, I think, is what I want to
bring out: there is a difference between the meaning of a sentence
(its sense) and what it makes sense to say. According to Rhees, this
is the sort of shift that Wittgenstein makes when moving from his
earlier to his later work. He is less interested in asking "What is
the meaning of a sentence?" and more interested in asking "What
is it to say something?" In uttering, "This is my hand," you might
think that I was simply offering a bit of trivial information.
However, the more likely reaction to my behavior would be to
quickly fish around for a context in which it would make sense for
me to say, "This is my hand," and say it so that it *wouldn't* count as
a piece of trivial information. For example, you might think to
yourself: this idiot thinks that I think that he doesn't have a hand.
The point to stress here is that although the Verification Principle
might work to account for the meaning of the sentence "This is
my hand," it does nothing to help us understand why uttering it in
this context is so creepy.

Even when given reasons for the purchase of the piston
engines, the reasons are strange. The strangeness, I think, stems
from the fact that Mrs. Smoker's answer to the question "Why did
you buy that?" *is* connected in all the right ways to this question,
though it cannot be accepted (by us) as an answer. For, given the
cost of living, and the fact that these ladies are of the working-
class (and so must spend their money wisely—this is why being
working-class is significant here), one buys a piston engine only if
one is in need of one. To be sure, that it would be on sale at the
time one needed to purchase such a thing would be a matter of
good fortune—one worthy of note. But, one doesn't buy such a
thing *simply* because it is a bargain! That the engines are gift-
wrapped makes things even stranger. For, though one *might* buy a
piston engine on sale knowing that one will most certainly need
one in the near future, one wouldn't normally go the extra step and
have the thing gift-wrapped. And so, even granting that reason is

---

[5] Rush Rhees, "Wittgenstein's Builders," in *Discussions of Wittgenstein* (New York:
Schoken, 1970), p. 80.

at work, the assumption doesn't go very far in making the exchange between these women intelligible.

Wittgenstein in his later work seems to have abandoned the Verification Principle, which he claims to have never held in the first place. Now, why he would abandon something that he never held is itself a bit curious, but be that as it may, he appears to abandon it and introduces another: the Meaning-as-Use Principle.[6] This principle says: "For a *large* class of cases—though not for all—in which we employ the word 'meaning' it can be defined thus: the meaning of a word is its use in the language." This could go far in helping explain away the worry about Mrs. Gorilla's and Mrs. Smoker's contradictory statements. For instance, we might say that it has become customary among these women to use a phrase of the form 'No, . . . P' when asked whether one has been P-ing. So, when Mrs. Non-Gorilla asks, "Been shopping?" the appropriate response (if one has in fact been shopping) is "No, . . . been shopping." If this is the accepted form of response, then we might say that the sentence 'No, . . . been shopping' means "Yes, I've been shopping" or something like this. The phrase gets its meaning here by its being *used* to confirm that one has been shopping.

But, what of the other statements in the dialogue? For example, when Mrs. Non-Smoker says, "You can't eat that *raw!*" she appears to be using it to inform Mrs. Smoker of a simple fact about eating such things as piston engines. Mrs. Smoker replies, "Oohh, I never thought of *that.*" Of course, neither have we, but our never having thought of it is connected to our never having thought of eating piston engines to begin with, let alone cooked! Why has Mrs. Smoker not thought of it? How is Mrs. Non-Smoker using the sentence "You can't eat that *raw!*"? Is it really being used to *inform* Mrs. Smoker? Why would she need to be informed about that?

To better see how the distinction—between the meanings of sentences and what it makes sense to say—may be of some help here, let me take the analysis in a slightly different direction. Looking at all of this from the audience's point of view, for

---

[6] Ludwig Wittgenstein, *Philosophical Investigations*, *Third Edition*, translated by G.E.M. Anscombe (New York: Macmillan, 1958), p. 43.

instance, we might speculate that Mrs. Smoker says what she does in order to provoke from us a laugh. Fine. But this doesn't explain how she takes *herself* to be using the sentence. It only explains how the skit's writers are using it. Now, if we say that it is really only this use for which we need an account—that is, an account of the writer's use—I am reminded of a curious remark that Wittgenstein later makes in the *Philosophical Investigations*. He writes:

> When I say that the orders "Bring me sugar" and "Bring me milk" make sense, but not the combination "Milk me sugar," that does not mean that the utterance of this combination of words has no effect. And if its effect is that the other person stares at me and gapes, I don't on that account call it the order to stare and gape, even if that was precisely the effect that I wanted to produce. (498)

Here, it appears that he is saying that there are cases in which I may use a sentence to produce a certain effect, but nevertheless my *using* it to produce this effect does not count as the *meaning* of the sentence. And so, he suggests that the meaning of "Milk me sugar" is not the order "Stare and gape at me!" even though my using the former is to get you to stare and gape at me. Of course, in being reminded of this passage, I am also reminded of my time spent in the U.S. Navy, when such sentences as "Milk me sugar" were used from time to time, especially while in port, and were just packed with meaning—though I will not go into this here. I mention it only because it is important to note that he is not saying that "Milk me sugar" is *inherently* meaningless. As my Navy experience has taught me, it is easy to invent contexts in which such a sentence has a life. I think that Wittgenstein would agree. What is important about this passage is that Wittgenstein is telling us that even though the skit's writers *use* (*via* Mrs. Non-Smoker) the sentence "You can't eat that *raw!*" to produce laughter in the audience, for all that we should not count the *meaning* of this sentence to be the order "Laugh at what I am saying!" We should emphasize Wittgenstein's saying that for a *large* class of cases the use determines the meaning. It just so happens that our piston engine skit is not a member of this class.

The difficulty, as I see it, is that neither the earlier Verification Principle nor the later Meaning-as-Use Principle work to explain what is going on in the piston engine skit, though I do think that they hint at an explanation. In what remains of the chapter, I want to explore what I take to be the hint, and offer a very brief sketch of what an explanation might look like.

Meaning and Practice

In *Remarks on Colour*, Wittgenstein writes:

> When someone who believes in God looks around him and asks "Where did everything that I see come from?" "Where did everything come from?" he is not asking for a (causal) explanation; and the point (*Witz*) of his question is that it is the expression of such a request. Thus, he is expressing an attitude toward all explanations.[7]

In this passage, the *point* (*Witz*) of the believer's question can be also translated as the *joke* of his question. That is, his expressing what he does in the form of a certain sort of question is a kind of joke. Here, the *funny* of the joke is akin, if not identical to, the *wonder* of the absurd. In other words, the absurdity one senses when lighting upon the difficulty in contemplating the origin of reality itself is a reaction that is much like the humor one senses when lighting upon the punch line of a joke. A natural reaction to both can be laughter. He continues:

> What I actually want to say is that here too it is not a matter of the *words* one uses or of what one is thinking when using them, but rather of the difference they make at various points in life. . . . *Practices* give words their meaning. (58e, paragraph 317)

Notice that here he seems to sidestep the very notion of the use of words, as well as sidestepping the notion of the meaning of a

---

[7] Ludwig Wittgenstein. *Remarks on Color* (Los Angeles: University of California Press, 1978), p. 58e, paragraph 317.

sentence being what one is thinking while using the words, made famous by David Hume.[8] What he focuses on instead is the idea that the import of words is "the difference they make at various points in life." Connected to this is his saying that "practices give words their meaning." The ideas of *making a difference* and *practice* are certainly compatible with both the Verification and Meaning-as-Use Principles, but there seems to be something more here. What that is exactly is admittedly unclear. Even so, I will suggest as I did above that here Wittgenstein is drawing the line between the *meaning* of a sentence on the one hand, and what it makes sense to *say* on the other. I will now take a closer look at this difference before bringing our brief examination to a close.

In *On Certainty*, Wittgenstein considers the following sorts of cases:

> Suppose that I were the doctor and a patient came to me, showed me his hand and said: "This thing that looks like a hand isn't just a superb imitation—it really is a hand" and went on to talk about his injury—should I really take this as a piece of information, even though a superfluous one? Shouldn't I be more likely to consider it nonsense, which admittedly did have the form of a piece of information?[9]

By 'nonsense' here, Wittgenstein does not appear to have in mind the idea that the sentence is *meaningless*. The sentence "This is my hand" is no doubt meaningful. But suppose, in line with what Wittgenstein says in the above passage, that I walk into a doctor's office having injured my hand and say, "Hey doc, I've injured my hand." So far, so good. But, now suppose that as I say this, I extend my hand and continue, "Oh, and *this* is my hand." Such a remark may be followed by the doctor's asking, "Did you hit your head, too?" As Wittgenstein says, it would be strange to take this as a piece of superfluous information, though one could do that. Rather, it would very likely be taken as a sign of my having some-

---

[8] I have in mind Hume's Ideational Theory of Meaning. See, for instance, David Hume's *An Enquiry Concerning Human Understanding* (Oxford: Clarendon, 1990), Section II, pp. 20–22

[9] Ludwig Wittgenstein. *On Certainty* (New York: Harper Torchbooks, 1969), p. 60e.

thing more seriously wrong with me than an injured hand. The idea here, I think, is that where it makes sense in this context for me to say "Hey doc, I've injured my hand," it does not make sense for me to say "This is my hand." The sentence just doesn't have a life in this context. To be sure, I can imagine contexts in which it would make sense to say it (again, I am reminded of my Navy days), but my visit to the doctor's office here isn't one of them. What is determining what it makes sense to say? Practice! By this Wittgenstein seems to mean the practice or the way of people in a community. He doesn't mean it in the sense that we do when we tell a kid to go and practice scales on the piano. As he puts it in *Philosophical Investigations*, he is considering a people's form of life: "to imagine a language is to imagine a *form of life*" (p. 8e, paragraph 19).

We might think of the ritual of greeting, or the telling of what brings one to the doctor, as language games. This is what Wittgenstein famously called them. "Here," he says (again, in *Philosophical Investigations*), "the term 'language-*game*' is meant to bring into prominence the fact that the *speaking* of language is part of an activity, or of a form of life" (p. 11e, paragraph 23). The things people do in communal life, their practices, underwrite what it will make sense to say. That seems to be very different from the conditions that underwrite the meanings of sentences (truth conditions, for example).

A bit later in *On Certainty*, Wittgenstein writes:

> This is certainly true, that the information "That is a tree", when no one could doubt it, might be a kind of joke and as such have meaning. A joke of this kind was in fact made once by Renan. (p. 61e)

And, he even produces a joke about a philosopher (G.E. Moore?):

> I am sitting with a philosopher in the garden; he says again and again "I know that that's a tree," pointing to a tree that is near us. Someone else arrives and hears this, and I tell him: "This fellow isn't insane. We are only doing philosophy." (p. 61e)

The statement "That is a tree" in the second passage is akin, I think, to "This is my hand" in the first and to "I know that that's a tree" in this last passage. That Wittgenstein would feel compelled to tell the onlooker that his philosopher friend is not insane but only doing philosophy is important—he wouldn't want the onlooker to react to his friend as the doctor reacts to the patient in the above injured-hand case. These cases, I think, help to illuminate our piston engine case (and show that my initial impulse to borrow René Magritte's "This is not a pipe" was not far from the mark).

Along the lines of the cases Wittgenstein introduces above, we might say that what strikes us as funny about Mrs. Non-Gorilla's reply (to the question of why she bought the piston engine) is that it is not really a reason for buying the engine after all, even though it takes the form of one. To be sure, we *could* count it as a *lousy* reason for buying it, but then we shouldn't be laughing at Mrs. Gorilla, as much as we should be pitying or rebuking her (for being so shallow or so stupid). And, we could take "No, . . . been shopping" as a customary response to the question "Been shopping?" but if we did, again we shouldn't find this funny, as much as we should find it an interesting custom. But, these aren't strangers with strange customs! They are working-class women at the park, who live somewhere in England (at least, this is the premise of the skit). Rather, the joke arises in its not being a response at all, even though it takes the form of one. Although we are led to believe (at first) that we are watching the social interaction of women in the park, who express interest in what the others have done, and so on, the joke is that we are not watching anything of the sort. And though the scene at first appears ordinary enough, at the end, along with Mrs. Smoker and Mrs. Non-Smoker, we walk off dazed and confused, reminded of something Hamlet tells Horatio: "There is more in heaven and earth, Horatio, than is dreamt of in your philosophy." Alas, Monty Python has pulled back the curtain. For, none of the philosophical theories of meaning will do. They have made Wittgenstein's point! A complete analysis of what these women say in terms of syntax, semantics, truth-conditions, use, and so on, will not capture what it is about their exchange that makes us laugh. There is simply more going on in the park than there is dreamt of in our philosophy. For whatever it is that is left over after we have accounted for meaning, which some will say is all there is to account for here, it is the leftovers that work their magic on us. It is the stuff that Horatio's philosophy cannot account for that seems to matter here.

5

Why Is an Argument Clinic Less Silly than an Abuse Clinic or a Contradiction Clinic?

HARRY BRIGHOUSE

Monty Python's Flying Circus drove numerous young people of my generation into philosophy. Having been driven into philosophy and stayed, I'm startled to notice how many references to philosophy in Monty Python have some basis in the reality of philosophy as a profession. The Bruces' Philosopher's Song (also known as the Australian Philosophers' Song), for example, is simultaneously a comment on the incongruity of an Australian accent (regarded by elitist Britons as crass and un-intellectual) combined with something as serious and highbrow as philosophy, and a tribute to the enormous influence that Australian philosophers had over English-speaking philosophy at the time, and still have.

Perhaps most striking of all to a practicing philosopher is the "Argument Clinic" sketch (*Monty Python's Flying Circus*, Episode 29, "The Money Programme"). The customer enters the Argument Clinic, after a false start with Mr. Barnard in the abuse room:

> **MR. BARNARD:** What do you want?
> **CUSTOMER:** Well, I was just . . .
> **MR. BARNARD:** Don't give me that, you snotty-faced heap of parrot droppings!
> **CUSTOMER:** What?

MR. BARNARD: Shut your festering gob, you tit! Your type really makes me puke, you vacuous, toffee-nosed, malodorous, pervert!!!

CUSTOMER: Look, I CAME HERE FOR AN ARGUMENT, I'm not going to just stand . . . !!

MR. BARNARD: OH! Oh I'm sorry, but this is Abuse.

He then finds Mr. Vibrating in the argument room:

CUSTOMER: Ah, is this the right room for an argument?
MR. VIBRATING: I told you once.
CUSTOMER: No you haven't.
MR. VIBRATING: Yes I have.
CUSTOMER: When?
MR. VIBRATING: Just now.
CUSTOMER: No you didn't.
MR. VIBRATING: Yes I did.
CUSTOMER: You didn't.
MR. VIBRATING: I did!
CUSTOMER: You didn't!
MR. VIBRATING: I'm telling you I did!
CUSTOMER: You did not!!

Slyly evoking the English pantomime tradition, the professional arguer simply contradicts every statement that the man seeking the argument makes.[1] The customer objects that

CUSTOMER: I came here for a good argument.

---

[1] This is not the only time the Pythons evoke this tradition; consider the more explicitly philosophical sketch in episode 27 of *Monty Python's Flying Circus* ("Whicker's World") in which Mrs. Premise and Mrs. Conclusion find themselves arguing about the meaning of Jean-Paul Sartre's 'Roads to Freedom':

MRS. PREMISE: . . . Well this is the whole crux of Jean-Paul Sartre's *Roads to Freedom*.
MRS. CONCLUSION: No, it bloody isn't. The nub of that is, his characters stand for all of us in their desire to avoid action. Mind you, the man at the off-license says it's an everyday story of French country folk.
MRS. PREMISE: What does he know?
MRS. CONCLUSION: Nothing.

MR. VIBRATING: No you didn't; no, you came here for an *argument*.

CUSTOMER: An argument isn't just contradiction.

MR. VIBRATING: It can be.

CUSTOMER: No it can't. An argument is a connected series of statements intended to establish a proposition.

MR. VIBRATING: No it isn't.

The customer goes on to draw the distinction as follows: "Argument is an intellectual process. Contradiction is just the automatic gainsaying of anything the other person says."

What Kind of Argument Would You Like?

The sketch works for numerous reasons. It seems absurd to "try out" an argument clinic, especially when, as any British viewer at that time knew, any normal person could get abuse and contradiction for free, just by calling a tradesperson or trying to buy something out of the ordinary at a department store (most older Britons of the time would have found the cheese shop sketch only a *slight* exaggeration of their experience). The idea that someone is able to turn on and off the habit of irritated contradiction at will is also funny. One of the things that makes the sketch work is that the professional's understanding of what an argument is fits well with a certain ordinary-language understanding of "argument." But in *that* sense of argument it is so easy to have one that it is hard to imagine anyone paying for one. The customer who wants

---

MRS. PREMISE: Sixty new pence for a bottle of Maltese Claret. Well I personally think Jean-Paul's masterwork is an allegory of man's search for commitment.

MRS. CONCLUSION: No it isn't.

MRS. PREMISE: Yes it is.

MRS. CONCLUSION: Isn't.

MRS. PREMISE: 'Tis.

MRS. CONCLUSION: No it isn't.

MRS. PREMISE: All right. We can soon settle this. We'll ask him.

MRS. CONCLUSION: Do you know him?

MRS. PREMISE: Yes, we met on holiday last year.

to engage in something akin to a verbal game of chess wants his ideas to be taken on, thought through, and refuted, in an intellectually stimulating process. He wants, in other words, something like a philosophical argument, but, unphilosophically, has failed to specify what he wants.

The professional contradictor does, in fact, display an ability to argue in this sense: he correctly distinguishes 'argument' from 'good argument' and rightly points out that an argument can consist of mere iterated contradiction. But his arguing about the argument just makes it even more frustrating for the client. He will not engage in a true argument about anything substantive.

Philosophers like the sketch for at least two reasons. First, argument is just about all we are good at: it is not at all uncommon for a philosopher to exclaim dismissively "but that's an empirical, not a philosophical, issue," and by that they mean that evidence is irrelevant: argument is the only guide to the truth. Second, frankly, the idea of a world in which our narrow range of skills find a market like the market for accountants and hairdressers strikes us both as delightful and absurd; we fantasize that in that world we might make more money.

But the sketch also poses a puzzle. As I mentioned, viewers at the time would have known that contradiction could be accessed for free just by walking into any shop or workplace. Why, though, would someone go to an argument clinic for a "good" argument? What the client wants is for someone to show him what is wrong with his own beliefs and reasons for those beliefs. Why would he pay for *that*? Doesn't it seem, as I said earlier, absurd?

One possible reason would be, simply, for intellectual stimulation: a kind of work-out for the mind, or mental game of tennis. But there is another, rather different, reason, which I shall spend the rest of this chapter explaining. It is, in short, this: that *only through a process of argument with other people can most of us hope to come to have true beliefs about matters of any complexity*. In explaining this, I am going to focus on my own area of expertise within philosophy, which is moral philosophy. But I think the claim is true in other areas of philosophy, and even beyond philosophy.

The *Philosophical* Argument and Reflective Equilibrium

What constitutes a philosophical argument? How does somebody go about constructing one? What, in other words, would the client be getting if he got what he wanted, at least if he got it from a philosopher? Assuming that most readers have a limited exposure to professional philosophy, I want to describe how philosophers go about making arguments, focusing on a particular method popularized by the American philosopher John Rawls (1926–2002), known as *reflective equilibrium*.[2]

Philosophy is the systematic study of questions, the answers to which cannot be determined simply by gathering observational data about the world and making hypotheses about those data. "What is on the telly?" is not a philosophical question, because ultimately it has to be addressed through observation. "What is the nature of knowledge?," by contrast, is philosophical. Without experiences we could not address it, but its answer does not rest on observation. Philosophical questions may well have determinate answers. There is a truth about them. But theoretical, rather than empirical, reason is the means to arriving at the truth. My own particular interest is in moral philosophy, the field within philosophy that asks questions about how we should live our lives, and what constitutes goodness. It addresses large general questions such as "What makes a flourishing human life?"; "Does the moral value of actions lie in their consequences or in the motives behind them?" and "Are states of affairs or the characters of persons the ultimate bearers of value?" and also much more specific questions such as "Is abortion morally wrong?" and "Is it ever right to lie?"

These questions simply cannot be answered by gathering empirical, or scientific, evidence. So how do we try to work out the answers to them? Philosophy rejects appeals to authority. Good philosophers never offer anything like "As the great thinker Arthur "Two Sheds" Jackson argues . . ." as *support* for their claims (although they might preface an explanation of what is *wrong* with Arthur's views with a comment on his greatness). So they can't

---

[2] John Rawls, *A Theory of Justice* (Cambridge, Massachusetts: Harvard University Press, 1971).

resort to *The Holy Bible*, the Ten Commandments, or the sayings of Spike Milligan, profound as they are. Such appeals replace the question "What is moral?" with "Why are Spike Milligan's, or *The Holy Bible*'s, sayings morally authoritative?" But we can't answer that question without establishing what is moral in the first place. So we might as well have started with that question.

Since neither authority nor empirical evidence is decisive, how do we do it? As suggested above, the method that most contemporary philosophers use is what Rawls called *reflective equilibrium*. This method invites us to approach questions about morality, and philosophical questions generally, in the following way. Taking up a topic like justice, or punishment, or lying, we first list our considered judgments about specific *particular* cases, and look at whether these all fit together consistently. Where we find that they don't fit together we reject those judgments in which we have least confidence (for example, those in which we have reason to suspect there is an element of self-interest pressing us to that particular judgment). We also list the general principles, or rules, we judge suitable to cover cases, and look to see if those principles fit together as well, again rejecting the principles in which we have least confidence. Then we look at the particular judgments and the principles in the light of one another—do *they* fit together? Do some of the principles look less plausible in the light of the weight of considered judgments, or *vice versa*?

Of course, all that this method gives us is, at best, a set of judgments that fit together; what philosophers call a *consistent* set of judgments. But if we engage in the process collectively, in conversation with others who are rational like us, we can have increasing confidence in the truth of the outcomes. Other people can bring out considerations we had not noticed; they can alert us to weaknesses in our own judgments; they can force us to think harder and better. If we converge on conclusions about particular cases with people with whom we otherwise disagree a great deal, we should have even more confidence in our judgment. We can't ever be certain that we have arrived at a final, true view of justice, or punishment, or lying. But this method at least gives us a way of making some progress.

What exactly do I mean by "judgments about particular cases" and "principles"? An autobiographical comment which, I'm afraid, does not reflect particularly well on me, will help. In the late 1970s I held a view that, I think, was quite common among British teenagers with my political outlook, which was that there was no reason to grant free speech to racists, or anyone with anti-social views, and that it was entirely fine for the government to censor offensive films. So, the principle I held was something like this: "Governments should have the power to censor expression when it meets some objective criteria for being anti-social." One morning I turned on the radio and heard Jimmy Young (a DJ) announce that he was soon going to be talking to a Church of England vicar who was trying to have a new film, "Rimbaud," banned from his local cinema. My reaction was outrage—"How dare this busy-bodying minister try to shut down a film about the great homosexual French poet Arthur Rimbaud?" (Here we have a judgment about an individual case: it is wrong to censor *this* film). When the discussion began, however, it turned out that the vicar objected not to the film's portrayal of homosexuality, but to its excessive violence. The film was, in fact, entirely devoid of reference to homosexuality or poetry, and had I heard the vicar without having been confused about his topic, I would have agreed with every word he said (the judgment about the individual case I *would* have had: "It is fine to censor *this* film"). The film was, of course, called "Rambo," not "Rimbaud," and starred Sylvester Stallone (who would have been an eccentric, not to say Pythonesque, choice for Rimbaud). The two judgments are not strictly speaking inconsistent, but what the incident brought home to me was that my real reason for defending one rather than another film from censorship was not that one met some objective standard of anti-sociality, but that one reflected my values and the other clashed with them. In other words my judgment did not reflect the principle I brought to the cases, but self-interest of a certain sort; the same sort of self-interest that had, incidentally, led only a year or two earlier to calls for censoring *Monty Python's Life of Brian.*

Suppose You Were Attached to a Dead Parrot: The Role of Thought Experiments

How do we isolate our judgments about particular cases? Usually we are not so lucky as to be forced by a disc jockey to think things through. There are several methods of isolating our particular judgments, but I am going to focus on one of the most prominent, what philosophers call the *thought experiment.* Thought experiments tend to be very unrealistic inventions, in which the theorist imagines a situation in which implementing a principle has an unacceptable consequence, or in which two judgments that we previously thought were consistent in fact conflict. Often the thought experiment is supposed to be analogous to a real life case in all relevant respects, but shows up the inapplicability of some judgment to the real-life case. The most famous, and in my view the greatest, thought experiment in moral philosophy is Judith Jarvis Thomson's "violinist" case, in her article "A Defense of Abortion."[3] Thomson makes an analogy between the case of abortion in which the prospective mother has conceived as a result of rape, and the following case: a famous violinist is dying of a rare blood disease, which can only by cured by having you (the reader) hooked up to him for a certain amount of time (say nine months) so that he can use your body to cleanse his liver. No one else will do—because, say, you and he are the only people in the world with a certain blood type. A Society of Music Lovers takes it upon itself to kidnap you and hook you up to the violinist. When you awake you find yourself able to unhook yourself and walk away. Thomson asks whether the violinist has the right to your body in this manner, and assumes that most of her readers will say "no." But, she says, what is the difference between this case and the case of abortion, where the pregnancy arose from rape? The prospective mother is being used by the fetus, and only she will do for its purposes. She is not in that situation out of choice: she was forced into it by someone else (not, admittedly, the fetus, but nor did the violinist force you into being hooked up to him). So, abortion, at least in the case of rape, is not wrong.

Thomson deploys other thought experiments to show that abortion is permissible in a much wider range of cases, but I want to focus on what this, very limited, thought-experiment actually shows. When I teach Thomson's article I find that most of the students who oppose abortion are not persuaded that there is anything acceptable about abortion. But in fact Thomson's article is

---

[3] Judith Jarvis Thomson, "A Defense of Abortion," *Philosophy and Public Affairs* 1 (1971), pp. 47–66.

less directed at showing there is a right to abortion than to showing something quite different: that whatever is wrong with abortion has nothing to do with the right to life of the fetus. Whereas supporters and opponents of abortion rights frequently argue over whether the fetus has a right to life, Thomson concedes at the start that it does. Her thought-experiment is so striking because the violinist, who is supposed to be analogous to the fetus, is an adult, with all the rights and moral standing that adults typically have. When we say that we are entitled to walk away from the violinist, we do so in the knowledge that he is an adult who certainly has a right to life, and that he will die if we walk away, and, crucially, that even though he will die we will not be violating his right to life. Opponents of abortion believe the fetus has a right to life, and that the violinist has a right to life. They are not forced by Thomson's thought experiment to give up the view that abortion is wrong, even in the case where pregnancy arises from rape. But, if they want to say that it is permissible to walk away from the violinist, they are forced to look for some other grounds than the right to life of the fetus for justifying the wrongness of abortion. In my own experience I find that students are, like Mr. Vibrating, quite ingenious. They can almost always find other grounds for supporting what they believe, but what they have given up is the central slogan of the anti-abortion movement: "right to life." Sure, fetuses have rights to life, but that cannot be why abortion is wrong.

I've dwelled on this example, because it neatly displays both the power and the limits of thought-experiments. Good thought experiments are powerful because they can force us to interrogate judgments we had previously simply assumed, and show them to be groundless. But they are also limited. By themselves they do not support substantive conclusions about what is right and wrong, but only show that certain kinds of reasons support (or fail to support) such conclusions.

Moreover, we have to recognize that individually and collectively we are subject to all sorts of biases and prejudices that we cannot readily filter out about these matters. We are reluctant to see our own behaviors as systematically wrong, and, like it or not, we have a tendency to normalize the values of our own social framework. For example, a world in which women are systematically barred from using certain occupational skills is one in which they will tend to be seen both by men *and women* as less capable of exercising those skills. We all, now, see what was wrong with slavery or witch-burning, but when these practices were in force they were seen as normal by nearly all involved. So reflective equilibrium, when conducted as a variant of personal meditation, gets us only so far. Getting to the full truth requires that we have an array of interlocutors: people with different perspectives who can challenge our biases and help us to transcend the limits of our own efforts. When women entered the debate about women's status in society they presented arguments and perspectives that were not previously in play, and which the men involved in the debate may not have been able, or at least may not have bothered, to imagine. The wider the participation in reflective equilibrium, the more likely the process is, other things being equal, to lead us toward the truth.

This brings us back to the Argument Clinic. One's own perspective on moral, and other, matters is necessarily limited. This doesn't mean that one is completely stuck in one's own perspective; one can, and should, think as far beyond it as one can. But often, one needs help: someone or, preferably, many people, to present alternatives, with whom one can then uncover agreement and disagreement. Mere contradiction, entertaining as it is to a pantomime audience, simply does not serve this purpose.

This philosophical point also tells us something about Monty Python's humor and why many people find both Monty Python and thought-experiments ludicrous when they first encounter them. Good thought experiments have a great deal in common with good absurd sketches, of the kind the Python team excels in (and, I think, the kind of creativity required to produce them is very similar). They both depend on an internal logic, which may look absurd from the outside. So the Pet Shop owner in the Parrot Sketch (*Monty Python's Flying Circus*, Episode 8, "Full Frontal Nudity") has at his fingertips a huge array of alternative possibilities to the Norwegian Blue being dead; and the customer has an equally rich array of ways of making the point that the parrot is, in fact, dead. The structure of the sketch depends on this contrast, and the pieces of the sketch have to fit together. Thought experiments and Python sketches also both depend on a connection with the world. The thought experiment has to be connected in a way that isolates the intuitive judgments that are at issue;

the absurdist sketch has to connect with some aspect of the audience's experience enough so that it is possible to suspend disbelief for the duration of the sketch. And, in fact, some sketches are themselves rather like thought experiments; they say "Of course, this couldn't happen or isn't going to happen. But let's ask what would make sense if it *did* happen." The "Argument Clinic" works better than it otherwise would precisely because, as I am arguing, argument—much more than mere contradiction or abuse—engages us aesthetically as well as intellectually.

Far from being absurd, then, it is entirely sensible to go to an argument clinic (as the client understands it). If one has strong ideas about parrots, it may even make sense to go to Michael Palin's pet shop. If we are committed to uncovering the truth about matters of human value or other matters of great complexity, we usually need other smart, good-willed, and intellectually serious people to alert us to perspectives and reasons we would not have been able to conjure up on our own. If more people sought argument clinics the world would be a better place, and not only because philosophers would be richer.

6

A Very Naughty Boy:
Getting Right with Brian

RANDALL E. AUXIER

How I Was Saved

et's start by just facing it. We're all sinners—not me so much as you, because I've actually done pretty well, but I could stand a bit of regeneration and I can see that *you* are in real trouble with you-know-Who. He told me so Himself, last night, over a bottle of Two-Buck-Chuck. He likes cheap wine because, well, He loves a bargain. Here is the point. I have a message for you from Him, so listen up: "You are to regard the following essay as revealed, on peril of your eternal soul" (and if you are reading this, I'm sure the peril is quite real). I don't ask any more of you than would any other inspired being.

How came I to possess such particular favor with He-Who-cannot-be-named? I was a delinquent of fourteen, wandering down a street in Memphis, when a small band of renegade Baptists sidled up to me, sincerely inquiring as to the likely destination of my soul.[1] I said I was late to meet my dealer. They were undeterred. I told them he would be armed and dangerous, and that he was a Methodist. That just encouraged them. They said that if I would pray a simple prayer with them and ask Brian into

---

[1] I don't want to single out Baptists for ridicule. Some of my best friends were once Baptists. And I have enough ridicule to spread among many deserving factions, each convinced that the others are bound for Hades. This special conviction is my cue that God wants me to make fun of them.

my heart, my life would be changed, Brian would take away my sins and save me a seat on that Great Greyhound to Chicago (you can't go to hell or heaven without a layover in Chicago). I could see these were no ordinary Baptists. These fellows *had* something. That was long ago, and many things have been revealed to me since, including the actual code for the Microsoft Operating System, which I now know to have come directly from Satan. I stand before you today an altered man, yes, some of it was surgical, but some came by direct action of the Almighty. If you care for your soul, turn back.

God Is Dead
(and I'm Not Feeling so Good Myself)

Alright, I can see *your* priorities. Let me play, then, Virgil to your Dante, Socrates to your Plato, Pontius Pilate to your Biggus . . . well, never mind. Let's examine the remarkable, sinless life of Brian Cohen (Maximus) in light of certain philosophical and theological worries. And regarding such worries, God is on top of the heap, so let's get right to that. This may be objectionable to some. Perhaps I'm bound for the infernal region. Handily, my Baptist friends believed that once you are saved, you'll *always* be saved, and they have even been known to toss out those who disagree (although I was never clear whether *that* is enough to get a person "unsaved"). It seems the Baptists can send you *on your way*, but not precisely to hell, so they, along with most Protestants, seem to have signed a sort of non-proliferation of damnation pact, abdicating the nuclear option for the soul. The Roman Catholics wisely retain their weapon stock, leaving them the only remaining super(natural)-power. But as I mentioned, *I* got saved by the Baptists and I am not going to look a gift-Deity (or badger) in the mouth. *You* are quite another matter. You may need to go and find your own Baptists. Mine are probably in heaven by now. But it is your soul I am most worried about, as you will see.

So, God. In 1882, Friedrich Nietzsche (1844–1900), in an especially foul mood, published the following infamous words (except they were in German):

Have you not heard of that madman who lit a lantern in the bright morning hours, ran to the market place and cried inces-

santly: "I seek God! I seek God!" As many of those who did
not believe in God were standing around just then, he pro-
voked much laughter. "Is God lost?" one asked. . . . "Or is he
hiding?" "Is he afraid of us?" "Has he gone on a voyage?
Emigrated?" [I thought God was non-migratory.] The madman jumped into their midst. . . . "Whither is God?" he cried.
"I will tell you. *We have killed him*, you and I. All of us are his
murderers. But how did we do this? How could we drink up
the sea? . . . [a dozen more such questions] . . . Do we hear
nothing yet of the gravediggers of God? . . . God is dead. God
remains dead. And we have killed him.[2]

Nietzsche was never renowned for his lightness of heart. It is not
easy to distinguish the philosophical from the theological sense in
this little narrative. Until recently both theologians and philosophers were plenty occupied with the Big Guy, so how to tell the
difference?

One might think, "no theologian would proclaim the death of
God," but in the 1960s a bunch of theologians got a wild hair and
did just that, and started wringing their hands over what becomes
of theology afterwards.[3] It was a silly time. They mostly went
away, some not by their own choosing. So what is Nietzsche on
about, and what makes it philosophy?

In the passage, the crowd of unbelievers is laughing at the man
who would be sincere. Make no mistake, this is all about laughing
at God, and what perils to the soul accompany this activity. What
kills God is the laughter—or at least, laughter kills the *cheerless* God
sought by those whose dominant religious passion is wrapped in
pathos. Few have contributed more to laughing at such a God (and
His followers) than the loyal Pythons, but they begin by having
God (a less austere one) laugh at such believers. In *Monty Python
and The Holy Grail*, addressing the believers adopting the "correct"
pathos, God says: "Oh, don't grovel . . . do get up! If there's one
thing I can't stand it's people groveling!!" When Arthur apolo-

[2] Friedrich Nietzsche, *The Gay Science* (New York: Vintage, 1974), p. 181 (translation slightly modified).
[3] See Thomas J.J. Altizer, *The Gospel of Christian Atheism* (Philadelphia:
Westminster Press, 1966); Altizer and William Hamilton, *Radical Theology and the
Death of God* (Indianapolis: Bobbs-Merrill, 1966).

gizes, God rebukes him: "And don't apologize. Every time I try to talk to someone it's sorry this and forgive me that and I'm not worthy . . ." and "It's like those miserable psalms. They're so depressing. Now knock it off."[4] This is the sort of situation into which Nietzsche's "madman" steps, as a pathetic follower (or so he is *taken* to be by those laughing). The laughter is the clue that whatever reverence the solemn God once commanded has lost its grip. This may be the "madman's" point, of course.

This Deity Is Bleedin' Demised

Nietzsche is quite right. If that God ever really existed, He is dead now. That so many people find the Pythons funny is Nietzsche's justification. The God of our Victorian foreparents doesn't frighten us now nearly so much as a Stephen King novel, although His followers (God's, not King's) are still numerous enough and in themselves *plenty* scary and increasingly desperate in an unbelieving world. Stephen King's followers are scarier when one sits near them at dinner, although they get on nicely with Nietzsche's people, since they all wear black, chew with their mouths open, and happily endure the interminable ramblings of self-indulgent writers who need editors far more than followers. The old God has been reduced now to a weapon of mass destruction, wielded by those angry about His death. Yet, to have a personal relationship with the dead God, one must supplement the historic pathos with a peculiar narcissistic psychosis.[5] This psychosis I will call "the Comic," following a usage by Henri Bergson (1859–1943), which I will explain in a moment. For now, grant that reflection upon the difference between the *history* of the pathos of Christianity and its modern transformation into a psychosis is very much a philosophical matter, not a theological one, and this is what Nietzsche was foreseeing.

Philosophy is reflection upon *all* experience and aims at self-knowledge, *including* religious experience and ideas like "God." Theology, by contrast, is reflection upon religious experience and ideas, undertaken in faith that such experiences do exist and such

---

[4] Graham Chapman, *et al.*, *Monty Python and the Holy Grail (Book)* (New York: Methuen, 1980), pp. 23–24.
[5] Freud describes the problem in *The Future of an Illusion* (New York: Norton, 1927).

ideas do refer to realities beyond themselves. This makes theology a more specialized activity. If you are already offended by what I have said, you'll prefer theology. But there may still be a God never dreamed of in your theology, and He (or She, or It) may be laughing at you. On the far side of theology, you don't know very much; even Dr. bloody Bronowski doesn't know very much.[6]

That "far side" is where philosophical consideration of God finds itself after a couple of World Wars and a Cold War. Thus, where the faith can no longer be assumed, one moves past theology into philosophy. While we might be tempted to build an "alternative theology" based upon the Pythonic revelation, indeed, *sorely* tempted (forgive me Brian), instead we need to grasp how the Pythons enter the philosophical world precisely on the assumption that (the old) God is dead, or at least might be (I mean, maybe he's not dead yet, but will be any moment). At the end of the infamous passage quoted above, Nietzsche's madman says "I have come too early. My time is not yet. This tremendous event is still on its way."[7] If his time was not yet in 1882, certainly by 1979 (when *Monty Python's Life of Brian* was filmed) the days had been accomplished. The Pythons speak of God and all this hilarity is not only tolerated, it drowns out the rage of those "serious" Christians.

Yet, laughing at God is dicey business any time. As I said, I'm right with Brian, and I am here to help *you* get right; I think it may be too late for Nietzsche. Even the Mormons, with their wise doctrine of salvation for the dead, show no interest in reclamation of the retiring little guy with the migraine that wouldn't quit. In some ways, however, Nietzsche's seriousness touches upon a characteristic of all that is comic. We can use it here.

So Brian Cohen (Maximus) stands continually before new incarnations of the same crowd as Nietzsche's madman, asking the same sorts of questions. But Brian's pathos is different from the madman's; Brian has the sincerity of the divine idiot.[8] Recall

---

[6] Dr. Jacob Bronowski, author of *The Ascent of Man* (Boston: Little, Brown, 1973), which is the text version of a TV series produced by the BBC. Bronowski, who "knows everything," was a mathematician, statistician, poet, historian, teacher, inventor and a leader in the Scientific Humanism movement.

[7] Nietzsche, *The Gay Science*, p. 182.

[8] Nietzsche associates Jesus himself with the psychological type of the divine idiot, and means it as praise for Jesus. See *The Anti-Christ* (Harmondsworth: Penguin, 1969), Section 29.

the following exchange, when Brian finds himself obliged to prophesy:

> **Brian**: Don't you, eh, pass judgment on other people, or you might get judged yourself.
> **Colin**: What?
> **Brian**: I said, 'Don't pass judgment on other people, or else you might get judged, too.'
> **Colin**: Who, me?
> **Brian**: Yes.
> **Colin**: Oh. Ooh. Thank you very much.
> **Brian**: Well, not just you. All of you. . . . Yes. Consider the lilies . . . in the field.
> **Elsie**: Consider the lilies?
> **Brian**: Uh, well, the birds, then.
> **Eddie**: What birds?
> **Brian**: Any birds.
> **Eddie**: Why?
> **Brian**: Well, have they got jobs?
> **Eddie**: Who?
> **Brian**: The birds.
> **Eddie**: Have the birds got jobs?!
> **Frank**: What's the matter with him?
> **Arthur**: He says the birds are scrounging.
> **Brian**: Oh, uhh, no, the point is the birds. They do all right. Don't they?
> **Frank**: Well, good luck to 'em.
> **Eddie**: Yeah. They're very pretty.
> **Brian**: Okay, and you're much more important than they are, right? So, what are you worrying about? There you are. See?
> **Eddie**: I'm worrying about what you have got against birds.
> **Brian**: I haven't got anything against the birds. Consider the lilies.
> **Arthur**: He's having a go at the flowers now.[9]

All one needs is a literal-minded group who neither believes nor disbelieves, asking obvious questions. Religious sincerity crum-

---

[9] See *Monty Python's Life of Brian*.

bles. The same could be done to any preacher in his pulpit any-where, but none will do it. Yet when fire-and-brimstone evangel-ists ply their trade on college campuses, sometimes this scene is replayed. More often the listeners are beset with the countervail-ing pathos, opposing the pathos of the evangelist. Throughout *Monty Python's Life of Brian*, *detachment* from pathos pushes the plot and generates the humor. The story depends not upon mocking God, Jesus, or even Brian, but upon holding oneself at a distance, not allowing the countervailing pathos of opposition to take hold—Nietzsche called this countervailing pathos *ressentiment*.[10] And how is the latter pathos avoided? One can rise above it, as would an *Übermensch*, but that isn't funny; or one can idiotically fall below this dialectic, a sort of divine *Untermensch*. Brian doesn't claim to know anything. He would be glad to, but he doesn't. He is a well-meaning moral idiot, just like nearly everyone else. When questioned, he shifts ground and finally gives up, like anyone with common sense.

The Plumage Don't Enter into It

Thus, the death of God is not *simply* the end of a certain concept of God, nor of the power of that concept to fill us with fear. The death of God is the onset of a detachment from the entire ques-tion of God, and common sense telling us that *no one* actually has the answers to questions like "is there a God?" Those who pos-sess such detachment by native temperament find Pythonic reli-gious humor pleasing, while those who do not find it troubling, offensive, or even blasphemous. Common-sense detachment from impossible questions leads us to tend our *mortal* souls, leaving the immortal soul, if there is one, to its own fortunes.

Today we need not be as upset about all this as Nietzsche. He thought that killing off this old God means humans would have to bear God's burden—and would be unequal to the task. But I think we are probably up to the chore, which is part of the reve-lation I received when I asked Brian into my heart. Yet there real-ly is a "moment of decision" Brian puts to his hearers: "shall I

---

[10] See Nietzsche, *Ecce Homo and On the Genealogy of Morals* (New York: Vintage, 1967), pp. 36–37, 40, 73f, and so on.

shun this, be offended by this, condemn this?" If the still small voice in the back of your brain says, as mine did: "no, *if* there is a God, He's surely enjoying this too, and if not, bugger Him," then you are open to salvation of the sort Brian brings. Of course, this is salvation *from* the pathos of religious authorities who would ruin your cheer with their dreary pronouncements of Hellfire, with a thinly veiled confidence in the absolute truth of their own convictions (concealing an utterly unconscious fear that they may be wrong). Their confidence is difficult to distinguish from mere pride, but it is best not to judge, since, as Brian taught, you might get judged yourself if you do it. Better to laugh. They can't do much about that—at least, not any more.

According to Henri Bergson, "the Comic" just is anything overly stiff that holds itself opposed to the flow of experience, and when its rigid bearing is noted by others, laughter results. The person who is "comic" has at least two very important characteristics. First is this mechanical inelasticity, this rigidity amid what should be a flowing present. Second, a "comic" person is invisible to himself *as* comic, does not realize he is being rigid. As Bergson says, "the comic person is unconscious. As though wearing the ring of Gyges with reverse effect, he becomes invisible to himself while remaining visible to all the world."[11] Hence, the art of the straight man affects sincerity, rigidity, unself-conscious pathos—and the Pythons, especially Chapman and Cleese, are among the best straight men comedy has ever produced. But for the pathetic follower of the dead God, comic rigidity is no affectation, it is a mode of existence. So the issue is not *whether* religious fundamentalists are utterly comic, the crux of the matter is whether anyone will point it out so that we can all laugh. But your soul is still in jeopardy, so don't laugh yet.

We have more to say of rigidity and the comic, but please grant that it is far more difficult to be funny about things that are already funny, like the Pythons, because funny stuff isn't rigid and comic. In such situations one needs recourse to the lower types of humor: puns, off-color jokes, ethnic slurs, or, at the very bottom rung, politics. We are not scrupulous people. Let's do politics.

---

[11] Henri Bergson, *Laughter* (New York: Macmillan, 1911), pp. 16–17. The ring of Gyges is a Greek legend (see Plato in *The Republic*, Book II) about a ring that turns the wearer invisible, bringing absolute power and some very naughty behavior.

Romani Ite Domum

It is hard to be the only remaining super-power. One's empire is always getting a bad rap. But there is no pleasing some people, as both Jesus and Brian taught. Bring people the aquaduct, sanitation, roads, medicine, education, order, peace, and even the public baths and good wine, and what do you get? Just complaints about little foibles that come along with it—a taste for ocelot spleens and jaguar's earlobes, or blood pudding and Branston Pickle. British humor has a connection to Roman stoicism, for the humor works in inverse proportion to the degree in which the humorists' culture is repressed: the more repressed the conquerors, the greater the comic possibilities, which is one reason why British humor seems almost surreal to the American ear (one can hardly be more repressed than the British). But get one thing straight: It's *their* empire, not ours, even when we have temporary administrative responsibility.

On a recent trip to Britain I discovered to my (very American) dismay that the British are unimpressed with American wine. I was poking around in a good wine store in Oxford and finding little or nothing American to drink. I affected my best British accent (the secret is to speak without moving the upper lip, the rest takes care of itself, with some practice), and inquired after some wine from California. The clerk (pronounced "clark") lilted back: "'aven't got any; tried it once, can't sell the stuff." He had spam, though. I had thought they made some pretty good wine in California, and here it isn't even taken seriously. And if you pour what the Brits know about wine-making into a thimble, it wouldn't even be half empty. No matter. Obviously I am a colonist. Having worn out the bit about "taxation without representation," I'm looking now for the headquarters of the American People's Front. What have the lousy British ever done for us?

And here's the lesson of empire. Empire takes mettle. It isn't for nancies or pleasure-loving creatures of comfort like Australians and the Americans. Empire requires one weapon: organizational genius. And of course, an unfailing sense of what is and is not important. So the *two* weapons of empire are organizational genius and an unfailing sense of what is and is not important. *And* perfect confidence in one's own superiority. So, the *three* weapons of empire are: organizational genius, an unfailing sense of what is and is not important, and a perfect confidence

in one's own superiority. I mean, *nobody* expects a perfect confidence in one's own superiority. "Great race, the Romans," says
Michael Palin, hanging from the ceiling in chains the Romans
granted him the privilege of wearing. But the same might be said
of the British. It takes an astonishingly blithe attitude toward suffering (your own *and* other people's) to keep hopping in your boats
and invading every place you can even land, not to mention constantly having to spank (for their *own* good) the troublesome
Dutch and French and Spanish who are without even the decency
to bring British civilization to other lands. No, the Aussies and
Yanks don't have that in them.

To illustrate, it is far, far more important that Brian be made
to conjugate his Latin correctly than that he be silenced from saying "Romans Go Home." The true threat to empire is people who
refuse to learn the *lingua franca* correctly. Was I not, after all, asking after American wine in the Queen's own English? When in
Rome. . . . History is a stubborn and harsh teacher. Right up to
my own middle school years we were still learning, at the tip of a
blade, to conjugate Latin. The language had been dead for five
centuries. Now *that's* an impressive cultural imperialism. People
will be learning the Queen's English everywhere for another two
millennia, minimum. Some things come and go, some come and
stay. Latin and English are of the latter sort. The Romans and the
Britons, kindred spirits and stoically convinced of the unlimited
power of self-mastery, are confident that when they have impart-
ed their cultural forms to lesser people, that's all that can be done
for our betterment.

Having borne the superior man's burden, a Roman or a Briton
may freely stare in incomprehension at the ridiculous behavior of
his empire's foreign subjects. Yes, the foreigners have silly beliefs
and customs; it hardly matters. But let them misuse the mother
tongue and, well, they're in for a good thrashing. It is little known
that the actual cause of the American Revolution was an intense
desire on the part of the British to teach table manners to the
colonists. Not the Battle of Yorktown but our utter incompetence
at eating peas off the convex curve of a fork led the British to give
up on civilizing us. We would have to improve ourselves after
1783.

But our superior masters, Roman or British, ask no more of us
than they ask of themselves—not one of the Queen's native sub-

jects can possibly fail to see his own Latin teacher in Cleese's centurion, nor fail to see himself in Brian's own cowering submission to correction. Romanes eunt domus? I think not. A hundred times on the blackboard and no blood pudding. And of course, if Americans had anything like the British confidence of civilized superiority, they wouldn't make such a fuss about being the greatest nation since 1066. Americans go on so much about it just because they *know* it isn't true. Don't be misled by a few simplified spellings, you self-appointed purveyors of American superiority. You know you love the Queen. You *know* you do. Praise Brian for the self-loathing Canadians. With them around at least Americans can feel superior to one other passel of British subjects. Now have some back bacon and return to your seat.

But there is more to it. One thing that is utterly lost on American audiences is how the Pythons use British class-consciousness as a continual source of contextual humor. Apart from the social situations themselves, the class consciousness is mainly conveyed by the various accents adopted by the Python characters, all the way from Terry Jones's shrillest cockney up to John Cleese's Oxbridge titter. It is no accident that the individual Pythons tend to occupy roles that cast them within the same class range of British society (with *some* small social mobility). But a lot of their posture towards all things British has to do with the re-enactment of their *own* class forms, made comic. It is the very rigidity of British class consciousness that creates the comic context.

And here we draw closer to the true secret that was revealed to me by God. The British understand the Romans so well because they built an empire to rival Rome's own—not only by organizational genius, or an unfailing sense of what is and is not important, or by a perfect confidence in their own superiority, but also by sheer self-mastery and utter repression of all emotional weaknesses. So, four weapons. Five is right out. And the unexpected gift that accompanies these repressions is, surprisingly, an ability on the part of Romans and Britains to laugh at *themselves*. Americans simply don't possess this capacity, at least not *qua* American. The British, like the Romans, are fascinated with how well they can mock themselves. Americans, lacking the needed detachment, become unconscious of their own pathos. The Americans may laugh *at* the British, but not at themselves, and which is the greater virtue? This is why Americans could never have built the empire they now enjoy at the beneficent *noblesse oblige* of their British cousins (shame that the French got that phrase when the British own the virtue). Americans do not *want* to suffer for the sake of imparting higher culture to a barbaric world. They want to make money and B movies and live in Florida. Only their own comfort, security and wealth moves them in any serious way. Yes, yes, democracy, freedom, things of that nature, but it's not like we will hop in our boats and go off to create it (not really). The British and the Romans willingly ordered their societies in ways as repressive to themselves as to those they conquered for the *sake* of civilizing the world, and without a moment's doubt that they were the ones to do it. But of course, this is funny, is it not, or more precisely, "comic"?

Are they able to laugh at themselves *because* their sense of superiority is so little threatened by seeing how comical it is? Or are they actually superior *because* they have always been able to laugh at themselves? This is too great a question. Neither God nor Brian has revealed this bit to me.

A Good Spanking

You may doubt that anyone, even a writer with a special revelation, could now tie together all this business about God being dead and the comic and politics and empire, but you underestimate the power of Brianic salvation. Your lack of faith is appalling. I should give you all a good spanking. Like an alien craft catching my fall from the tower of my own babbling, comes the saving stroke of an Italian pen.

The idea of laughter as blasphemy is nicely joined to its class context near the end of Umberto Eco's *The Name of the Rose*, a historical novel set in 1327. An old Spanish monk named Jorge, the librarian of a remote abbey, booby-traps the very last copy of Aristotle's (now) lost treatise on comedy. Jorge is unable to bring himself to destroy the blasphemous book (he is a librarian after all), or allow anyone to *read* it (I always suspect librarians of secretly not trusting me with their books, and really wanting them all for themselves). Thus, he poisons the pages so that anyone will die from the sin of reading it. William of Baskerville, Eco's protagonist, a sort of medieval Sherlock Holmes (and proper

Englishman), asks the old librarian in the climactic scene: "What frightened you in this discussion of laughter? You cannot eliminate laughter by eliminating the book." The old monk answers, in a speech that would make even John Calvin proud:

> No, to be sure. But laughter is weakness, corruption, the foolishness of our flesh. It is the peasant's entertainment, the drunkard's license. . . . laughter remains base, a defense for the simple, a mystery desecrated for the plebeians . . . laugh and enjoy your foul parodies of order, at the end of the meal, after you have drained jugs and flasks. Elect the king of fools, lose yourselves in the liturgy of the ass and the pig, play at performing your saturnalia head down. . . . But here, here [indicating Aristotle's book] the function of laughter is reversed, it is elevated to art, the doors of the world of the learned are opened to it, it becomes the object of philosophy, and of perfidious theology. . . . [T]he church can deal with the heresy of the simple, who condemn themselves on their own...provided the act is not transformed into plan, provided this vulgar tongue does not find a Latin that translates it . . . in the feast of fools, the Devil also appears poor and foolish, and therefore controllable. But this book could teach that freeing oneself of the fear of the Devil is wisdom. . . . Look at the young monks who shamelessly read the buffoonery of the *Coena Cypriani*.[12] What a diabolical transfiguration of the Holy Scripture! And yet as they read it they know it is evil. . . . The prudence of our fathers made its choice: if laughter is the delight of the plebeians, the license of the plebeians must be restrained and humiliated, and intimidated by sternness.[13]

Quite an un-British speech. This man clearly has no sense of humor. We see, now, why *your* soul is in such peril. You have been

---

[12] "Cyprian's Supper," is an anonymous parody from the fifth or sixth century in which many biblical characters, from Adam to St. Peter, take part in a great banquet and are satirized with brief, sharp verses." See the Associated Press story in *The Clarion Ledger* (March 26th, 2005) and http://www.clarion-ledger.com/apps/pbcs.dll/article?AID=/20050326/FEAT05/503260355/1023.

[13] Umberto Eco, *The Name of the Rose* (New York: Warner, 1984), pp. 576–78.

very naughty indeed. You *shamelessly* watched *Monty Python's Life of Brian* just like one of those young monks, and you *knew* it was evil, not because it was funny, but because it unfolds according to the best principles of the comedic art. There is something very twisted about its being so *good*. So long as humor remains a mere ethnic joke of the working class told over too many beers, it can be tolerated, but raised to a standard of educated taste, even to the level of philosophy, it is more threatening to authorities, religious or political, in Jorge's view. Such humor undermines the efforts of our serious "betters" to shepherd us toward order—unless of course (and this is what Jorge misses) those "betters" are Roman or British. If our "betters" are these psychotic Christians of the Falwell type, who cannot ever laugh at themselves, then yes, the comedy becomes a palpable threat as the humor becomes more intelligent. In the case of *Monty Python's Life of Brian*, the *better* the film is at depicting the times of Christ, the more diabolical is the effect to pathetic followers of the dead God. *Monty Python's Life of Brian* is, by the estimate of all the Pythons, their best film.[14] Yet the British do not worry (much).[15] How can this be sac-religious unless one has already taken the immortal soul too seriously?

Now let's consider *your* soul. You apparently have two souls. The soul you *know* about is human, mortal (as far as you can tell), and inhabits this world, this life only. This is the soul which "animates" your physical existence, brings you to life, moves your body, fuels your consciousness. The immortal soul, if there is one, is a sort of sojourner in this world, it doesn't much like your body (and if you look in the mirror I'm sure you'll see the reasons), and frankly can't wait to get the hell out of Dodge (or Hampstead, in fact, especially Hampstead). If these two souls are really the same, it isn't obvious. So which soul is in peril? Must you lose one to save the other?

---

[14] Even though *Monty Python's The Meaning of Life* won the jury prize at Cannes. See *The Life of Python*, BBC/A&E, executive producers Elaine Shepherd and Amy Briamonte (2000).

[15] See Robert Hewison, *Monty Python: The Case Against* (New York: Grove Press, 1981). Shortly after the film was released, Cleese and Palin debated Malcolm Muggeridge and the Bishop of Southwark on the BBC2 discussion program *Friday Night, Saturday Morning*.

Getting Right with Brian (Just in Case)

There was a morose philosopher named Blaise Pascal (1623–1662) who, in spite of his dreary mood, can help you. We have seen the extent of your sin. You laughed. You may think this not your worst sin, but if so, you just aren't listening. I almost think you must be British. Anyway, Pascal thought too much, *way* too much, and left behind his fragmentary putterings which were gathered together and published by still gloomier admirers, and *that* takes some doing.[16] One of these fragments received the number "233," and contains what is called "Pascal's Wager." I won't ruin your dinner with Pascal's words, but I'll adapt his wager to your current dilemma, according my own less moribund, er, umm . . . "idiom Sir?" Yes, that's it, idiom; thank you Patsy.

So you *know* you have a finite soul. You also know that infinite things exist, like numbers. But here is a curiosity: "Infinity" is by definition a number, yet no one knows *what* it is, or much about it—for instance, whether it is odd or even. Yet, every number *must* be either odd or even. Don't get your knickers in a twist. You don't *need* to know, but you see it's possible for you to know *that* something *exists* without knowing *what* it is. Your immortal soul is analogous. It may exist even if you don't know what it is (and of course, the same for God, but never mind Him). And if you have an immortal soul, you have already wagered it: you laughed, not once but repeatedly during *Monty Python's Life of Brian*. I firmly suspect you saw it more than once; you probably have the video somewhere, don't you? You have wagered. Now what do you stand to lose and gain? If you have an immortal soul and the dead God isn't *quite* dead, isn't an ex-God, is only stunned or resting, you lose all. But if the dead God never was God, and you do have an immortal soul, then you don't really know if you've gained or lost, since that really depends on whether God finds Monty Python funny—in short, if God is British, you're okay—your laughter even counts as worship of such a God, you are among the elect, and will receive a fine German car in paradise (since it is paradise, it won't be a *British* car). What I mean by "British" is that God is of the sort who not only can take a joke, but positively

---

[16] Blaise Pascal, *Pensées* (New York: Modern Library, 1941), Fragment 233.

laugh at Himself. You have wagered your immortal soul, if you have one, on the chance that God is British. Does that make you worried or what?

Now you may *have* no immortal soul (I mean others, yes, but not *you*), and in that case the bet is really off. Might as well enjoy yourself—where was the Castle Anthrax exactly? But let's suppose you have one, so it's down to God being British. We need some way to decide. The evidence is a bit ambiguous. I mean, the sinking of the Spanish Armada and Trafalgar seem to suggest God *may* be British. But it's hard to be sure. We only know He isn't Spanish or French. God might still be German, but here Nietzsche helps, since the "madman" was unable to find him there. If God is German, He is hiding or afraid of us or has emigrated (in which case He might still be British by naturalization). Since God was drinking Two-Buck-Chuck with me, He isn't Italian. If God is Russian, everyone is screwed, starting with the Russians. No point in worrying over that. We might go on by this process of elimination that philosophers call "induction" until the salmon goes bad, but let's use a handier method. Philosophers call it "deduction," which is induction for lazy, impatient people.

(1) If God is not British, you are screwed (since you laughed at Brian).
(2) If God is British, you're saved.
(3) God is either British or not British

This last proposition (3) is where the cheating occurs. It's called the Law of Excluded Middle, which is a fancy name designed to distract you from it's real nature, which is The Law of I Shall Finish this Thought by Tea Time. If (1) is true, indulge your mortal soul for whatever time it has left. I know you watched *Monty Python's Life of Brian* and you laughed—this hasn't actually been revealed to me, I'm doing induction. You're still reading this. Only three possibilities present themselves: (a) you watched the movie and laughed (like a Roman soldier); (b) you are *going* to watch the movie and laugh (which amounts to the same as (a)); or (c) you have nefarious intentions toward me and everyone like me. In case you haven't noticed, if a's and b's are screwed for *watching Monty Python's Life of Brian*, imagine how it will be for *me*. So if you have evil intentions toward my lot, have a little faith in your cheerless God and let Him take care of me and my ilk. Your "God" has already fed Graham Chapman to Lucifer and the rest of us can't be so far behind. Be patient and have the courage of your convictions. So I *know* the rest of you are A's or B's, which means either God is British or it's too late for you.

I realize you want some modicum of hope that God is not only *not* French, but actually *is* British. Here is the hope. The strongest competitor for God's nationality is, well, American. If ever a bunch of undeserving people was touched by divine favor, it's the Americans—even luck seems eliminated as a competitor. Now, if God is an American, you're a goner. And frankly, most of the evidence, with the exception of Viet Nam and Iraq, points to an American God. But consider: isn't it right that *only* a British God could have thought up America? America is to Britain what Disneyworld is to, well, America. It's an impossible gift, beyond human imagination, to be allowed to be British and to see what your entire culture would look like if it were a cartoon. It is true that America could never be as funny to the British as they are to themselves, but it runs a fair second. Yes, God is British and when the Britons had everything else God could give them, and became bored with it, the Supernatural Make-a-Wish Foundation for declining empires waved a wand. Poof. America. And here we are: watching Monty Python, not exactly getting it, but laughing at it just as cartoon characters would laugh at us if they could see us watching them on the telly. And if you must know, that is *why* the penguin was on top of it. The penguin was an American spy, not Burmese. It also explains the bomb.

You can get off your knees now. Brian's saving work is done. You've been naughty, but God is not an American and your mortal soul is healthy. Your immortal soul, if you have one, has my assurance that God is not angry, and that your enemies will all die at some point. I could be wrong of course. Now go away, or I shall taunt you a second time.[17]

---

[17] I would like to thank Tom Alexander and Aaron Fortune for their silly and unhelpful advice about this essay.

7
Monty Python and the Holy Grail: Philosophy, Gender, and Society

REBECCA HOUSEL

We're Knights of the Round Table
We dance whene'er we're able.
We do routines and chorus scenes
With footwork impeccable.
We dine well here in Camelot
We eat ham and jam and Spam a lot.

—Knights, *Monty Python and the Holy Grail*

Mynd You, Moose Bites Kan Be Pretty Nasti . . .

his chapter examines the historical and philosophical context and significance of Arthurian legend and Grail romances to uncover the serious roots of this very funny film, *Monty Python and the Holy Grail*. Aristotle (384–322 B.C.) said, "The roots of education are bitter, but the fruit is sweet." Humor is always rooted in truth, which is exactly why it's so amusing. Looking at the intriguing, yet serious, undertones of *Monty Python and the Holy Grail* will enrich any audience experience. Now let's move on before this book's editors decide to sack the author or—worse—forty specially-trained, Ecuadorian mountain llamas decide to take over.

Why the Pythons Chose Arthur
and the Grail

Monty Python and the Holy Grail is the top-rated comedic film in
Great Britain according to the British Press Association, and the
film ranks highly with American audiences, too. In fact, the popularity of the film in America has spilled over into other entertainment venues, notably the musical based on the film, *Spamalot*,
directed by Mike Nichols and written by Eric Idle. As they would
later do with their controversial film *Monty Python's Life of Brian*,
the Pythons chose a subject iconic in Western popular culture.

King Arthur and his Knights of the Round Table stand tall as
chivalric heroes in popular culture. The legend arose during a time
in Europe when there were four distinct and powerful mythological strands: the classical Roman, classical Greek, Germanic, and
Celtic strands. Arthurian and Grail romances developed during
1150 to 1250 A.D., with the help of Chretien de Troyes, Wolfram
von Eschenbach, and Sir Thomas Malory. Each of these authors
crafted different renditions of the quest for the Holy Grail over
the course of approximately one hundred years. Like all mythology, these romances reflected their time by assimilating various
cultural notions from the four mythological strands. The cultural
tapestry of Arthurian and Grail romances is woven from a patriarchal warrior society and what Joseph Campbell, famous for his
scholarly work on world cultures and religions, called an "earth-
oriented, mother-goddess society," with an overlay of
Christianity.[1] The romances represent the idea of the individual
and the individual path, an idea derived from the four mythological strands. They also combine the Christian notion of community with an emphasis on rules and laws. The result is a powerful
and patriarchal cultural stew.

The Pythons, however, changed the recipe. They wrote and
produced *Monty Python and the Holy Grail* in the early 1970s in the
midst of a growing movement for women's liberation. In 1968
Britain legalized abortion, followed by the United States' legaliza-
tion of abortion in 1973 and France's two years later. Britain's Sex

---

[1] Joseph Campbell, *Transformations of Myth Through Time* (New York: Perennial
Library, 1990), p. 218.

Discrimination Act of 1975 also gave women greater equality. Yet in that same year the movement faced resistance in the United States, for example in the Hyde Amendment of 1976 (which cut federal funding for abortions) and in increased criticism of foreign aid for programs tolerant of abortion. Still, women were gaining political power, with nineteen women elected to the U.S. Congress in 1975 and 604 elected to state legislatures in the same year. Much as the Arthurian legends reflect the cultural and political currents of their time, *Monty Python and the Holy Grail* reflects these developments.

But there is a twist. Arthurian legend has traditionally been used to maintain and endorse patriarchal ideas and attitudes. From the days of King Edward of Britain in 1286 to the modern Boy Scout movement (its founder, Britain's Sir Robert Baden-Powell, even inscribed Arthurian legend as historic fact in his Boy Scout manual's *Knight's Code*) the legend has trumpeted the importance of male gender in society. With Monty Python, however, the connective tissue between the world politics of the women's movement and Arthurian legend in the film is flipped. The Pythons use Arthurian legend to speak to the *absurdity* of patriarchy and its reverberations in the twentieth century.

Some of these reverberations are philosophical. The Pythons are infamous for their use of philosophy and, in particular, for their attention to analytic philosophy. *Monty Python and the Holy Grail* has a strong thread of analytic philosophy—a philosophical program that analyzes individual statements. It endorses a kind of atomism—the idea that an idea can be understood best by breaking down the whole to its separate parts, and examining the relationships among the parts. Atomism opposes the philosophical idea of holism, according to which the whole is primary and greater than the sum of its parts. Joseph Campbell finds holism at the core of mythic stories about the hero. Such stories feature a theme of transcendence through which the hero journeys from duality to an underlying singularity and unity with the universe.[2] Parmenides (around 515 B.C.–450 B.C.) perhaps set the stage for this kind of quest, famously writing that "All is One. Nor is it divisible, wherefore it is wholly continuous."

---

[2] Joseph Campbell, *The Power of Myth* (New York: First Anchor, 1991), p. 57.

However holistic, Grail romances specifically highlight the significance of the individual's path. Arthur and his knights receive the call to search for the Holy Grail, and each knight decides to seek the Grail by taking separate paths. The search is not conducted by a group, but by separate individuals—a circumstance that allowed the Pythons to disentangle and highlight different aspects of patriarchal society.

Come On, You Pansy!

Traditional masculine ethics are based on an abstract idea of morality—outside of relationships and emotions.[3] This abstract notion of right and wrong leaves no room for negotiation. Negotiating is more common to feminine ethics or care ethics. Care ethics holds that relationships—and not abstract principles—are the motivating factors in moral development.[4] Consider the scene in which King Arthur, played by Graham Chapman, and his faithful, coconut-clacking servant, Patsy, "ride" through the wood and come upon the Black Knight. The Black Knight, played by John Cleese, battles the Green Knight in defense of a footbridge, and Arthur is duly impressed.[5] Naturally, he invites the Black Knight to join his quest for the Grail. But the Black Knight refuses and challenges Arthur as he and his entourage attempt to cross the footbridge.

Enter masculine ethics. The Black Knight must protect the footbridge, regardless of who tries to cross. There will be, so far as he and his masculine ethics are concerned, no negotiation, no exceptions, no exploration of gray areas and examining relationships from different angles. The Black Knight is compelled by his duty to this idea ("None shall pass," he intones) and this idea *only* as it functions in the moral abstract. Relationships, in particular, don't matter. Arthur's protest that he is "King of the Britons," is

[3] The notion of a "masculine ethics" is based on the "ethics of justice," a concept developed in turn by Harvard psychologist, Lawrence Kohlberg.
[4] See Carol Gilligan, *In a Different Voice: Psychological Theory and Women's Development* (Cambridge, Massachusetts: Harvard University Press, 1982).
[5] In Arthurian tradition, the Black Knight is the Thunder Knight, killed by Yvain in Chretien de Troyes's account. See Campbell, *Transformations of Myth Through Time*, p. 237.

of no consequence to the Black Knight. *"None,"* after all, "shall pass."

Once they begin their battle, Arthur promptly chops off the Black Knight's left arm. "'Tis but a scratch," claims the Black Knight, refusing to back down. His aggressive masculinity is an absolute component of his ethics, and will not be compromised by inconveniences such as missing limbs or extreme pain. To give in to those would only amount to "crying like a girl." That's for "pansies."

Soon, the Black Knight is a fountain of blood standing on a single leg. Yet he continues to goad Arthur—who watches this spectacle without suffering a scratch—into the breach. "Come here!" the Black Knight yells. "What are you going to do, bleed on me?" Arthur asks sarcastically. "I'm invincible!" replies the Black Knight. "You're a loony," replies Arthur, speaking as much to the Black Knight as to the masculine ethics that he struggles to maintain in his defeat. Even without a leg to stand on, he continues to taunt Arthur and Patsy as they cross the bridge and continue their quest: "Running away, eh? You yellow bastard, come back here and take what's coming to you. I'll bite your legs off!"

We Have Found a Witch. May We Burn Her?

Another scene opens with flagellating monks in the manner of Ingmar Bergman's *The Seventh Seal*. The monks walk purposefully in a line through a village street as Arthur and Patsy arrive to witness Sir Bedevere's widely-known expertise in science and logic. But Bedevere appears to be known for something else as well.

First, Bedevere is confronted by a group of villagers who have dressed up a young woman to look like a stereotypical witch. Bedevere examines the woman and takes testimony about her alleged mischief from the villagers. One, played by John Cleese, explains that this witch turned him into a newt. "She turned you into a newt?" Bedevere asks, and there follows a long, puzzled silence. "I got better," Cleese's villager sheepishly explains. Bedevere's logical gymnastics are no match for these villagers' stories, but he grants that the woman may yet be a witch. To know for sure, he explains, she must be weighed. She may be a witch only if she is made of wood and weighs the same as a duck (because both ducks and wood float on water). Impressed by this faulty logic, the villagers follow Bedevere to his grand scales (much like the scales of justice) to weigh the young woman against a duck. If the scales balance, the young woman must be made of wood, and is therefore . . . a witch.

But it is not Bedevere's logical loops that impress King Arthur. Once again (remember the Black Knight) Arthur is easily impressed. As he observes the wise Bedevere in action, the homo-erotic subtext to this story of a witch burning is suddenly no longer subtextual. The male bonding begins as Arthur invites Bedevere to join the quest for the Holy Grail; Bedevere drops to his knees and grovels in submission, and Arthur unsheathes his very large sword which he taps on Bedevere's shoulders, thus dubbing him Sir Bedevere. As these bonds fall into place, however, the angry mob, eager for a witch burning, has dragged the young woman off screen and, despite the fact that she seems to weigh more than a duck, are surely up to no good. But these realities are of little concern for Arthur and Bedevere, now infatuated with each other, their shared sense of masculine ethics, and their shared quest for the Holy Grail.

We Have but One Punishment. . . . You Must Tie Her Down on the Bed and Spank Her

Arthurian legend and sadomasochism? Consider Sir Galahad the Chaste, played by Michael Palin. On his journey, he is lured into the Castle Anthrax by a Grail-shaped beacon and confronted with the unspeakable terror of a bevy of most-willing and unchaper-oned beauties. Here the film addresses the theme of the individual's path—the crux of all the Grail romances. Seeking individuality, these stories suggest, has a greater reward than following the desires of others. So imagine Galahad the Chaste's predicament.

Slowly, he warms to the idea. The women have requested that Galahad punish each and every one of them by tying them to a bed, then spanking, and then engaging in oral sex, that epitome of male sexual desire. But just as Palin is being led off to the bathing area to prepare for his tasks, he is intercepted by Sir Launcelot, played by John Cleese, who arrives at the castle with his knights to save Galahad from such unholy temptation. After all, on this most holy of quests, Launcelot counsels, Galahad must maintain his devotion to the search and the common good. The idea is an old one in Arthurian legend and in masculine ethics as well: males engaged in their duties must not become "disengaged" on account of such temptations.[6] As early as the Old Testament, in which Eve tempts Adam with an apple, women are portrayed as temptresses. Women, rebirth, and the feminine are often associated with the primitive and ancient symbol of the snake to indicate some aspect of deceit, such as having a "forked-tongue." The feminine is also associated with mystery, unpredictability and, therefore, danger.[7]

Castle Anthrax is as deadly as its name. It is full of poisonous, deceitful women eager to tempt the righteous and good men of the world, throwing up false grail-shaped beacons to lure unsuspecting, innocent men to their lair. Again, the image of the snake is a clear parallel as a poisonous and sly hunter who uses wiles, like projecting a Grail-shaped beacon, to capture "prey," or unsuspecting knights, like Sir Galahad the Chaste.

True, Galahad resists Launcelot's efforts to save him. "Oh, let me go and have a bit of peril," Galahad pleads. No, Launcelot insists, "It's unhealthy!" "I bet you're gay," Galahad responds, as he adds one more layer of meaning to the scene and the film. In Arthurian legend, Launcelot saves Guinevere after she is abducted by the lord of an enchanted castle. Yet Launcelot, Arthur's greatest knight, is also a fool for love and embarks upon a passionate affair with Guenivere following her rescue. The story makes use of a typical medieval hero-trial, what Campbell calls, in his *Transformations of Myth through Time*, the "Trial of the Perilous Bed" (p. 235). The trial always entails a treacherous bed that the knight must dominate in full armor. With Launcelot, the dangers of the bed involve being pelted by arrows (symbolic of a reverse-rape) and attacked by a ferocious lion. Yet with Cleese and Palin, the "Trial of the Perilous Bed" becomes the women of Castle Anthrax (indeed, Cleese uses the words "peril" and "perilous" throughout their exchange). Launcelot, moreover, is anything but a fool for love (unless it's love for Galahad himself). Why else

---

[6] Joseph Campbell, *Transformations of Myth through Time*, p. 239
[7] Joseph Campbell, *Masks of God: Occidental Mythology* (New York: Arkana, 1991).

would he drag Galahad away from the beautiful women demanding his services?

Er, Well . . . the Thing Is . . .
I Thought Your Son Was a Lady

Parzival was a knight of the Round Table. His Grail adventure speaks to individuals about seeking the truth from within. As Campbell notes, Parzival's failure was due to his listening to others rather than himself. Finding the true self is what the Grail represents. During the twelfth century marrying for love was not common. Marriages were arranged based on social class, material possessions, and money—not love. Listening to one's heart was not particularly popular in the shame culture of the twelfth century, where honor took priority over the self. The Pythons, of course, knew this cultural and literary history well when they introduced their audience to Prince Herbert, played by Terry Jones.

Prince Herbert is sorrowfully sitting in his tower room awaiting his wedding to Princess Lucky, whose father owns large tracts of land in Britain (much to the joy of Prince Herbert's father, played by Michael Palin). Prince Herbert's father, the "King of the Swamp Castle," has arranged the marriage despite Herbert's protestations. Perverse as always, the Pythons cleverly present the reverse of what was typical in the twelfth century, where a woman would be forced into a loveless marriage. The feminine Prince Herbert despairingly writes a note describing his distress and appealing for rescue, which he fastens to an arrow and launches in a romantic gesture from his tower window to find its destiny. Well, at least the arrow comes *close* to finding its destiny. First it finds the chest of Concorde, the coconut-clacking servant of Sir Launcelot, played by Eric Idle. As Launcelot reads the note from the arrow, still stuck in Concorde's chest, his eyes "light up with holy inspiration." A sub-quest! There is nothing quite like a damsel in distress to provide the necessary heterosexual matrix for masculine display. Prince Herbert, though he enjoys musicals and notices curtains, is no damsel. The note only indicates a need for a rescue from the "Tall Tower of Swamp Castle" and nothing more. Launcelot is about to enter his "idiom" as he leaves the wounded Concorde, and rides off into the sunset to save . . . well, he doesn't quite know who yet—hopefully, the distress is attached to some fair damsel and Launcelot's own masculinity will be saved (especially after that scene with Sir Galahad at Castle Anthrax).

"The whole sense of the courtly idea was pain of love," Campbell states (*Transformations of Myth through Time*, p. 213), and in fact the Pythons plan on plenty of pain in the upcoming scenes. Launcelot, now in his idiom, ferociously makes his way through the guards at the door and the wedding guests—even kicking the bride in the chest! He slashes his way to the tower in a masculine frenzy of swords and bloodied bodies—anything for a damsel in distress. And there she is, sitting at the window. He kneels, presenting himself while averting his eyes. "Oh, fair one," he says, "behold your humble servant, Sir Launcelot, from the Court of Camelot. I have come to take you..."—at this point he looks up and his voice tails off—"... away ... I'm terribly sorry. ...." Prince Herbert responds with glee, "You've come to rescue me?" Launcelot reluctantly replies, "Well ... yes ... but I hadn't realized. ..."

Poor Launcelot! The harder he tries to be a patriarchal paragon of masculinity, the more he appears to be just the opposite. Not to worry. Just as Prince Herbert is about to launch into song, the swamp king, a hairy, bearded man in a beastly fur coat, interrupts. Homo-social bonding ensues as the king and Launcelot decide to descend the stairs for a drink. Yes, the Pythons take the pain of courtly love in a deadly serious manner.

The action continues with Launcelot once again striking out at guests before the king of Swamp Castle announces, much to Launcelot's dismay, that since Prince Herbert is dead and Princess Lucky's father is also dead, Launcelot and Lucky will be tying the proverbial knot. Launcelot is saved from this profusely heterosexual act, however; Concorde arrives suddenly carrying an injured but living Prince Herbert, who fell from the tower window (with his father's help). Launcelot's sword proves impotent after all, as the more feminine characters of Herbert and Concorde usher in a musical number affirming their presence. Launcelot moves toward a swashbuckling escape by attempting to swing from a rope through a glass window. Once again, Launcelot proves impotent, stopping short of the window while swinging pathetically in mid-air, "Excuse me ... could somebody give me a push." As the

French guard says in the final scene, "You couldn't catch clap in a brothel."

Gender misidentification, exaggerated masculinity, homosocial bonding, the heterosexual matrix, and phallic allusions abound in the preceding scenes with Prince Herbert and Sir Launcelot. Feminist ideas are clearly woven into the intricate fabric of the historical, literary, cultural, philosophical, and mythological tapestry of this brilliantly funny Python film.

Yes, but What About the Killer Rabbit?

There's no time here to examine the killer rabbit, brave, brave Sir Robin and his minstrels, or the uncompromising Knights who say "Ni!" Yet beneath the humor these sketches also bear the imprint of the struggles—involving philosophy, gender, and social politics—that make *Monty Python and the Holy Grail* as much a document of the 1970s as a satire of medieval life and culture.[8]

---

[8] My thanks to George Reisch and Gary Hardcastle for their excellent editing efforts on this chapter and to William Irwin for inspiring philosophical discussions.

8

Against Transcendentalism: *Monty Python's The Meaning of Life* and Buddhism

STEPHEN T. ASMA

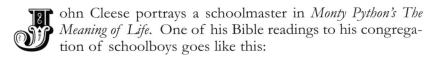ohn Cleese portrays a schoolmaster in *Monty Python's The Meaning of Life.* One of his Bible readings to his congregation of schoolboys goes like this:

> And spotteth twice they the camels before the third hour. And so the Midianites went forth to Ram Gilead in Kadesh Bilgemath by Shor Ethra Regalion, to the house of Gash-Bil-Betheul-Bazda, he who brought the butter dish to Balshazar and the tent peg to the house of Rashomon, and there slew they the goats, yea, and placed they the bits in little pots. Here endeth the lesson.

Cleese then turns to his chaplain (Michael Palin) who rises to lead the congregation in prayer:

> Let us praise God. Oh Lord, oooh you are so big. So absolutely huge. Gosh, we're all really impressed down here I can tell you. Forgive us, O Lord, for this dreadful toadying and barefaced flattery. But you are so strong and, well, just so super. Fantastic. Amen.

Headmaster Cleese then addresses the schoolboys with a series of general announcements, including the importance of "Empire Day, when we try to remember the names of all those from the

Sudbury area who gave their lives to keep China British." Almost
forgetting, and clearly resenting its intrusion on these more important matters, Cleese turns to one boy, Jenkins, for just enough time
to deliver a message from home: "Oh . . . and Jenkins . . . apparently your mother died this morning." Over Jenkins's tears, Palin
briskly resumes business by leading a hymn to match his earlier
prayer: "Oh Lord, please don't burn us," it goes. "Don't grill or
toast your flock, Don't put us on the barbecue, Or simmer us in
stock. . . ."

This sketch is emblematic of a philosophical mood that one
finds throughout Monty Python's work. But it sparkles in *Monty
Python's The Meaning of Life*. This movie is filled with *reductio ad
absurdum* arguments that reduce traditional positions to absurdity
by drawing out their logical conclusions or by juxtaposing them in
the context of our deeper (usually ethical) convictions. Here, the
complete insensitivity of the Headmaster and chaplain to one of
the deepest injuries that can befall a young boy (the death of his
mother) is compounded by the elaborately useless verbiage of religious orthodoxy. The thing that's needed most in response to little Jenkins's loss, some humane compassion, is completely truant
in these rituals and authority figures. So it goes throughout *Monty
Python's The Meaning of Life*—not just the cruel humor but also the
suggestion of a causal connection. The Headmaster and chaplain
are not just insensitive people who happen to be running a religious boarding school. They are in fact insensitive *because* their
religion has led them to lose perspective and compassion.

Much of *Monty Python's The Meaning of Life* is a critique of
ridiculous and dangerous distractions that dehumanize us. Among
them are religious ideology, class distinction, science, medicine,
education, and corporate greed. The film displays the myriad ways
that humans alienate each other and also alienate themselves from
their own happiness. In the section titled "Birth," for example, we
see the way that modern medicine objectifies and abstracts a
patient into a meaningless afterthought that gets significantly less
consideration than the expensive equipment that fills the "fetus-
frightening room." The "machine that goes '*ping*'"—as the
Python-doctors call it—is more valuable than the mother and
newborn child. Their humanity has been crowded out by profit-
driven corporate healthcare and sterile technology. As the
Pythons' depiction of life's cycle continues (into the section titled

"Growth and Learning") we see institutional education deadening the spirit of young people. Even sex education, illustrated vividly by "teacher" Cleese and Patricia Quinn, becomes a dry pedantic exercise that simply affords the abusive tutor one more excuse to berate and scold his students. All these comments, moreover, come on the heels of the film's surrealistic "short feature presentation" depicting a mutiny by the oppressed workers of the Crimson Permanent Assurance Corporation. Despite the transformation of their office building into a fierce, seaworthy battleship, and their swordfight victories over their corporate foes (including the Very Big Corporation of America), they meet an inglorious end as they sail off the edge of the earth into oblivion.

For all that, however, the film is not despairing. A thread of optimism runs through it and serves as an alternative to the portrayed estrangements. To see this, I'll explain how the movie offers a sustained critique of transcendentalism, a way of looking at the world that connects and unifies the film's sketches.

Is There *Really* Something Called 'Transcendental Metaphysics'?

Transcendentalism is a theory embraced by thinkers as diverse as Plato, St. Augustine, and Vedantic Hindus. It posits the existence of two worlds instead of one. The physical world we live in is, according to the transcendentalist, a corrupt copy of a more perfect world. My slowly degenerating body, my material lap-top computer, my faltering democracy, and my entire sensory experience, to take a range of examples, are all just fleeting shadows when compared to the ideal and perfect realm believed to exist by transcendentalists. This ideal and perfect realm is populated by ideas (like "Justice") and perfect beings (like "God," "angels," or even purified "souls") that are higher and better—and serve as blueprints for—our usual, mundane realm of imperfect ideas and beings. This is not an obscure or uncommon theory. The vast majority of religious humans, both East and West, embrace some form of transcendentalism. If you believe that God is in his heaven, that He created the physical universe and is in some sense above and beyond his creation, then you are a transcendental thinker. Palin's chaplain who gushes, "Oh Lord, oooh you are so big. So absolutely huge. Gosh, we're all really impressed down here I can tell you," is a transcendentalist through and through.

In Hindu philosophy the transcendental being is called Brahman. Brahman is the permanent eternal reality that serves as the stable principle underlying the fluctuating world of material nature. The cosmos is always changing and becoming something new and different, but Brahman is the divine unity behind this veil of changing appearances. And in the same way that the cosmos has a persistent unchanging reality that is hidden from view, so too each human has a persistent unchanging reality hidden within. In the West we call the hidden reality within us the "soul" and in the East it is called "atman." This view of humans as a combination of body and soul is frequently called "dualism." My body may change its material composition from one year to the next (even one day to the next), but a soul or atman remains the same over the course of these changes and provides my source of personal identity (my self) over time. Hindu philosophers (especially in the *Svetesvatara* and *Katha* Upanishads) recognize the common metaphysical functions of these permanent realities, Brahman and atman, by claiming that they are actually one and the same substance or being. In other word, the permanent hidden soul or atman inside me is actually a piece of God or Brahman itself. A bit of Brahman is living inside me as my divine soul and through moral perfection and wisdom I can release this soul (my true self) after death to rejoin its transcendent origin. According to Hindu orthodoxy, my own moral weakness and persistent stupidity prevents the estranged bit of Brahman within me from reaching its "home," and damns my soul to return again and again in subsequent lifetimes (reincarnation). Hindu scriptures liken the eventual metaphysical reunion (after countless lifetimes) to a drop of water returning to the ocean or a tiny spark returning to the eternal conflagration. And this final communion will be eternal bliss.

The belief in a soul, whether in its Eastern or Western version, is transcendentalist because it posits another reality beyond this mundane world of sensory experience. It suggests that my true self is some intangible undetectable being, having a similar metaphysical tint as God, that will eventually go to live in a world beyond.

In *Monty Python's The Meaning of Life* the poor Yorkshire father (Palin) who explains to his abundant brood that "every sperm is sacred" is also a transcendentalist. The father is forced to sell his fifty-some children to science for "medical experiments" because God, according to Roman Catholicism, commands that sexual intercourse be for the exclusive purpose of procreation. As a result, there are just too many mouths to feed. Explaining the reason for the family's predicament, the Yorkshire father says of the Church "Oh they've done some wonderful things in their time, they preserved the might and majesty, even the mystery of the Church of Rome, the sanctity of the sacrament and the indivisible oneness of the Trinity. But if they'd let me wear one of those little rubber things on the end of my cock we wouldn't be in the mess we are now."

This is no mere critique of organized religion and its inflexible dogmatic positions. A deeper critique is lurking here, too. No one, whether Catholic, Hindu, or Muslim, or whatever, would submit themselves to the decrees and directives of organized religion if they did not already accept a transcendental commitment and further accept that an earthly institution is the trustworthy authority on or manifestation of those eternal transcendental truths. This is clear when the father concedes to his dejected children that the Church may not see his transgression of the rules (a transgression lobbied for by the jeopardized children), but God will see everything. There's no escaping transcendental justice.

The father of this family (and the transcendental moralist, generally) is so focused on upholding the abstract intangible rule of God, that he causes immeasurable misery and suffering in *this* world—the world that contains his own flesh and blood, his children. The transcendental divine world beyond this mortal coil is so compelling that it takes priority over or *overrides* this world and its attendant values.

A similar example of this transcendental override can be seen in the classic Hindu epic the *Bhagavad Gita*. The *Gita* tells the story of a military leader named Arjuna who finds himself leading an army against an opposing legion of his kinsmen. On the battlefield, just before combat, Arjuna confides to his chariot driver (the divine being Krishna in disguise) that he is morally conflicted about the impending battle. Why should he kill his cousins? Indeed, why should he kill at all? These deep apprehensions plague Arjuna's mind in the beginning of the text, and the remainder of the scripture is a series of arguments and revelations that

Krishna offers to inspire Arjuna into battle.   First, Krishna explains, Arjuna should kill his enemies because God says so—on the grounds of simple, straightforward, divine authority.   Like Abraham in the West, Arjuna must demonstrate his devotion to the sacred, transcendental powers.

The second explanation that Krishna offers involves the realities of the Hindu caste, or class, system. Arjuna was born into the ksatriya class, which means that it is his sacred *duty* to fulfill the actions of a warrior. Social caste was understood in cosmic terms, and the harmony of the universe itself was tied to the social harmony of each caste fulfilling its function or destiny. Without the execution of our sacred duties, the world itself slouches toward chaos.

Finally, Krishna attempts to assuage Arjuna's guilt over murdering his kinsmen by pointing out that it is only the physical body that gets destroyed. The soul, or atman, of his kinsman is divine and eternal and will not perish on Arjuna's sword. In fact, the atman will only be liberated by the killing of the body. The *Gita* explains: "This physical body is perishable. But the embodied soul is described as indestructible, eternal and immeasurable. Therefore do fight. Neither the one who thinks it kills nor the one who thinks it is killed knows the truth. The soul neither kills nor gets killed. The soul is never born nor does it die at any time. It has neither past nor future. It is unborn, ever existing, permanent and ancient. . . . Just as a man discards worn out clothes and puts on new clothes, the soul discards worn out bodies and wears new ones" (*Bhagavad Gita* [Bantam Classics, reissued 1986], pp. 18–22).

What's So Wrong with Transcendental Thinking?

Under this transcendental override, common sense, human compassion, peaceful diplomacy, and even the evidence of one's senses are all overridden by Arjuna's eventual acceptance of a transcendental God whose unfathomable commands require Arjuna to kill the enemy. The transcendental position here actually claims in essence that killing someone is doing them a favor (because it releases their transcendental self). If we put John Cleese in the role of Krishna and Michael Palin in the role of Arjuna, we'd have a classic Python sketch. Instead of trying to convince a fellow that his dead parrot is still alive or that his empty cheese shop really has cheese, we'd have God convincing a warrior to see killing as an act of helpfulness.

The meaning of life for the transcendentalist is hidden from the perceptions of common sense. Sometimes it is not just hidden but seemingly contradictory to life itself. As Monty Python often reminds us, transcendental values and the overrides they require can be comical, dangerous, or both. In the section of the film titled "Death," the Pythons skewer the traditional idea of a transcendental soul that travels after death to a transcendental place (heaven) to enjoy eternal, transcendental bliss. The sketch shows the absurdity of the idea by simply imagining this heaven in concrete detail. After dying from a bad dish of salmon mousse, a group of souls enter a reception area in paradise. "Welcome to Heaven," a hostess says as she greets them. "There's a table for you through there in the restaurant." She then wishes them "Happy Christmas" and explains that "it's Christmas every day in Heaven." For the transcendentalist (of both East and West), the return home of the transcendental soul to its transcendental realm is the very zenith and purpose of all life—it is the true meaning of life. Yet here, the Pythons lampoon it as a nauseating Vegas-style dinner-theater. Soon, an unctuous, overly tanned, sequin-tuxedo-wearing Graham Chapman takes the stage to sing, with hyper-white teeth, an unbearably maudlin song celebrating the good fortune of heaven's elect. Up here, "it's nice and warm and everyone looks smart and wears a tie." But there's more, including "great films on TV . . . *The Sound of Music* twice an hour, and *Jaws I, II, and III.*" All this, every day, over and over.

With this reduction *ad absurdum*, the Pythons vividly suggest that the ultimate culmination of transcendentalism is ridiculous and hardly worth striving for. Much like Palin's and Cleese's heartless school administrators and Palin's sacred-sperm counting father, the sketch reveals how the appeal of transcendentalism collapses under its own weight. Far from being desirable, the fruits of transcendentalism seem not only cloying (Las Vegas-style) but dangerous and dehumanizing. This was exactly what the historical Buddha said about the reigning Hindu philosophy of his time. Much as the Pythons urge in *Monty Python's The Meaning of Life*, the Buddha argues repeatedly that belief in a soul or a God or anything eternal and otherworldly actually *interferes with* our more immediate and pressing responsibilities to each other as human beings.

Remember from the *Gita* (but also see the earlier *Upanishads*) that Hindu orthodoxy maintained a transcendentally mandated social caste system (wherein a cosmic class hierarchy manifested itself in all subsequent generations of this earthly realm); a transcendental divine soul (atman); and a transcendental God (Brahman) who would be the ultimate blissful repository of enlightened souls. The Buddha (Siddattha Gotama, 563–483 B.C.E.) didn't like any of these standard Hindu ideas and explicitly argued against them throughout his original scriptures. These are known as the *Tipitika* scriptures, written in the language Pali. One of these scriptures, the *Agganna sutta*, criticizes the traditional caste story that Brahmins were born of God's mouth while the sub-servient caste, the Sudras (including the lowest Untouchables) were born from his lowly feet. Buddha counters this longstanding prejudice, and deflates the mystification, by pointing out that all the Brahmins, warriors, craftsmen, and servants that he knows were all born the exact same way—from their mother's wombs! In addition, the Buddha noted that since virtue and vice are easily witnessed in all the castes (not just the Brahmin priestly class), there is no real ground for saying that one caste is inherently better than another. Open your eyes, he suggests, and you will find Brahmin scoundrels as well as Untouchable saints. A more earthly law of value, of observable ethical goodness, should therefore trump the old transcendentalist hierarchy.

Yet the Buddha saved most of his logical acumen for a career-long attack on the Hindu idea of the soul. He aimed not to be some nihilistic kill-joy, however, but to break the romantic obsession with eternal unseen realities which Indian culture had embraced—the kind of romanticism which, in scriptural form, led Hindu Gods (like Krishna in the *Gita*) to pronounce that killing is acceptable because this mortal life is only illusion anyway. Death and even human suffering is not as troubling for the transcendental thinker because this short illusory life will be infinitely outweighed by the next world—where we're going to find perfect joy, and *Jaws I, II* and *III*, forever and ever, amen.

The Buddha finds all this buoyant brightness rather suspicious. As did Wittgenstein, who traced the source of philosophical confusions to careless uses of language, Buddha thinks that language has gone on holiday. What does it mean to be perfectly happy? In the *Potthapada sutta* (*Digha Nikaya*), Buddha retells a debate he had with some "philosophers and brahmins" who believed that "the soul is perfectly happy and healthy after death." The Buddha says:

> I asked them whether, so far as they knew it or perceived it, the human world was perfectly happy, and they answered "No." Then I asked them: "Moreover, can you maintain that you yourselves for a whole night, or for a whole day, or even for half a night or day, have ever been perfectly happy?" And they answered: "No." Then I said to them: "Further, do you know a way or a method, by which you can realize a state that is altogether happy?" And still to that question they answered: "No." And then I said: "Sirs, have you ever heard the voices of heavenly beings who had realized rebirth in a perfectly happy world, saying: 'there is a right path, a true path, which is in human capacity to follow, a path to the world of unfailing bliss, for we ourselves by following it have come to this world of bliss'?" They still answered: "No."[1]

The Buddha concludes from this Socratic questioning, that, while their mouths are moving and words are coming out, these philosophers and Brahmins are really speaking a kind of nonsense. They're like carpenters who build staircases for mansions that they've never seen, and for which they have no dimensions or measurements. They labor, but their misunderstanding of what they do renders their work absurd.

Why must transcendentalists so misunderstand what it is they strive for? The real point of the Buddha's argument is metaphysical. Why can't you be perfectly happy? Why can't you even be happy for more than a few hours? Because happiness is inherently impermanent (*anicca*). Like all other feelings, happiness comes and goes, and like all other things in the world, it cannot last. Treating a moment as if it were a thing to be possessed *ad infinitum* is a regular human tendency. But it is regularly in error. Even for those who enjoy Vegas-style dinner theater, two or three hours

---

[1] Digha Nikaya, Potthapada Sutta in *The Buddha's Philosophy of Man: Early Indian Buddhist Dialogues*, edited by Trevor Ling (Everyman's Library, reissued 1993), p. 34.

may be a treat. But days and years and centuries would seem more *a propos* of hell than heaven.

Upon close inspection, Buddha shows, paradise crumbles. The atman, on the other hand, is a no show. The Buddha thinks that atman is nowhere to be found except in the literary inventions of Hinduism and the confusions of its followers. Buddhism, contrary to all dualistic theories, asserts that we are not made up of two metaphysically different parts, a permanent spirit and an impermanent body. Buddhism breaks with most religions, East and West, by recognizing that we are each a finite tangle of qualities, all of which eventually exhaust themselves, and none of which, conscious or other, carries on independently. All humans, according to Buddha, are composed of the five aggregates (*khandas*); body (*rupa*), feeling (*vedana*), perception (*sanna*), dispositions or volitional tendencies (*sankhara*) and consciousness (*vinnana*). If the Buddha was standing around in the battlefield setting of the *Bhagavad Gita*, he would certainly chime-in and object to Krishna's irresponsible claim that a permanent soul resides in Arjuna and his enemies. Show me this permanent entity, the Buddha would demand. Is the body permanent? Are feelings permanent? What about perceptions, or dispositions, or even consciousness? The Buddha says "If there really existed the atman, there would be also something that belonged to this atman. As however, in truth and reality, neither an atman nor anything belonging to an atman can be found, is it not really an utter fool's doctrine to say: This is the world, this am I; after death I shall be permanent, persisting and eternal?" (*Mijjhima Nikaya*) Buddha examines all the elements of the human being, finds that they are all fleeting, and finds no additional permanent entity or soul amidst the tangle of human faculties. There is no ghost in the machine.

What's So Grotesque about That?

In their rejection of transcendentalism, Buddhism and Monty Python converge in their celebrations of the grotesque. The Python crew seems to relish the disgusting facts of human biology and they take every opportunity to render them through special effects. Throughout *Monty Python's The Meaning of Life*, blood spurts, vomit spews, babies explode from birth canals, decapitated heads abound, and limbs putrefy. Theravada Buddhism also celebrates the revolting, treating it as a meditation focus for contemplating the lack of permanence. The transcendentalist consoles herself with the idea that this physical body may decay and perish, but an eternal soul will outlast the material melt-down—not so for the Buddha.

In an attempt to undercut human vanity and demonstrate the impermanence of all things, Buddhist scriptures are filled with nauseating details about rotting carcasses and putrid flesh. In the *Anguttara Nikaya*, for example, the scripture asks, "Did you never see in the world the corpse of a man or a woman, one or two or three days after death, swollen up, blue-black in color, and full of corruption? And did the thought never come to you that you also are subject to death, that you cannot escape it?" (III, 35)

When I was at a monastery in Southern Thailand, I chanced upon some reproductions of "dhamma paintings" from the mid-nineteenth century. These pictures were from a Chaiya manuscript discovered nearby, and they depicted, in detail, the "Ten Reflections on Foulness" (*asubha kammatthana*). The paintings illustrate the various uses of corpses as objects for contemplating impermanence. Following the great Theravadan philosopher Buddhaghosa's *Visuddhimagga* text ("Path of Purification"), the artist rendered decaying corpses in rather comprehensive stages of dismemberment and putrification. According to Buddhaghosa, staring at a bloated corpse will be particularly useful to me if I'm feeling overly attached and arrogant about the shape and morphology of my body. If instead I'm feeling snobby or bigoted about my skin's color or complexion, I should focus on the livid corpse that ranges from green to blue-black in color. Or, if I mistakenly feel that my body is my own, I am to rectify this error by meditating on a worm-infested corpse (*puluvaka*). As Buddhaghosa explains, "The body is shared by many and creatures live in dependence on (all parts and organs) and feed (on them). And there they are born, grow old, and die, evacuate and pass water; and the body is their maternity home, their hospital, their charnel ground, their privy and their urinal." Buddhist "mindfulness" (meditational awareness) about the body is being aware of its transience, its brevity, its fugacity. The physical body is slowly macerating, and to try to hold onto it or recompose it is a pipedream.

The single issue that invited comment from film reviewers when *Monty Python's The Meaning of Life* was released was its wallow in the grotesque. One exclaimed that the film's "ramshackle bouts of surreal physical comedy—a clotted mass of frenzied bodies, debris, mud, and gore—induce feelings of revolt and despair."[2] In light of the film's critique of transcendentalism, however, this reviewer got it just backward. Far from despairing, the Pythons aimed to smash the deceptive veneer of puritanical snobbery that devalues the flesh and overvalues the invisible spirit. Like Buddhism, Python asks us to "say yes" to our true nature, filled as it is with impermanence and unpleasantness. At first this may seem jarring and disturbing, but in the long run it is preferable to self-deception through figmentary transcendent reality.

Buddha's rejection of a permanent transcendental soul is known as the *anatta*, or "no-self" doctrine (and the companion doctrine that rejects the idea of a permanent God is called *paticca samuppada*, or "dependent arising," because it denies the need for any transcendent uncaused cause). The most important Buddhist critique of the transcendental soul finds place in *Monty Python's The Meaning of Life*. It is the idea that belief in unseen, eternal, and divine realities ultimately distracts us from our own humanity. Transcendentalism dehumanizes us by feeding selfish craving. If we embrace a worldview that pivots on the idea that we will attain immortality, then we are going to be overly concerned with our soul's protection and its future fate. We become more concerned with saving our own souls than valuing and attending to the needs of those around us. Simply put, belief in a soul and a heaven of blissful happiness actually makes you less ethical in this life.

The rejection of souls, heaven, and God, does not lead, as so many critics contend, to bleak egoistic nihilism. Many transcendentalists foretell a gloomy picture without the security of otherworldly meaning, predicting rampant hedonism (pure pleasure seeking) or nihilistic apathy. The Buddha disagrees and thinks that these life patterns are to be avoided as much as otherworldly dogmatism. The extremes, excesses, and general sufferings of the hedonist strategy and the nihilist strategy are revealed in the film.

---

[2] David Denby, *New York Magazine* (April 4th, 1983).

Terry's Jones's Mr. Creosote, for instance, is the giant embodiment of the crass pursuit of sensual gratification. After gorging
himself on multiple servings of food and wine at a fancy French
restaurant, his unchecked desire for the pleasures of chocolate
puts him over the edge. Though he claims he can eat no more,
Cleese easily seduces him with a single, small, "vaffer-thin" chocolate mint. Mr. Creosote then begins to inflate and he soon
explodes, showering the restaurant in his blood and entrails.
Obviously, such hedonism and self-gratification is not an appropriate fall-back for those who reject transcendental metaphysics
and ethics. Nor is it appropriate to give oneself over to despair or
indifference. The folly of that is illustrated in the movie's gruesome portrayal of a liver transplant. After Graham Chapman
starts the bloody business of removing this poor chap's liver in his
dining room, his partner, Cleese, chats up the man's wife (Terry
Jones in drag) in the kitchen. Cleese asks if she too would give up
her liver, but she replies, "No . . . I don't want to die." Cleese per-
severes and introduces her to Eric Idle, who steps out of her
refrigerator and commences a musical tour of the sublime immen-
sity of the universe and the tiny insignificance of her life:

Just remember that you're standing on a planet that's evolving
And revolving at nine hundred miles an hour,
That's orbiting at nineteen miles a second, so it's reckoned,
A sun that is the source of all our power.
The sun and you and me and all the stars that we can see,
Are moving at a million miles a day
In an outer spiral arm, at forty thousand miles an hour,
Of the galaxy we call the Milky Way.

The Universe itself keeps on expanding and expanding
In all of the directions it can whizz
As fast as it can go, at the speed of light you know,
Twelve million miles a minute, and that's the fastest speed
    there is.
So remember when you're feeling very small and insecure
How amazingly unlikely is your birth
And pray that there's intelligent life somewhere up in space
Because there's bugger all down here on earth.

"Makes you feel so sort of insignificant, doesn't it?" Cleese and Chapman ask. "Can we have your liver then?" She gives in— "Yeah. All right, you talked me into it"—and the two doctors set upon her with their knives.

Just as Mr. Creosote succumbs to sensual overindulgence, this housewife opts for a groundless underindulgence. Just because she realizes she lives in an almost infinitely large universe, that is no reason for her to think that her life is worthless in itself and not worth continuing. This is what the extreme nihilist does (indeed, this is what nihilism is all about), and the Python crew is showing us the absurdity of it. Life does not become meaningless once you give up the idea that you are playing a role in a transcendentally planned drama. The values of family, work, love, understanding, simple pleasures, and peace, don't go away once you reject transcendent meaning. Nor does the woman's natural desire for self-preservation and the avoidance of suffering evaporate once she realizes her own finitude.

Transcendental dogmatism is dehumanizing, but so are the opposing extremes of hedonism and nihilistic skepticism. The Buddha made this point explicitly when he argued for a Middle Way between all opposing extremes. Just as one should find a middle way between the slaveries of excessive indulgence and excessive asceticism (self-denial), so too one must avoid embracing both absolutist worldviews (like Palin's toadying transcendentalist chaplain) and relativist worldviews (where all values and meanings are leveled or negated). The Buddha's Middle Way doctrine seeks to reclaim human values and meaning by avoiding overly rigid blind faith and also avoiding distracting speculations about matters that are remote from lived experience.

Back Down to Earth

So, what are these more down-to-earth human values that must be rescued from transcendental flights-of-fancy and nihilistic negativity? In light of the film's critique of transcendentalism, the extremely modest list of values offered at the end as final "answers" to the meaning of life make good sense. They are introduced by Palin (in drag) as he interrupts the Vegas-style celebration of perpetual Christmas. "Well, that's the end of the film," she announces. "Now here's the Meaning of Life." She opens an envelope and reads, "Well, it's nothing special. Try and be nice to people, avoid eating fat, read a good book every now and then, get some walking in, and try and live together in peace and harmony with people of all creeds and nations."

This rather modest sounding list makes perfect sense if we no longer pine for some more grand transcendental meaning. Once we dispatch both the otherworldly values (toadying to God and conserving our sperm, for example) and the otherworldly "realities" which ground those values (soul, heaven, God), then matters of meaning become markedly more pragmatic and demystified. Like Buddha's philosophy, the essential goals in life become attempts to realize moderation, actualize one's potential, and reduce suffering. When we try to make issues of ultimate meaning more melodramatic than this, we end up with the distracting and dehumanizing edifices of transcendentalism.

The Buddha offers us Four Noble Truths that can be used to fight these temptations and distractions. First, he says "All life is suffering, or all life is unsatisfactory (dukkha)." This seems pessimistic at first, but he's simply pointing out that to have a biological body is to be subject to pain, illness, and eventually death. To have family and friends means that we are open to inevitable loss, disappointment, and also betrayal. But more importantly, even when we feel joy and happiness, these too are transient experiences that will fade because all things are impermanent.

Second, the Buddha says "Suffering is caused by craving or attachment." When we have a pleasurable experience we try to repeat it over and over or try to hang on to it and turn it into a permanent thing. Sensual experiences are not themselves the causes of suffering—they are inherently neutral phenomena. It is the psychological state of craving that rises up in the wake of sensations which causes us to have unrealistic expectations of those feelings—sending us chasing after fleeting experiences that cannot be possessed.

The Third Noble Truth states that the cure for suffering is non-attachment or the cessation of craving. In the *Samyutta Nikaya* text, the Buddha says that the wise person "regards the delightful and pleasurable things of this world as impermanent, unsatisfactory and without atman (any permanent essence), as a disease and sorrow—it is he who overcomes the craving" (12:66).

And the Fourth Noble Truth is an eight-fold path that helps the follower to steer a Middle Way of ethical moderation. Following the simple eight-fold path, which contains simple recommendations similar those listed at the end of *Monty Python's The Meaning of Life*, allows the follower to overcome egoistic craving. Perhaps the most important craving that must be overcome, according to Buddha, is the craving for immortality. The Buddha claimed that giving up transcendental tendencies would help us to better see the people all around us who need our help. We would become more compassionate, he argued, because we would not be distracted by cravings for the "other world."

Mind the Mindfulness

As the Pythons suggest, however, not all dehumanizing distraction comes from "above." Often, we lose sight of compassion and humane living by drowning ourselves in a sea of trivial diversions. In existential terms, we lose our "authentic self" in the unimportant hustle and bustle of everyday matters. Consider again the executives of the Very Big Corporation of America. Later in the film, we learn that just before they were attacked by the mutineers sailing the Crimson Permanent Assurance they were having a meeting about "Item Six on the Agenda, the Meaning of Life." The board chairman, Graham Chapman, turns things over to Michael Palin: "Now Harry, you've had some thoughts on this." "That's right, yeah. I've had a team working on this over the past few weeks," Palin explains in his best American accent:

> What we've come up with can be reduced to two fundamental concepts. One, people are not wearing enough hats. Two, matter is energy; in the Universe there are many energy fields which we cannot normally perceive. Some energies have a spiritual source which act upon a person's soul. However, this soul does not exist *ab initio*, as orthodox Christianity teaches; it has to be brought into existence by a process of guided self-observation. However, this is rarely achieved owing to man's unique ability to be distracted from spiritual matters by everyday trivia.

The other Board members sit quietly through Palin's impressive and important report. But, they need clarification about one of the more important points: "What was that about hats again?" one of them asks.

Distraction reigns again in Part IV, *Middle Age*, when the hyper-pleasant, smiley, and vapid American couple (Palin and, in drag, Idle) are served up a "philosophy conversation" in the form of flashcard prompts. The waiter (Cleese) tries to get the insipid couple started on their philosophy conversation by asking, "Did you ever wonder why we're here?" They fail utterly to stay on topic. "Oh! I never knew that Schopenhauer was a philosopher," Idle exclaims. Palin responds, "Yeah. . . . He's the one that begins with an S.

WIFE: "Oh."
HUSBAND: "Um [pause] . . . like Nietzsche."
WIFE: "Does Nietzsche begin with an S?"
HUSBAND: "There's an S in Nietzsche."
WIFE: "Oh wow! Yes there is. Do all philosophers have an S in them?"
HUSBAND: "Yeah I think most of them do."
WIFE: "Oh! Does that mean [the popular singer] Selina Jones is a philosopher?"
HUSBAND: "Yeah, Right. She could be. She sings about the meaning of life."
WIFE: "Yeah, that's right, but I don't think she writes her own material."
HUSBAND: "No. Maybe Schopenhauer writes her material?"
WIFE: "No. Burt Bacharach writes it."
HUSBAND: "There's no S in Burt Bacharach."

If we combine this tedious conversation and the Boardroom's fascination with hats, the results of Palin's research begins to make sense. Human beings must "create" their "souls" day-by-day (rather than simply discover them, ready made) through "a process of guided self-observation." The great enemy of this process, these sketches show, is distraction.

This is a conception of the soul that the Buddha could agree with. It embraces impermanence, avoids transcendentalist metaphysics, and accepts the view that we must actively cultivate our "souls." This is the point of Buddhist "mindfulness" (*sati*)—a powerful meditation that cuts through the dehumanizing distractions. There's nothing mystical or particularly fancy about it. You can do it in your daily activities as well as in isolated contemplation. It just requires you to focus your mind and senses in the present moment, and to resist the mind's natural tendency to wander off into the past or future, to replay events or imagine scenarios that fill our minds with worries, regrets, hopes or cravings. Mindfulness is a state of awareness that comes from training and discipline, a state that shuts out the drifting distractions of life and reveals the uniqueness of each present moment. In doing this careful attending, one can become more present in his or her own life. Mindfulness helps to rehumanize a person by taking their head out of the clouds. And according to Buddhism it reconnects us better with our compassionate hearts by revealing other human beings as just human beings. Once the distractions of trivia, or theoretical, transcendental, or ideological overlays are removed, we may become better able to know ourselves and compassionately recognize ourselves in others. We may even come to learn that, in fact, we should all wear more hats. But we will only know for sure if we are less distracted and more mindful.

9

Is There Life After *Monty Python's The Meaning of Life?*

STEPHEN A. ERICKSON

uestions regarding the meaning of life have haunted humanity, for these sorts of questions yield little in the way of sustainable answers. Little, that is, unless we answer them by way of belief systems that are quickly taken for granted, becoming merely conventional and soon thereafter artificial: in short, through doctrines that are seldom satisfying.

It is therefore no surprise that the script of *Monty Python's The Meaning of Life* proved to be enormously frustrating for the Pythons, so much so that it was their last major project together. Like religions themselves, the questions surrounding the meaning of life separated them, rather than brought them together. In the words of John Cleese, "The script lacked a central idea."

But what would a central idea have looked like? Might it have been a specific one, like the idea that eating—or not eating—fish reveals life's meaning? And to whom? The fish? Their consumers? Not very likely in either case. Something more general then? Perhaps a vantage point from which to understand competing accounts of life's meaning? This sounds more promising, but also quite abstract and not at all comical. One doubts the Pythons would have pursued this. But we could pursue it, especially if the Pythons' failure to do so may have been part of what flawed *Monty Python's The Meaning of Life*. So let us look at some competing accounts of life's meaning, accompanied, naturally, by Monty Python.

Life, the Journey: The Axial Answer

Especially in the West, life has been understood as a journey—
from bondage to liberation, appearance to reality, confusion to
insight, or darkness to light. Liberation, reality, enlightenment, or
light are the destination, the goal. Our purpose in going there is
to *be liberated*, to be made fully *real* and *enlightened*. According to
many religions, the *meaning* of life is to get to this place. This kind
of thinking is identified in philosophy as *axial* thinking, and we
can talk in this context about the axial journey and about axial
time, the temporal dimension of this journey. The German
philosopher Karl Jaspers (1883–1969) coined this term in the
twentieth century, construing the last 2,500 years or so as the playing out of the Axial Age and its picture of human life.[1]

This all sounds like very serious stuff. One can't help but wonder how to go about making such a journey. And here the Python
humor has its bite. As it turns out, the undertaking of "salvation"
has, it seems, been handed over to institutions, chief among them
organized religions, that have laid down rules and regulations to
guide people to the "place of light." As the Pythons were aware,
institutions tend to institutionalize, rather than serve, their customers. They engaged especially the Christian way of approach-
ing the meaning of life, within which earnestness, sacrifice, and
suffering are the pious pathways to premium seats at the
"Heavenly Concert," the greatest show off earth. The Pythons
saw this Christian approach as not only numbing, but misdirected,
and their humor helped dislodge it from its place in human life.
Even if it *were* true, they felt, it needn't be so priggish and pious.

As with much Python humor, the Pythons made the point by
juxtaposing desperately high stakes—life's very meaning—against
the silly, narrow-minded, squalid people purporting to institutionalize this meaning and dispense it to the assembled membership.
So we have for example the British headmaster in *Monty Python's
The Meaning of Life*, John Cleese's Humphrey Williams, making the
following announcement to his young male students in a late-nine-
teenth-century British (and, correspondingly, Christian) boarding
school:

---

[1] Karl Jaspers, *The Origin and Goal of History* (New Haven: Yale University Press,
1968).

Now, two boys have been found rubbing linseed oil into the school cormorant. Now, some of you may feel that the cormorant does not play an important part in the life of the school, but I would remind you that it was presented to us by the Corporation of the town of Sudbury to commemorate Empire Day, when we try to remember the names of all those from the Sudbury area who so gallantly gave their lives to keep China British. So, from now on, the cormorant is strictly out of bounds! Oh, and Jenkins, apparently your mother died this morning.

This is dark humor at its best, making us simultaneously gasp, wince, and laugh. Its point, of course, is that little Jenkins's church (of a piece, as it is, with his school), the institution charged with comforting Jenkins in what will be one of the most difficult times of his life—charged, in fact, with providing his life, and his mothers', with a meaning sufficient for Jenkins to continue his life—has less concern for his emotional needs than it has for the school's (apparently wooden) cormorant. So much for *this* institution as a guide to the meaning of life.

But the Python critique goes deeper, to a critique of this axial approach to the meaning of life itself, the approach that regards the meaning of life as a journey to some destination. It's worth reminding ourselves that Monty Python emerged with, and hastened along, what was at the time called "the countercultural revolution." To what culture was it counter? "Mainstream" is a very insufficient answer to this question. The counterculture (more recently termed "postmodernism") sought to break down hierarchies and reverse traditional priorities. The Pythons fit this agenda almost as if they invented it on their own. The "spiritually" high and mighty, particularly the pompous, were parodied, especially if they had little to offer beyond platitudes they did not live by. And an audience of quite ordinary people, the supposed sheep of the flocks, were laughed into seeing the institutions around them, especially the supposed "meaning purveyors," as silly or empty, or hilariously both.

Amidst very serious political issues, matters of sexual liberation, and the unencumbered pursuit of experiences, then, a *metaphysical* revolution had been underway as well. Its enemy, in fact, was the axial way of understanding the meaning of life: life as a journey, more a pilgrimage, in which *here* does not matter as much as *there*, and *now* does not matter as much as some upcoming *then*. This journey suggested—no, *mandated*—targeted travel, thus conjuring the notion of postponements and delays requiring discipline and restraint, strict itineraries, painful detours and fixed resting places. Exceptional patience, along with the ability to read and obey a map, would be needed. One ought always to be in purposive transit, monitored from lowest position in the company, organization, or institution, so to speak, to its highest executive rank: chairman of the "bored." And who could not fail to become stilted and bored, having to go through all the rigmarole—a favorite target for Python spoof—to get to the top, to membership on the oh-so-privileged board, in the first place? Since there was said to be no salvation outside of the company, there could be no escape, no exit from earnestness, in any case. Such was the burden imposed by an axial reading of the meaning of life.

As part of the counterculture, Monty Python helped break down mystifying hierarchies and eliminate a culture of deference. It was now okay to fart in church. The service stank anyway, and the bishop was no better positioned, knew no more than anyone else. What mattered was not getting to the pearly gates on time but *being here now* and enjoying unrestricted explorations. And who was to say anyway that any one thing was more fulfilling than any other?

It would not be ridiculous to say that the meaning of life is simply to enjoy this life we have. After all, lots of fun and funny things, interesting experiences and adventures, happen during it. Seriousness about life, on the other hand, can make it far less enjoyable and make us susceptible to tunnel-vision and even a little boring. A good argument might be presented that we should just live our lives, hopefully be able to live them *up*, and not think too much about any destination or purpose. It's one thing to strategize for more money and thereby more of the "good things of life," but it's another to brood and brood over "what it all means."

Death and (the Meaning of) Life

Consider the fish swimming in the tank at the beginning of *Monty Python's The Meaning of Life*. Among other things, they note their fellow fish, Howard, being eaten outside of the tank. But they make no connection between that event and their own likely fates, and they wonder, casually if not benightedly, what life is all about. Have they missed something? Have we?

Considerations of death provide an alternate account of the meaning of life. There are, of course, at least two ways to regard death. It can be an event that happens (mostly to others) at some indeterminate time or other, or something that will happen to me, at any time, and might very well result in—might *mean*—my very and altogether permanent extinction. But this second alternative has an even stronger form. It is found in the philosopher Martin Heidegger (1889–1976) and, more generally, among philosophers who have been labeled *existentialists*. On this stronger rendition, you understand something in terms of its *end*, that towards which it moves, and which might at least in some cases be called its *goal*. So to understand your life you must also understand your death. That, after all, is where your life inexorably leads.

One has to be careful here, for "end" and "goal" are not the same thing. For example, starting as an "assistant" professor I became an "associate" professor and am now a "full" professor. If and when I retire I will become an "emeritus" professor. But now things get tricky. Whether I retire or not, someday I am going to be a "dead" professor. That is my end, like it or not. This last step on the professorial ladder does not sound appealing in the least, for I will have become a compatriot of Howard the fish. This could hardly be called my goal.

On the other hand, Socrates says that the art of living, philosophy itself, is "learning how to die," meaning that death is at least our only *obvious* ending point and its attainment is even a goal of sorts. The Socratic implication is that knowing this might help us live a fuller and a better life in the meantime. The analogy is imperfect, but if you *know* that you only get three weeks in Paris and presumably will never return again, you will probably take more advantage of your time there.

Socrates is close to saying that death is actually part of life, if it is where life leads, so to know how to live fully you must know how to die properly. This doesn't mean learning how to load a gun or knowing which poison is painless. But it does mean learning what will be lost through our death and the extent to which the things that will be lost matter. Supposedly we will come to see that nothing will always be with us, for we will not be able to remain permanently with anything. Those things that really *do* matter in life we will then be more prone to linger with and devote ourselves to. We have all heard of trivial pursuits; this should help us achieve trivia avoidance.

Heidegger and some of the existentialists take this one step further. Their claim is that each of us has our own unique and special possibilities in life. The meaning of our lives is largely found through pursuing these opportunities. But we must first know what in fact they *are*, and knowing that death is part of our life—at least in the sense of telling us that nothing, including ourselves, lasts forever—is supposed to reveal our own unique and special possibilities to us. On the basis of this revelation we can then pursue the meaning of our lives. This meaning may have more to it than these special possibilities of ours, but they are essentially part of it.

Philosophy as an Answer

We've considered the Christian version of the axial answer to the meaning of life as well as the perspective invited by impending death. But we might be accused of overlooking an obvious candidate: philosophy. Philosophy was described by the ancients not only as *knowing how to die*, but as *the love of wisdom*. What do the Pythons have to say about philosophy?

The fish at the beginning of *Monty Python's The Meaning of Life* do not connect death with *what life is all about*, with what life *means*. Similarly, the couple examining the philosophy menu in the restaurant in the film show no more than the most idle of curiosities regarding philosophy:

> **WAITER**: Good evening! Uhh, would you care for something to . . . talk about?
> **MR. HENDY**: What is this one here?
> **WAITER**: Uhh, that's 'philosophy'.
> **MRS. HENDY**: Is that a sport?
> **WAITER**: Aah, no, it's more of an attempt to, uh, construct a viable hypothesis to, uh, explain the meaning of life.

MR. HENDY: Oh, that sounds wonderful. Would you like to talk about the meaning of life, darling?

MRS. HENDY: Sure. Why not?

WAITER: Philosophy for two?

MR. HENDY: Yup. Uhh,— uh, h— how do we—

WAITER: Oh, uhh, you folks want me to start you off?

MR. HENDY: Oh, really, we'd appreciate that.

WAITER: Okay!

MR. HENDY: Yeah.

WAITER: Well, ehh, . . .

MR. HENDY: Mhmm.

WAITER: . . . look. Have you ever wondered . . . just why you're here?

MR. HENDY: Well, we went to Miami last year and California the year before that, and we've—

WAITER: No, no, no. I mean, uh, w— why we're here . . . on this planet.

MR. HENDY: Hmmm. No.

WAITER: Right! Aaah, you ever wanted to know what it's all about?

MR. HENDY: Nope.

MRS. HENDY: No. No.

If wisdom were to result from consuming philosophy—which the menu has on offer—you would think that their interest would be keen and their appetite great. Shouldn't they be almost passionately involved in ordering? Could you ever be more voraciously hungry, excited or intensely careful, if what you were ordering was *wisdom*?

What this scene suggests is that just as religion had, for many, become conventional and humdrum in its forms and rituals, deadening in fact, philosophy, especially in the Pythons' England, had become very removed, sophisticated and "picky." It appeared on the menu, but aroused next to no excitement. Above all it was patronizingly detached from those questions that really mattered, the most central of which remains: *what is the meaning of life?* Rather than pursuing wholeheartedly the meaning of life, thereby seeking true wisdom, philosophy had become a very refined and detached examination of what are humanly irrelevant bits and pieces of this and that, impressively articulated trivia.

What an awful situation! Religion, the supposed vehicle of *answers*, seems to have gone stale, offering anesthetized or outrageous answers to people who, claiming to believe in them, nonetheless act as if the proposed answers are not worth a passing nod, let alone living by. And philosophy, supposedly the major vehicle for *asking* life's fundamental questions, appears as an arcane, sophisticated domain for "cultured" people, initiates in command of a specialized, often formal, vocabulary.

Something needs to be done. Stale answers to life's questions can make us forget the questions. If passed down through generations without consideration of the questions they are said to resolve, answers can become anaesthetizing. They can put us to sleep. In becoming merely conventional formulae, such dogmas render us spiritually unconscious, all in the name of awakening us to reality.

Liberating Laughter

The Pythons offer zany and irreverent comedy that can liberate us. We can distinguish the joyful laughter that comes over us when we feel happy from laughter that arises from the often sudden and intense recognition of an incongruity, the flash of awareness that "things don't add up." This is especially the case when words and actions move in different directions. In the space this opens up, a Pythonesque space, a newfound freedom becomes available.

Consider the following situation. Preaching abstinence, the minister, we discover, is attached to an intravenous tube that leads to a down-turned whisky bottle. Meaning in his sermon to say, "drinking is sinful," he slurs "thinking is simple." And in the course of his remarks he says a great number of all too simple things. We laugh, but at the same time we are opened to a space once closed. The minister's bumbling benightedness and hypocrisy open a door previously shut, perhaps not even known to have been there, and we are liberated to think without fetters, or maybe for the first time. What is going on here? An unrecognized, but nonetheless stifling obligation to passive acceptance is lifted. The preacher's slurred remark that "thinking is simple" invites open questioning. The minister and what he represents is all too simple, even simpleminded, and we come to believe that questioning itself—maybe a little drinking, too, who knows?—is liberating and not routine. This might well get us out of the trap of packaged solutions to problems that, however crucial to our lives, we didn't quite know existed. We gave the problems away to supposed experts.

Liberation can, of course, be *from* and *for*. If freed *from* pieties and dogmas, we can become free *for* questioning. The latter is, perhaps, most important. According to the German philosopher Immanuel Kant (1724–1804), the questions regarding life's meaning define our humanity, and if we do not expose ourselves honestly to these questions we not only betray our humanity, we impoverish it. In part, and precariously, the Pythons understood this, making these questions (and their far more ridiculous, though conventional, answers) available to a larger audience. At times their laughter in its most delightful aspects was something simply for its own sake. This is, quite curiously, related to the thinking of philosophers like Friedrich Nietzsche (1844–1900) and Jacques Derrida (1930–2005), whom we will discuss briefly.

For Kant, philosophy boils down to the pursuit of three questions: What can I know? What should I do? And, for what may I hope? These questions, further, come down to just one: What is it to be human? (More exactly, Kant asked *What man is*, but the word 'man' is now in disrepute for seeming to exclude large portions of the human race—women, girls, boys, infants, and sissies, just to mention a few.)

It is not hard to see that the closer these questions regarding knowledge, obligation and hope are fused, the more they become aspects of the one simple question we are asking: What does life *mean*? The meaning of life thus becomes a journey toward our most realistic hopes, reflecting what we know we ought to be doing.

But of course this very picture of life, the axial journey, itself turns out to be funny if in fact there is no intended goal to living at all. If there is no true destination to life's journey, the various elaborate accounts of life's meaning—and their attendant practices and rituals—look silly. And the Pythons often revel in this silliness, regardless of whether the laughter they provoke is an important cathartic on the way to "real meaning" or simply silliness for silliness's own silly sake. Nietzsche and Derrida both counsel hearty, healthy laughter. Really enjoy life, it is suggested, and keep in mind that you don't need God, a mission, or metaphysics to do this. Maybe what you actually need is to free yourself of these very notions. Maybe only then can you laugh wholeheartedly, without disappointment, false expectations or deluded hope.

And Now for . . . Comedic Eliminativism

We noted above that Python, as part of the counterculture, helped initiate a sort of questioning. But what about today, decades after the counterculture movement? Can the Pythons evoke the same questioning laughter in a much younger generation? Comedy is often disguised philosophical commentary, for it can vividly present the gap between what is, what makes sense, and what ought to be. Most comedic commentary, however, only states the *is*, leaving the rest to imagination. Such commentary pervades the Pythons.

But might the Pythons (along with other of postmodernism's unwitting forerunners) have accomplished emotionally and in advance a major "postmodern" mission: the user-friendly—and also user-funny—domestication of "the death of God," that is, the loss of God as a source for the meaning of life? This death could then be comfortably absorbed. And as "God" went down, so, as suggested above, would an inseparable companion and fellow-traveler: the notion of the meaning of life as a journey from here to someplace better.

The Pythons have zanily guided us along this path, across this delightfully shallow water, from the need for deep things to the shallows of neat-because-silly things. It is no secret that the Pythons played especially well to intellectuals. Could this have been because it brought them *down* to earth, but in vocabulary and vignettes that were *up* to their standards? And when the Pythons brought such people to the point where they could not tell up from down, all could laugh. It was laughter stemming from knowing that neither mattered. It was neither here nor there. Was this perhaps because the weight of axial journeying had been lifted?

The Pythons scrambled lots of things—people and situations. Maybe we must simply be humored into enjoying this. Ludwig Wittgenstein (1889–1951) once remarked that those who seemed to have solved the riddle of life seldom had anything to say regarding what the riddle was. But Wittgenstein did not say that these liberated and "enlightened" ones didn't laugh. Maybe that is exactly what they did. I'd like to suggest that their laughter was the very solution to that riddle of life they had pursued.

This may come as a bit of a shock. But the fact that the meaning of life is not what it seems does not mean that, for the Pythons, there is no meaning to life. Nor, on the other hand, is there any indication in the Pythons that there is something we might call "the meaning of life."

I'd suggest that the Pythons help us to glide *through* the seriousness of theological atheism, *past* the mortuary of existential despair, to what some might call eliminative "comedyism." There is no such word, but since we do need it, we'll just go ahead and use it.

Eliminative *materialism* is the view from which my analogy is drawn. And it is fairly well known. It simply—well, of course, nothing in the philosophy industry is simple—involves replacing words in your vocabulary that commit you to mind-body dualism, René Descartes's (1596–1650) old problem, with words that do not. If you are thorough and complete in your switchings and really get the hang of these replacement words, the mind-body problem bothers you much, much less. If you come to forget the words these replacement words replace, you probably can no longer figure out what the mind-body problem actually is, except through some pretty serious scholarship. And you're going to need a philosophical dictionary.

Eliminative comedyism is much the same, except it is found less in replacement vocabularies than in altered reactions and responses. Is a major dimension of the "real" journey of life from piety to laughter? Thinking about it, neither too long nor "deeply," what in fact could be meaningless about this? As the Pythons might suggest, such a conception is worth a chuckle or two. And such chuckles might serve as unexpectedly helpful hints regarding life after the meaning of life.

Aspects of Pythonic Philosophy

"No score, but there's certainly no lack of excitement here . . ."

10

God Forgive Us

STEPHEN FAISON

In *Monty Python and the Holy Grail*, King Arthur (Graham Chapman) and his Knights of the Round Table get into all sorts of comic trouble as they search for the sacred article. Why do they seek it? They have been commanded by God. According to the animated God, people have lost the sense of purpose to their lives. Arthur is to search for the Holy Grail and in doing so provide much needed inspiration to others.

On the first leg of their journey Arthur and his knights reach a castle. Arthur announces himself to the guards as "King of the Britons," and invites their master to join his holy mission. Unfortunately the spokesman for the castle guards (John Cleese) is not British. Even worse, he's French! The Frenchmen snicker at Arthur's invitation, and when the King threatens to enter by force in the name of God, they hurl nonsensical insults, then livestock. King Arthur is frustrated because his God, wearing a kingly crown, really did order the quest, and Arthur expects others to be moved by his holy authority. The reaction of Cleese and his mates illustrates how silly the mission seems to those who do not share Arthur's beliefs. In order to accept Arthur's claim, they must believe that God would command such a mission and enlist English "pig-dogs" to accomplish it. The Frenchmen are skeptical, to say the least.

Scenes pertaining to religious belief in *Monty Python and the Holy Grail*, *Monty Python's Life of Brian*, and *Monty Python's The*

125

Meaning of Life raise the issue of God's character, his behavior, and
the role he plays in our lives. The need to speculate about God's
relationship with us almost seems unnecessary given the existence
of the Holy Bible. The Bible not only contains alleged first-hand
accounts of God, but actually features appearances by God
Himself. The Christian theory of God establishes the deity
through its story of the creation and its aftermath. According to
the Christian narrative, a supernatural deity called God, "with
powers and abilities far beyond those of mortal men,"[1] created the
heavens and the earth and human beings and other less important
stuff. These human beings were given dominion over all living
creatures. Humans were also given immortal souls and free will to
choose good or evil. Of course, we screwed it up. Adam and Eve
disobeyed orders, and they and their descendants were punished
with mortality and condemned to toil the earth.[2] Sometime later
God issued a pardon in the form of His son, Jesus Christ, who
would take the rap for human disobedience. Human beings could
now receive salvation and eternal life in heaven, provided they
repent their sins, ask God for mercy, acknowledge Jesus as the sav-
ior and live a life of submission to God. Even then they cannot
be certain of admission to heaven, but can only hope to be judged
worthy.

The Christian account reveals a God who is in all ways perfect,
yet displays some suspiciously human characteristics such as jealousy and anger. This presentation seems strange until we consider the possibility that man actually created God in his image. This
alternative interpretation would explain why God exhibits these
unflattering human traits. Nevertheless, certain Church doctrines
are based on this truculent side of the Christian God, producing
numerous and sundry thou-shalt-nots and relating the consequences for failing to comply. The Pythons have fun with human
adherence to these doctrines and the fear they instill. God is
always present, always watching, always judging, and penalties are
severe. Arthur was quaking in his shoes at the mere appearance of
God; imagine how frightened he must be about what may happen
to him if he fails to accomplish his mission. By lampooning reactions to God's omnipresence in our lives, the Pythons compel us

[1] This phrase was appropriated by Superman in the 1950s.
[2] That is why work sucks, and always will.

to examine this relationship. Their gags perform a preliminary function of philosophy by challenging these doctrines, thereby setting the stage for critical analysis of certain assumptions and beliefs.

During this discussion we shall be assisted occasionally by Socrates, the central character in Plato's dialogues. Though Christianity is a revealed religion, significant aspects of Plato's philosophy were adapted to Christian theology. There is, however, an important relevant difference. The god Socrates describes in Plato's most popular dialogue, the *Republic*, is a rather abstract collection of perfect attributes detached from human affairs. The Christian God, on the other hand, represents the characteristics associated with fatherhood, and His human creations are described as His children. The Christian God is a loving provider and protector, but is also the ultimate authority, taskmaster, and disciplinarian. The Christian God is a personal god, intimately involved in the lives of His subjects. Christian doctrine expresses what it considers the proper relationship of God and human. Despite the kinship between Platonism and Christianity, Plato would probably agree with the Pythons that certain Christian doctrines and practices, when accepted and followed uncritically, reflect poorly on us and God.

In Alphabetical Order: Birth Control (and Other Intimate Matters)

In *Monty Python's The Meaning of Life*, a mill worker, played by Michael Palin, sadly announces to his numerous offspring that the mill is closed and there is no work. How will they survive? Palin must sell the children for scientific experiments. "Blame the Catholic Church for not letting me wear one of those little rubber things," he tells the youngsters. Neither he nor their mother (Terry Jones!) can use contraception if they are to remain Catholic, "part of the fastest growing religion in the world." He proceeds to explain, in song, what "we believe."

> Every sperm is sacred,
> Every sperm is great.
> If a sperm is wasted,

> God gets quite irate.
> Let the heathen spill theirs
> On the dusty ground.
> God shall make them pay for
> Each sperm that can't be found.

According to this belief, God takes a keen interest in whether or not people have children. Apparently children are the means through which God replenishes his army. The notion that He becomes "quite irate" whenever sperm is "wasted" implies that God insists that people have children even when they can no longer afford to feed them, and will severely punish those who take measures to avoid conception. The alternatives He permits are to cease having sexual intercourse or be swiftly kicked out of the religion.

As Palin's children reluctantly trudge to the laboratory, a peering neighbor (Graham Chapman) explains to his wife (Eric Idle!) that "as members of the Protestant Reformed Church, which successfully challenged the autocratic power of the papacy in the mid-sixteenth century, we can wear little rubber devices to prevent issue." In fact, Chapman continues, Martin Luther "may not have realized the full significance of what he was doing," but the consequences of his actions are that "four hundred years later, thanks to him, my dear, I can wear whatever I want on my John Thomas."

So the Protestant Reformation was actually about contraception and personal sexual liberation. "That's what being a Protestant is all about," Chapman declares, "That's why it's the church for me. That's why it's the church for anyone who respects the individual and the individual's right to decide for him or herself." Protestants and Catholics, whatever their differences, apparently agree that God is very concerned about whether or not a man wears a condom.

This scene illustrates that too much of God's presence in sexual affairs is likely to, shall we say, take the lead out of the pencil. When Chapman explains that each time Catholics have relations they have to have a baby, Idle does not understand the difference between Catholics and Protestants like themselves, because, "we have two children and we've had sexual intercourse twice." "That's not the point," Chapman responds. They could have "it" as much as they want, and furthermore Chapman could purchase products intended to enhance pleasure. Idle's temperature rises at the prospect, but he soon realizes, probably for the zillionth time, that all this talk about God is cold water on the fire.

This assertion of God's concern about reproduction suggests that He spends much of His time voyeuristically observing the sexual practices of His human creations. Before you accuse God of perversion, realize that He has little choice but to spy if He is to know which members of His flock are guilty of naughtiness. If the Catholic position is correct, God must watch sexual preliminaries for possible application of contraceptive devices. Even if Chapman's Protestant viewpoint is right, God still must go "undercover" to monitor copulation for unauthorized positions (any but missionary) and for the proper number of persons (two), sexes (one male and one female)[3] and marital status (married) of participants. God must also ensure that couples are not "doing it" too frequently or making too much noise during the proceedings, since these infractions would undermine the dignity and holy purpose of screwing. The Pythons ask us to consider the consequences of the belief that God cares about reproductive practices and sees everything. If so, then he watches our sexual activities. The attractiveness, endowments and skills of a given couple no doubt affects the quality of the viewing experience, but Christians must concede that all things considered, this is one of God's less onerous responsibilities.

Blasphemy (Name-Calling: With Sticks and Stones to Break Your Bones)

In Monty Python's Life of Brian an old man is to be stoned by a crowd impatient to hurl their rocks. The condemned man cries out that he only meant to compliment his wife's cooking when he said "that piece of halibut was good enough for Jehovah." As soon as the mob hears the name "Jehovah," one of them strikes the old man with a stone. The official in charge (John Cleese) chastises the offender and commands the group to allow the charges to be heard. When he further instructs them not to react

[3] The appropriately concerned reader may rest assured that God is aware of the aforementioned unions.

when hearing the name "Jehovah" until the proceedings are concluded, he too is struck. One of the offenders (Eric Idle) defends his action, saying to Cleese, "After all, you did say 'Jehovah,'" and Idle is also assaulted. Each time the name "Jehovah" is spoken, however inadvertently, rocks fly.

The uncivilized may view the stoning of blasphemers as despicable violence, but it is actually a religious duty. After all, the condemned man's statement that the halibut served was "good enough for Jehovah" clearly uses the Lord's name for some purpose other than reverence or worship. "What's a little blasphemy?" you may ask. The old man's statement may seem like a minor infraction, but remarks like this are the marijuana of blasphemy: they lead to more serious usage. For example, people who say "Jesus H. Christ" know Goddamn well that "H" is not His middle initial. And even though God is peeping, it is not appropriate to call out "Oh, God!" during sexual intercourse.[4] So, there is no such thing as a "little" blasphemy. Stoning, then, is an ancient form of intervention meant to save blasphemers from bringing down the wrath of God. The punishment may seem severe, but if stoning saved just one life, wouldn't it be worth it?

All seriousness aside, the Python's sketch encourages us to reflect upon how absurd the policy of punishing blasphemers becomes in practice, when an old man is to be stoned to death for complimenting his wife's dinner and others are battered for accidentally saying "Jehovah." Apparently God is highly offended by these slights. To accept this view the believer must suppose that God heard the old man's compliment and said to himself, "Well, I'll be damned. I provide the halibut, the seasoning, the fire, and the cook gets all the credit. All she did was shove the darn thing into the oven, which I also provide, by the way. I tell you, I don't get no respect." Believers eager to punish transgressors evidently judge the All-Mighty incapable of handling these insults Himself. According to this view, God sanctions stoning and perhaps enjoys the spectacle as much as the participants who treat them as amusements not to be missed.

Socrates would no doubt take a dim view of this treatment of blasphemy. Blasphemy is a form of impiety or sinfulness and includes any false representation of the gods. In Plato's *Republic*,

---

[4] A wink or nod is sufficient acknowledgment.

Socrates discredits the work of Homer which depicts the gods acting out of anger, jealousy or pettiness. Socrates contends that the gods, as perfect beings, do not so conduct themselves, and therefore any such portrayal must be false. According to Socrates's usage, blasphemy involves words which reflect negatively on the gods, particularly if such language is offered in the name of the gods. The condemned man in *Monty Python's Life of Brian* is not guilty of blasphemy properly defined, and the mob's definition has been inappropriately stretched to include simply uttering His name. To say that God authorizes punishment for such usage of His name is to portray God as arrogant and nasty. On Socrates's account, the stoning citizens are guiltier of blasphemy than those they punish since their actions, performed in God's name, present an image unbecoming to God.

Heaven (Capitalize for Effect)

Toward the end of *Monty Python's The Meaning of Life* three freshly dead couples are led to Heaven. They are greeted with "Merry Christmas" as they check-in at the front desk. Is it Christmas? Well, you see, every day is Christmas in Heaven. This seems reasonable since one might expect that in Heaven believers eternally celebrate the birth of Christ, who made their salvation possible. The guests are seated and the master of ceremonies (Graham Chapman) is introduced to the soft strains of "Silent Night." This is a "wonderful, warm and emotional moment," he says, and begins the song "Christmas in Heaven." The musical tempo increases and showgirls appear in red suits and caps. Chapman sings that in Heaven it snows above their heads but the weather is warm down below. There are great films on TV, toiletries and games, all that anyone could possibly desire. Surprised? As it happens, Christmas in Heaven is *Santa Claus* Christmas.

This scene presents Heaven as a place filled with earthly rewards, and is a comic depiction of the conflation of religious and commercial versions of Christmas. Some religious hymns describe Heaven as the land of milk and honey, with streets paved with gold. This conception of Heaven conveys that even Christians do not believe the religious life has sufficient intrinsic value to motivate moral behavior. The sketch suggests that believers do not actually renounce their sinful appetites for worldly pleasures, but hope that by restraining themselves on earth they will receive an unlimited supply of material goods and services in the afterlife. The scene implies that God, as the architect of Heaven, understands human nature and has material compensation waiting up there for His followers. If Heaven was not always this way, apparently even God could no longer bear to watch the disappointment of those who discover that their Heavenly reward amounts only to eternal communion with Him.

Bonus Material: The Origin of Monty Python's Christmas in Heaven Is Revealed for the First Time

Once upon a time people died. Believers ascended to Heaven to dwell in the house of the Lord (animated version from *Monty Python and the Holy Grail*) forever, while unrepentant sinners were immediately escorted (by the Grim Reaper from *Monty Python's The Meaning of Life*) to Hell. Heaven and Hell were structured to reward the saved and punish sinners. Since salvation is its own reward, those in Heaven spent eternity singing hymns and praying to God (led by Michael Palin's chaplain from *Monty Python's The Meaning of Life*). Since sin is its own punishment, Hell was designed (by interior decorator Graham Chapman) in a manner conducive to sin, thereby ensuring everlasting suffering. Inhabitants of Hell were furnished with gambling, liquor, and whores. An eternity of debauchery (and annoying parenthetical interruptions) would teach them a lesson they would never forget. Expensive material goods were purchased from Acme Decadence, Inc. to promote high-stakes wagering; the scorching climate encouraged the removal of clothing which facilitated fornication.[5] As everyone knows, nothing goes with gambling and whoring like booze. Unfortunately the plan backfired when, incredibly, the residents actually enjoyed their vulgar surroundings. Word of the "suffering" soon reached Heaven and all Hell broke loose. A

---

[5] The Devil was known to sneak about the gaming tables jabbing naked buttocks with his pitchfork.

group of trustees in Heaven (led by John Cleese) filed a class-action discrimination suit claiming that the sinners had received preferential treatment. The case was settled out of court and the afterlife stations were redesigned (by new decorator Eric Idle). Henceforth sinners would be mounted on rotisseries to roast forever, creating the Hell we have all come to know and love. The saved were awarded material compensation for renouncing worldly possessions on Earth. As a measure of good faith, the trustees agreed to maintain a prominent role for Christ (Terry Jones) in the new and improved Heaven. In an ingenious compromise, both sides promised that every day would be Christmas, and Santa Claus (Terry Gilliam, who did not want the part but failed his auditions for other roles) would deliver gifts to the faithful. That is how Christmas became merry!

Hell (Capitalized because Heaven Was Capitalized)

In *Monty Python's The Meaning of Life*, after dutifully praising God, the chaplain (Michael Palin) leads the congregation in the following song.

> O Lord, please don't burn us,
> Don't grill or toast your flock.
> Don't put us on the barbecue,
> Or simmer us in stock.
> Don't braise of bake or boil us,
> Or stir-fry us in a wok.

Apparently there is reason for even the faithful to live in a state of fear and trembling. Since all human beings are born into filthy sin and cannot cleanse themselves, their fate is determined by God. He is the final authority on sin and is accountable to no one. We cannot know how He will decide, and it would be imprudent to wait until Judgment Day to persuade the court. Therefore, the best approach for believers is to beg their loving God in advance for mercy. By having the song follow the prayer, the scene illustrates how ridiculous it is for Christians to worship a God they believe may at any moment capriciously chuck them all into Hell. In the Christian tradition Hell is presented as the final destination

for sinners who fail to repent. Nevertheless, as the scene demonstrates, the faithful live in terror that despite their righteousness,
they too may be judged unworthy and sentenced to burn forever
in the eternal flame.

     Socrates would reject that God behaves this way, and in the
Apology he explains why the virtuous need not fear death or the
afterlife. According to Socrates, death is either a state in which the
dead are nothing, with no perception of anything, or death is simply the relocation of the soul from one realm to another. If death
is the former, then it is like a dreamless sleep. If death is the latter, souls of the virtuous join those of great men and women
already deceased. Imagine abiding with the Queen of Soul,
Aretha Franklin, and the Godfather of Soul, James Brown.[6]

A Short but Grave Reflection about God and Hell (You Can Use This at Your Judgment-Day Trial to Defend Your Wickedness and Disbelief)

The Pythons' "Please don't burn us" song asks us to consider the
following. The righteous should have no fear of Hell. If God is
good and just, as believers claim, why would He condemn the
righteous to Hell? The concern that He could do exactly that
stems from the Christian portrayal of God as unpredictable and
wrathful. After all, God condemned the descendents of Adam
and Eve (us) before they were born. According to the Christian
tradition, Heaven is not a reward for faithful service, but a gift
from God which He may award or withhold. But if God con-
demns the righteous to Hell as well as the wicked, there is little
incentive to be righteous *for Heaven's sake*. The Pythons are able to
draw humor from these scenes because of the unspoken belief of
righteous yet "God-fearing" Christians. If the faithful and righteous must live in fear, God must be one bad-mutha-shut-yo-
mouth.

---

[6] Okay, so they're still alive. Chances are they're older than you are, so they'll be
dead when you get there. Happy now?

Justice (A Philosopher Is Observed)

In an early scene from *Monty Python and The Holy Grail*, a mob
intends to burn a woman whom they claim is a witch. How do
they know she is a witch? She looks like one. The mob's chief
representative, Eric Idle, confesses that they dressed the woman to
look like a witch, but nevertheless insists she is a witch.
Apparently clothes make the woman. A philosophical cleric,
played by Terry Jones, announces that there is a logical way to
determine whether the woman in question is actually a witch. He
leads them through the following (slightly abridged) line of reasoning:

> **JONES**: What do you do with witches?
> **IDLE/MOB**: Burn them!
> **JONES**: What do you burn apart from witches?
> **IDLE/MOB**: Wood.
> **JONES**: So, why do witches burn?
> **IDLE/MOB**: 'Cause they're made of wood?
> **JONES**: Good! How do we tell if she is made of wood? Does
> wood sink in water?
> **IDLE/MOB**: No, it floats.
> **JONES**: What else floats in water?
> **IDLE/MOB**: A duck.
> **JONES**: So, logically, if she weighs the same as a duck . . .
> **IDLE/MOB**: She's made of wood!
> **JONES**: And therefore?
> **IDLE/MOB**: A witch!

This scene presents how believers are willing to distort logic in
their zeal to execute what they perceive to be God's will. God is
drawn into the situation because witches are considered dangerous
since they have magical powers and practice sorcery. According to
religious superstition witches cannot command supernatural entities loyal to God, so their influence is limited to evil spirits. Since
witches conspire with these enemies of God, they are God's enemies, and God's enemies must be destroyed. The mob's determi-
nation to burn the witch, in His holy name, means they believe
that God is not able or willing to act and delegates authority to
humans.

A later scene from *Monty Python and The Holy Grail* asserts that
God not only sanctions the earthly destruction of His enemies,
but provides the instruments to do so. When the knights are confronted by the killer rabbit that has savagely attacked members of
the party, and more importantly, interfered with the mission
ordered by God, the rabbit must be annihilated, in His holy name.
As the knights prepare to unleash the Holy Hand Grenade, which
has been blessed for such use by God Himself, an assistant cleric
(Michael Palin) offers the following reading from the *Book of
Armaments*, Chapter 2:

> And Saint Attila raised the hand grenade up on high,
> saying "O Lord, bless this thy hand grenade,
> that with it thou mayest blow thine enemies to tiny bits,
> in Thy mercy." And the Lord did grin.

Evidently no job is too small when it comes to eliminating
God's opponents. God needs his defenders of the faith to overcome whatever sentiments they may have for killing women and
rabbits if His will is to be done. The case of the rabbit is not at
all ambiguous. This vicious little bunny was caught red-handed
(get it?) in the act of multiple assault and homicide and should be
terminated with extreme prejudice to prevent any further interfer-
ence with holy missions and serve as deterrent to other rabbits.
There is some doubt about whether the woman is actually a witch,
but it is better to err on the side of safety. The risk is greater if
the mob releases the woman only to discover later that she is a
witch, than to burn her only to learn that she was not. So *logically*
it is better to burn the woman on the chance that she might be a
witch. If the mob is wrong, there is no harm done. The woman
simply receives her Heavenly reward[7] ahead of schedule. Besides,
she might have been chucked into Hell anyway.

The mob of stoners in *Monty Python's Life of Brian* and the
knights that destroy the rabbit in *Monty Python and the Holy Grail*
believe that their actions are just because they are sanctioned by
God, which further implies that any action sanctioned by God is
for that reason just.

---

[7] Which, as you now know, is much better than it used to be.

The question raised by the Pythons of whether an act which seems unjust is nevertheless just if sanctioned by God is an ancient problem. In fact, the topic is the subject of a Socratic dialogue called the *Euthyphro*. Socrates meets Euthyphro in the city's center and learns that the young man has come to indict his own father because, Euthyphro insists, it is the pious thing to do. When Socrates challenges him to define piety, Euthyphro asserts that piety is that which is loved by the gods. Socrates asks whether a given act is pious because it is loved by the gods, or whether it is loved by the gods because it is pious. The same question is applicable to justice. Another way to put the question is to ask whether justice is determined by God and dependent upon God, or whether justice is embraced by God but independent of God. The former construction, which *Euthyphro*, the stoners and the knights evidently support, is problematic because it asserts that any action, no matter how monstrous it may seem, is just if authorized by God.

The examples of the witch and rabbit demonstrate why the character of God is so important. If God is angry and vengeful and orders the earthly destruction of His enemies, then it would seem that He is capable of ordering acts considered wicked. On the other hand, if God is perfect, and human characteristics and weaknesses are not applicable to Him, then wickedness cannot be performed in His name and cannot be attributed to Him.

Prayer (A Euphemism for Butt-Kissing and Begging)

In *Monty Python's The Meaning of Life*, Part II: Growth and Learning, the Python troupe has a little fun with church prayer. After some informational remarks by John Cleese, Michael Palin formally tells the congregation, "Let us praise God," and leads them in the following prayer, which they dutifully repeat.

Oh, Lord. Ooh, you are so big. So absolutely huge. Gosh, we're all really impressed down here, I can tell you. Forgive us, O Lord, for this our dreadful toadying. [Congregation] *And barefaced flattery*. But you're so strong and, well, just so super. [Congregation] *Fantastic*. Amen.

Believers are expected to constantly acknowledge the greatness of God. This form of prayer includes giving thanks to God for all He has given us. We are not only appreciative of the products and services we receive, but for our very lives, which persist only because of His will. Refusal to give thanks is not merely impolite, but the worst form of ingratitude. Even those in pain and misery must not appear ungrateful, for that too comes from God. These sorts of prayers imply that God wants and needs human praise, and never tires of hearing about His infinite might and goodness from His humble servants. Apparently God has an insatiable ego that centuries of worship have not satisfied and requires His followers to forever stand in awe of His magnificence. Believers must utter every word with passion or risk falling out of His favor and being, that's right, chucked into Hell. The congregation's acknowledgement of "barefaced flattery" conveys their recognition that God must be aware that they cannot continuously generate such worship with sincerity. In summary, prayer is an integral part of man's relation to God. Prayer is our means of giving thanks for His many wonderful blessings. Prayer is how we acknowledge His greatness and goodness. Finally, prayer is required and one had better perform this duty or risk being chucked into Hell.

The Pythons present a scene in *Monty Python and the Holy Grail* which confirms Socrates's view that a perfect God has no need of these displays of bowing and scraping. God appears in a cloud and Arthur and his men immediately drop to their knees. "Don't grovel!" God bellows, "If there's anything I can't stand, it's people groveling." When Arthur begins to apologize for groveling, God interrupts with, "And don't apologize! Every time I talk to someone, it's 'Sorry this' and 'Forgive me that' and "I'm not worthy.'"

In the *Euthyphro*, Socrates explains why God has no interest in this type of worship. Euthyphro claims that piety involves care of the gods, or service to the gods, which is performed through sacrifice and prayer. Socrates instructs that sacrifice and prayer cannot be wanted or needed by God since to sacrifice is to make a gift to God and to pray is to beg from God. A proper gift is that which another needs or wants. Since God is not in need or want of anything, we cannot give Him a gift. Since God has already provided all that we need, it is offensive and ungrateful to ask for more. Socrates adds that we sacrifice in order to beg more comfortably. So sacrifice and prayer are little more than trading and bargaining with God. God has no need or want of such commerce, so we should not conduct these practices, certainly not in His name.

The Christian God is a personal fatherly god, so it is not surprising that people approach God as children approach their parents for favors. A common prayer is the request for services in which the needy, or merely desirous, ask God to produce or prevent a certain outcome. The requests for services suggest that God's will is unstable, susceptible to pleading and weeping. Believers sometimes say that God can be moved by our prayers, but the Pythons encourage us to consider this belief. If God's wisdom is infinitely greater than ours, and all that happens is part of His master plan, why would He change His mind because we beg? If we believe the aforementioned, why would we beg?

It's little wonder that Christians make many claims about God that seem incredible, outrageous, and just plain silly. In the Bible, God creates the heavens and earth and gives his favorite creatures special privileges, but in a flash of rage takes it all back. God presents a fruit tree to Adam and Eve though they are forbidden to partake (some gift!), commands Abraham to sacrifice his son and heaps misfortune on Job. And there is plenty more drama where that came from. There is a contrasting image of the Christian God as loving and merciful, but the more turbulent characterization is responsible for the doctrines and practices lampooned by the Pythons. If biblical tales of an angry and vengeful God are meant to be taken literally, then Christians are sensible to take measures to avoid His wrath. It is often the case that religious beliefs are not arrived at and maintained through a process of careful reflection. Philosophy performs the service of critical analysis, but religious belief and superstition have been notoriously resistant to intellectual examination. Using humor to illustrate how ludicrous particular beliefs appear when their consequences are acted out for our benefit, the Pythons succeed in challenging us to question certain religious assumptions. That's not to say that belief in God should be extinguished, but if our behavior looks ridiculous when played for our entertainment, perhaps we should examine beliefs and practices attributed to God that seem so absurd.

11
Monty Python and David Hume on Religion

JOHN HUSS

66 Is God really real?" This is a perennial question for the philosophy of religion. Fortunately, the Pythons have answers to it. Perhaps too many answers. If we asked Arthur, King of the Britons, he would certainly testify that God exists, speaks English, and can't stand people groveling, averting their eyes, ceaselessly apologizing, and deeming themselves unworthy. Yet when we begin inquiring into *Monty Python's The Meaning of Life*, "there is some doubt" about whether God is really real, or, to put it more philosophically, there is doubt over whether God's existence can be established through a valid argument. There is a long philosophical tradition of constructing rational arguments for the existence and attributes of God, and an equally long skeptical tradition of deconstructing those same arguments. The Pythons have been exemplary participants in the latter tradition, either through parody, or by echoing in a funnier and more succinct way the skeptical arguments of such philosophical predecessors as Scottish philosopher David Hume (1711–1776).

Causes and Reasons

In the *Natural History of Religion* (1757), Hume made an important philosophical distinction between *causes* of and *reasons* for religious belief. By the *reason* for a belief, Hume meant an argument in its favor that appeals to shared norms of rationality, premises, and rules of reasoning that everyone can agree on. The *cause* of a belief is the particular set of environmental, historical, or personal circumstances that led an individual to hold the belief, whether or not it is rational to do so (we will return to a discussion of causes later in this chapter).[1] In Hume's day, there were a number of arguments for the existence and attributes of God—reasons to believe. He was highly critical of these arguments.

The Ontological Argument

An ingenious argument for the existence of God was concocted by St. Anselm, Archbishop of Canterbury (1033–1109). St. Anselm's argument, the Ontological Argument, was written in the form of a prayer, and began with the following lines:

> Oh Lord, ooh, You are so big, so absolutely huge. Gosh, we're all really impressed down here I can tell you. Forgive us, oh Lord, for this, our dreadful toadying. And barefaced flattery. But You're so strong and just so super. Fantastic. Amen.

So said St. Anselm. Well, not really. Actually this was the prayer of the school chaplain in *Monty Python's The Meaning of Life*. However, St. Anselm did advance a similarly superlative premise asserting God's greatness:

> God is that being than whom no greater being can be conceived.

Put another way, God is simply, by definition, the greatest conceivable being. (St. Anselm may have meant "possible" rather than "conceivable" but we will leave that point off to one side for the time being and return to it later). Ah, but what conclusion can be drawn from this premise? Does God, this greatest conceivable being, actually exist, or is he merely imaginary?

---

[1] David Hume, *Principal Writings on Religion: including Dialogues Concerning Natural Religion and The Natural History of Religion*. Edited with an introduction by J.C.A. Gaskin (New York: Oxford University Press, 1998). Having finished that, have a go at J.C.A. Gaskin, *Hume's Philosophy of Religion* (London: Macmillan, 1978).

St. Anselm was well aware of the freethinkers and skeptics who might doubt God's existence, but he had an answer for them. Imagine the greatest conceivable being: omnipotent, omnipresent, omniscient, omnivident, omnibenevolent, and omnivorous. Suppose, St. Anselm asks, that such a being didn't exist. Well, in that case, we wouldn't really be conceiving of the greatest conceivable being, now would we? For we can conceive of a still greater being, namely, one that has all of these traits, *and exists*. Therefore, if God, by definition, is the greatest conceivable being, he must exist. In fact, St. Anselm takes the argument one step further and says that God is an even greater being than we can conceive of.[2]

Get Me to the Argument Clinic!

We don't have to visit the Argument Clinic to see the problem with this argument (Yes, we do! No, we don't!). Instead, we can do what philosophers do and focus on the form of the argument. Let us forget for a moment that St. Anselm's argument is about God. Consider instead an argument of the same form, only in this argument we seek to establish the existence of Yeti. Yeti is defined as a Himalayan ape-like creature that leaves footprints in the snow. But suppose we tweak this definition as follows: Yeti is an *actually existing* Himalayan ape-like creature that leaves footprints in the snow. All that follows from this definition is that IF something is to count as Yeti, it would have to be Himalayan, ape-like, leave footprints in the snow, *and exist*. That's a big IF. It doesn't follow that Yeti does exist. In fact the camel-spotter of *Monty Python's Flying Circus* (Episode 7, "You're No Fun Anymore") before he became a camel-spotter, had been a Yeti-spotter, and never did actually spot a Yeti. Thus, we may here be dealing with a definition that goes unfulfilled by any real being. Likewise, directly or indirectly importing the property of existence into the definition of God, as St. Anselm did, leaves open whether there exists a being that fulfills that definition. Defining God as the greatest possible (hence existent) being leaves unanswered the

---

[2] Saint Anselm, "The Ontological Argument," in John Perry and Michael Bratman, eds., *Introduction to Philosophy*, second edition (New York: Oxford University Press, 1992), pp. 39–40.

question of whether there is any real being that fulfills the definition. We can certainly conceive of the definition going unfulfilled
without running into any logical difficulties. Hume summed this
up well in his *Dialogues Concerning Natural Religion*, when he wrote:
"Whatever we conceive as existent, we can also conceive as non-
existent" (p. 91). Thus, St. Anselm's argument fails to establish the
existence of God. Of course, its failure to do so does not dis-
prove God's existence either.

The Conceivable versus the Possible, Or, How to Confuse a Cat

Let us now return to the distinction between "conceivability" and
"possibility" mentioned earlier. Although for St. Anselm's argument I don't think it matters very much whether God is defined as
the greatest conceivable being or the greatest possible being, it is
nonetheless an important distinction in philosophy. On the one
hand, whether something is conceivable or inconceivable depends
very much on the thinker. For example, what is conceivable to an
intelligent man like the famous composer Arthur "Two Sheds"
Jackson (*Monty Python's Flying Circus*, Episode 1, "Whither
Canada?") is not necessarily conceivable to a Gumby brain special-
ist (see *Monty Python's Flying Circus*, Episode 32, "The War Against
Pornography"). Conceivability varies from one individual to the
next. On the other hand, not everything that is conceivable is possible. There is a certain sense of the term "possibility," namely
physical possibility, which is independent of the capabilities of
individual thinkers, and depends only on physical laws. For example, Luigi Vercotti (*Monty Python's Flying Circus*, Episode 10, untitled) can conceive of Ron Obvious jumping the English Channel,
digging a hole to Java, or running to Mercury. The fact that Luigi
can conceive of these things certainly does not make them possible, as Ron's failed attempts so laughably illustrate. While we're on
the topic, it should also be noted that conceivability and possibility often interact in interesting ways. For example, when something inconceivable to us turns out to be possible, we are often
quite baffled to see it actually happen. This fact was put to productive use by the Confuse-A-Cat team in jarring a listless pet cat
from out of its rut (*Monty Python's Flying Circus*, Episode 5, "Man's

Crisis of Identity in the Latter Half of the Twentieth Century"). Actually, in that episode, the Pythons take things even further. Some of the stunts pulled by the Confuse-A-Cat team were not only inconceivable, but physically impossible (although television makes anything look possible). As baffling as it is to see the inconceivable happen, it is even more baffling to witness something that is physically impossible! This is the stuff of miracles, but more on miracles later.

The Argument from Design, or, "All Things Dull and Ugly"

Another argument for the existence of God, a bit more intuitive than the Ontological Argument, is the Argument from Design. The Argument from Design says that the natural world provides evidence of creation by a rational God. What kinds of evidence are cited? Generally, evidence of order in the biological and physical worlds. Let us first consider the biological world. The biological variant of the Argument from Design states that the high degree to which plants and animals are adapted to their habitats and habits of life can hardly be due to chance. Besides, many of these adaptations are strikingly similar to the products of intelligent design by humans: the lens of an eye shares many features with the lens of a camera. Since human intelligence is known to be responsible for the design of man-made devices, by analogy, a divine intelligence must be responsible for the design of the far-more-complex adaptations of living things.

Now let us consider the physical world in general. The universe is chock full of orderly phenomena, as Eric Idle observes in "The Galaxy Song" from *Monty Python's The Meaning of Life*:

> Just remember that you're standing on a planet that's evolving
> And revolving at nine hundred miles an hour.
> That's orbiting at nineteen miles a second, so it's reckoned,
> A sun that is the source of all our power.
> The sun and you and me, and all the stars that we can see,
> Are moving at a million miles a day,
> In the outer spiral arm, at forty thousand miles an hour,
> of the galaxy we call the Milky Way . . .

The physical version of the Argument from Design states that all of this astronomical order and law-governed motion cannot have arisen due to chance, and therefore must have as its source a Higher Intelligence.

Today it is widely acknowledged throughout the world (and much of the United States) that Darwin's discovery of evolution by natural selection blew away the biological version of the Argument from Design. As the Pythons acknowledge in the title track to *Monty Python's The Meaning of Life*, "scientists say we're just spiraling coils/ Of self-replicating DNA." Blind variation in physical traits, some traits faring better than others in the struggle for existence, the encoding of traits in DNA, and their inheritance by offspring provide the basic ingredients for the evolution of adaptation by natural selection. A Divine Designer is not necessary to explain the presence of biological adaptations. Yet the physical version of the Argument from Design refuses to die. Many scientists and engineers today, while acknowledging that Darwin's discovery of evolution by natural selection has undercut the biological version of the argument, argue that the physical version of the Design Argument receives stronger and stronger support with each new theoretical advance in our understanding of the universe. Newton certainly thought so, as did Einstein, who wrote in *The World As I See It* (1934), pp. 267–68:

> Religious feeling takes the form of a rapturous amazement at the harmony of natural law, which reveals an intelligence of such superiority that, compared with it, all the systematic thinking and acting of human beings is utterly insignificant reflection.

This quotation emphasizes another dimension to the Argument from Design. Not only does the universe afford us evidence of the *existence* of God, but of His *attributes* as well. God possesses an intelligence that in some vague way is like human intelligence, only more super. Hume, a big Newton fan, and himself very much impressed with the orderliness of the universe, was very dismissive of this argument. For one thing, to invoke a Divine Intelligence to explain the origin of order in the universe doesn't seem to explain anything at all. It simply takes one mystery, the presence of order in the universe, and replaces it with something equally mysterious, a Divine Intelligence (in Hume's words, an "intelligent agent"). We might just as well ask where Divine Intelligence comes from. Clearly, Hume argues, this explanation gives no satisfaction. Yet even granting that the universe has a Creator, Hume was skeptical of the prospects of inferring His attributes from His creation. Where the orthodox Christian believer saw in nature evidence of God's moral righteousness, benevolence, and omnipotence, Hume saw evidence of moral indifference. Monty Python captured Hume's critique brilliantly on their *Contractual Obligation Album* in their mock hymn, "All Things Dull and Ugly":

> All things dull and ugly,
> All creatures short and squat,
> All things rude and nasty,
> The Lord God made the lot.
>
> Each little snake that poisons,
> Each little wasp that stings.
> He made their brutish venom,
> He made their horrid wings.
>
> All things sick and cancerous,
> All evil great and small,
> All things foul and dangerous,
> The Lord God made them all.
>
> Each nasty little hornet,
> Each beastly little squid.
> Who made the spiky urchin?
> Who made the sharks? He did.
>
> All things scabbed and ulcerous,
> All pox both great and small.
> Putrid, foul, and gangrenous,
> The Lord God made them all.

Hume believed that the Argument from Design did not derive its persuasiveness from observations of the imperfect world around us, but rather from weakly veiled appeals to church doctrine, which preached the existence of a single, all-powerful, eternal, and benevolent God. Our observations of the world are influenced by our prior beliefs about God. In other words, when we look out at the world, we aren't seeing evidence of God's attributes in the world, rather, we are simply seeing the world through God-colored glasses, selectively ignoring all things dull, ugly, rude, and nasty. Hume thought that not very much about God can be inferred from his creation. To underscore his point, he ventured a number of hypotheses equally compatible with the observations. Perhaps, he mused, the universe is the work of many Gods. Or maybe it was initiated by a deity who has long since abandoned it to its own devices.

There is a scene in Terry Gilliam's opening animation sequence to *Monty Python's The Meaning of Life* where God is shown vacillating between two possible earths, one spherical and the other cubical. Opting for the spherical one, he tosses it off to one side whereupon it promptly cracks open. Hume had invoked a similar image in *Dialogues Concerning Natural Religion* to emphasize that a number of different creation scenarios were consistent with our observations of the world around us:

> This world [for all we know] is very faulty and imperfect, compared to a superior standard; and was only the first rude essay of some infant Deity, who afterwards abandoned it, ashamed of his lame performance. (p. 71)

From the context of the passage, it is clear that Hume did not sincerely entertain this proposition or several of the others he mentions. Rather, he sought to illustrate that what we are able to observe of the world around us does little to illuminate such remote questions as the existence and attributes of the Creator, if there is one.

The Argument from Miracles, Or, "He's Been Taken Up!"

What religion would be complete without its miracles? Well, certainly not Christianity. One of the most important arguments for Christianity is founded on such miracles as the Virgin Birth, the

Resurrection, and the miracles performed by Jesus Christ and described in the New Testament by the Evangelists Matthew, Mark, Luke, and John. According to these accounts, Jesus brought about events completely outside the natural order of things, such as turning water into wine, raising Lazarus from the dead, healing the blind, the lepers, and even the impotent (the number of different kinds of miracles Jesus performed depends on which Evangelist you consult). What can we conclude from all this? A miracle is often cited as a sign that the person performing it is either Divine or Divinely empowered. Let's grant that only God can confer supernatural powers, and let's further assume that He would never give those powers to someone who would misrepresent Him. Then the words of a miracle-worker such as Jesus should be accepted as revelations of Divine Wisdom (a version of this argument may be found in John 3: 2). That, in a nutshell, is the Argument from Miracles.

This raises the question, was Brian Cohen divine? Let's take a look at his miracles. In *Monty Python's Life of Brian*, each "miracle" Brian performs leads to greater conviction on the part of his followers that his every utterance is Divinely sanctioned. His first miracle is to be "taken up" into heaven, only to be spotted in full sprint moments later. For his next miracle, he causes a juniper bush to bring forth juniper berries. Later he miraculously restores the power of speech to Simon, a hermit of eighteen years (by landing on his foot, that is). As evidence of Brian's divinity mounts, his words are received by the devoted throng as Divine revelation. His exasperated plea for the crowd to "fuck off" is treated as an invitation to ritual: "How shall we fuck off, O Lord?"

Of course, we know, as do Brian, Simon the Hermit, and everyone else who is not in a devotional stupor, that the purported miracles are nothing of the sort. Which of these events lies outside the natural order? Temporarily disappearing from view when running through a crowded marketplace? Juniper bushes bearing juniper berries? Yelping over a foot injury? The answer is none of the above. Eyewitnesses believe them to be miracles, yet clearly they are not. This is the starting point for a critique raised by Hume in his essay "Of Miracles."[3] Eyewitnesses are

---

[3] David Hume, "Of Miracles," in *An Enquiry Concerning Human Understanding* (Indianapolis: Hackett, 1977), pp. 72–90.

often wrong. And as weak as the evidence from the reports of eyewitnesses might be, it certainly gets no stronger as it travels through the grapevine, as anyone knows who has ever sent a story around a circle. Moreover, a miracle is by definition outside the natural order, and hence has the weight of every contrary event stacked against it. For every report of water being turned to wine, we have countless reports of water remaining water. The less probable an event is, Hume says, the more suspicious we should be of claims that it happened. From errors on the part of the witness, to mistakes or deception at each link in the chain of human testimony, there are countless ways that a report of a miracle could be mistaken. Ultimately, Hume says, the only condition under which we should accept someone's testimony of a miracle is if it would be even more miraculous if they were wrong!

It was central to Hume's philosophy that questions of existence, which he called "matters of fact," could never be settled by abstract reasoning alone (we saw this earlier in the critique of the Ontological Argument: a being cannot simply be defined into existence). Knowledge of what exists is always rooted in experience. Nonetheless, as is well-illustrated by the eyewitness accounts of Brian Cohen's "miracles," experience is a fallible source of knowledge. Hume readily acknowledged that we can be mistaken about what our senses are telling us.

The Cause of Religion, Or "Oh Father, Please Don't Boil Us"

Hume's examination of the Ontological, Design, and Miracle arguments found each of them severely lacking. Yet for all of his attention to the reasons for religious belief, Hume was convinced that elegant argumentation had little to do with why most people actually believed. To answer that question required an inquiry not into the *reasons* for religious belief, but rather its *causes*. In his *Natural History of Religion*, Hume fingered a rather simple and age-old cause of religious belief: fear.

Hume argued that people everywhere are afraid of the forces which affect their lives but are beyond their control. They call these forces Gods and seek to appease them through religious worship. Over time, the number of Gods has decreased, but the same story holds. In *Monty Python's The Meaning of Life*, the school chaplain leads the young lads in a hymn that essentially beseeches the Almighty not to cook and eat his loyal flock: "O Father, please don't boil us." And in *Monty Python and the Holy Grail*, God himself chastises King Arthur for his fearful groveling and supplication. These views of religion fit very well with Hume's analysis.

The Epilogue: A Question of Belief

Good evening, and welcome to the Epilogue! We have seen several arguments for the existence and attributes of God criticized (by Hume) and ridiculed (by Monty Python), but what are we to conclude from all this? In the end, not much. Both Monty Python and Hume seem to be in agreement that when it comes to questions at a remove from our experience—the origin of the universe, the existence and attributes of God, and while we're at it, let's toss in the afterlife—we are simply out of our element and any conclusions we draw will be sketchy at best. We would like to have useful empirical information on these questions, and the Pythons (in *Monty Python's Flying Circus*, Episode 36, "E. Henry Tripshaw's Disease") sure try, assembling, for example, a noted panel of the corpses of three professors to answer the question, "Is there life after death?" Their answers? No, no, and no. As for the existence and nature of God, after exposing the flaws in the positive arguments of others, Hume himself offered no clear answer, but rather counseled humility and suspense of judgment on such questions. For that matter, what good would an appeal to the authority of Hume do us anyway? His entire point was that *nobody* can be an authority on God. For their part, the Pythons suggested alternate ways of settling these questions. Why argue over the existence of God at all? Why not simply wrestle over it? And so we see, in *Monty Python's Flying Circus* (Episode 2, "Sex and Violence"), Monsignor Edward Gay, author of *My God*, square off against secular humanist Dr. Tom Jack, author of *Hello, Sailor*, to decide the question in the ring. In the end, God exists by two falls to a submission.

12
Madness in *Monty Python's Flying Circus*

MICHELLE SPINELLI

I mean, some people think I'm mad. The villagers say I'm mad, the tourists say I'm mad. Well, I am mad.

> —Kevin, a village idiot ("The Idiot in Society," *Monty Python's Flying Circus*, Episode 20, "The Attila the Hun Episode")

Some might say that "madness" is synonymous with Monty Python. After all, what makes the Pythons so funny is the extremes to which they take characters and situations. Everyday occurrences become ridiculous, bordering on the insane. But, how do the Pythons really see madness? How do they portray the mad? Can we learn anything from them about madness?

The Pythons' most comprehensive portrayal of madness is their sketch entitled, "The Idiot in Society" (*Monty Python's Flying Circus*, Episode 20, "The Attila the Hun Episode"). In it, the Pythons explore the role and character of the "village idiot," a term that can be traced back to the Middle Ages. "What is called the 'village idiot'," the philosopher and historian Michel Foucault (1926–1984) writes, "did not get married, did not participate in games, and was fed and supported by others."[1] In fact, the village idiot was considered quite mad.

---

[1] Michel Foucault, *The Essential Foucault: Selections from the Essential Works of Foucault, 1954–1984*, edited by Paul Rabinow and Nikolas Rose (New York: The New Press, 2003), p. 375.

But the Pythons, doing what they do best, use humor to turn our expectations upside down. In the sketch we are introduced to three village idiots, and all seem anything but mad. In fact, getting past appearances, they all seem quite sane. Arthur Figgis, an idiot and the focal point of the sketch, expresses his view of the idiot in society just as a sociologist might. He tells us that, "there is a very real need in society for someone whom almost anyone can look down on and ridicule." So, Figgis is not mad. Yet others see him as mad. What does that tell us about notions of madness?

Michel Foucault: Madness as a Social Construct

Foucault would say that madness is a social construct. Its definition is fluid, changing over time as culture changes. What we, as a society, understand to be madness one day is not what we might consider to be madness the next day. Nor, Foucault writes, does madness itself exist apart from its definitions: "Madness cannot be found in a raw state. Madness only exists in society. It does not exist outside the forms of sensibility that isolate it and the forms of repulsion that exclude or capture it."[2]

The madness of Monty Python's village idiot is not the same as the madness of the asylum inmate of the nineteenth century. The Pythons' idiot lives in *contemporary* society and is judged mad by *that* society, while the asylum inmate is judged, perhaps differently, by his or her own very different society. Once a definition of madness becomes available in a society, people within that society become free to use that definition to label individuals as mad. The label "village idiot," which imputes some kind of madness, is meaningless outside the society that created it, in much the way that 'hysteric' was common in Freud's day, but is no longer in ours.

Foucault developed his thesis that madness is a social construct in his *Madness and Civilization: A History of Insanity in the Age of Reason*, in which he examined the history of the Western world's interpretation of madness and the ways in which that changing

---

[2] Michel Foucault, *Foucault Live: Collected Interviews, 1961–1984*, edited by Sylvere Lotringer (New York: Semiotext(e), 1994), p. 8.

interpretation over time has resulted in changing conditions for the mad. Now, Foucault, of course, was French and perhaps thereby subject to all kinds of abuse in the name of the Pythons (remember the avalanche of insults hurled on poor Arthur by John Cleese's castle guard in *Monty Python and the Holy Grail*?). But it turns out that these French theories of madness are relevant to the Pythons' treatment of the topic. The dialogue we might construct between Foucault and the Pythons is even civil and productive. Understanding Foucault's theory of madness can help us understand the Pythons' interpretation of madness.

First, Foucault tells us that the modern history of madness in the West has been one of exclusion. The mad have lived on the periphery, often scorned and ostracized. But, up until the mid-seventeenth century, they were generally tolerated and allowed to roam freely. Individual families and townships took responsibility for them and, starting in the fourteenth century, a few were admitted to hospitals to exist among those who were physically ill.

In the early seventeenth century, European society actually became "strangely hospitable, in all senses, to madness."[3] This is the time when the "fool" played an important role in literature. In Shakespeare's *King Lear*, for example, it's the fool who illuminates what Lear cannot see for himself. Fools are used as literary devices—their madness has a purpose, and authors imbue fools with wisdom that is absent in other characters. During this period, Foucault writes, a *dialogue* existed between reason and unreason. The mad, being seen as curiously wise or simply comical, interacted with society. In those and other ways, society listened to them. Reason and unreason talked.

Things changed drastically for the mad around 1656, when what Foucault describes as the "Great Confinement" began. The dialogue abruptly ended, and a *monologue* of reason emerged. Around that time, starting in France, madmen began to be sequestered together in large internment houses. These institutions held not only the mad, but criminals, beggars, the sick, and others who were considered idle. The ability to work became very important in the newly industrial and urban society. As historian

---

[3] Michel Foucault, *Madness and Civilization: A History of Insanity in the Age of Reason* (New York: Vintage, 1988), p. 37.

Roy Porter puts it, "previously, the mad had exercised a particular force and fascination, be it as the holy fool, witch, or as a man possessed. Half-wits and zanies had enjoyed the license of free speech and the privilege of mocking their betters. Institutionalization . . . robbed madness of all such empowering features and reduced it to mere negation, and absence of humanity."[4] The mad, who were at the mercy of those with power, were silenced, deprived of autonomy, confined, persecuted, and punished.

In the eighteenth century, the mad began to be confined as a group, by themselves, in asylums. At this point, Foucault writes, madness acquired a new, medical definition. Madness, still subject to the monologue of reason, was now something to be studied. "The science of mental disease, as it would develop in the asylum, would always be only of the order of observation and classification. It would not be a dialogue" (*Madness and Civilization*, p. 250). In asylums there was an established hierarchy, with the "insane transformed into minors" (p. 252). Like children, the mad had to live under a set of strict rules. Those who deviated from the rules were punished.

In contemporary society, medicalization has persisted. Today, the mad are "mentally ill." They are to be diagnosed, treated, and managed by doctors—by psychiatrists and "medical professionals." Foucault refers to psychiatry as "condescending philanthropy" (*Foucault Live*, pp. 8–9) because society's dialogue with the mad remains a monologue. Psychiatrists speak to and about their patients, but they do not listen to the unreason articulated by them. Foucault writes, "What is called mental illness is simply alienated madness, alienated in the psychology that it has itself made possible."[5] Today, drugs are commonly used to "treat," "cure," or simply silence unreason. The mad, at least in the United States, continue to be excluded. Many are homeless or have been relegated to group homes, mental institutions, or prisons.

---

[4] Roy Porter, *Madness: A Brief History* (Oxford: Oxford University Press, 2002), p. 93.
[5] Michel Foucault, *Mental Illness and Psychology* (Berkeley: University of California Press, 1987), p. 76.

Pythonic Madness

Monty Python showcases the contradictions and ironies inherent in common stereotypes. In dramatically amplifying what we believe to be true, the Pythons force us to reconsider it. Or, they depict situations that are completely incongruous with what we believe, to the same effect. Consider the sketch, "Hermits,"[6] in which two hermits (Eric Idle and Michael Palin) serendipitously meet on the side of a mountain. Palin says to Idle, "Hello. Are you a hermit by any chance?" Idle responds, "Yes, that's right. Are you a hermit?" And, the two proceed to talk about what they're escaping ("the usual—people, chat, gossip"), the hermit lifestyle, the difficulties of properly insulating a cave, and fellow hermits ("Oh, well. Mr. Robinson's cave's never been exactly nirvana, has it?"). All the while other hermits pass by, greeting one another by name. At the conclusion of the sketch, Idle complains that he feels "cut off" because his cave is half way up the mountain. Palin responds, "Still, there's one thing about being a hermit, at least you meet people." "Oh, yes!," Idle agrees, "I wouldn't go back to public relations."

The irony is that these hermits engage in behavior contrary to that of "real" hermits, whom we take to be loners or misanthropes. Hermits are not mad, necessarily, but they do represent that aspect of madness, seclusion, or isolation that lies at the core of Foucault's analysis of madness. The Pythons give us hermits woven into the fabric of modern society.

So it goes with "The Idiot in Society," a sketch where the Pythons lead viewers to a similar conclusion about the mad. A voiceover tells us, "Arthur Figgis is an idiot. A village idiot. Tonight we look at the idiot in society." We first see Figgis sitting on a wall in a contemporary rural community. He has rosy cheeks, disheveled red hair, and wears a dirty smock and straw hat. He is the embodiment of madness as it existed, in Foucault's analysis, before the Great Confinement. This sketch is entirely modern, though. It is a mock documentary in which Figgis is a most serious and rational commentator. He speaks to us directly and rationally, and interrupts his analysis only when various members

---

[6] "Hermits," *Monty Python's Flying Circus*, Episode 8, "Full Frontal Nudity."

of the village walk by. Then, he makes funny noises, rolls his eyes, and moves his body in odd ways. When Mr. Jenkins, a fellow idiot, walks by, however, Figgis is his serious self again. He and Figgis are dressed exactly alike, a hint at where this sketch may be going. For the moment, however, Figgis has some work to do. "Oh, excuse me," he tells his interviewer. "A coach party has just arrived. I shall have to fall off the wall, I'm afraid."

Figgis is not the type of madman that Foucault traces through most of Western history: this madman has a voice. Not only does he have a voice, but he has an audience very willing to listen—us, the viewers. By speaking directly into the camera, Figgis needs no interpreter, no intermediary, no doctor to get his points across. He has direct access to us, and we are listening. In fact, we're eager to listen.

Most importantly, Figgis is keenly aware that he plays a role within society. He explains that "There is a very real need in society for someone whom almost anyone can look down on and ridicule." In fact, idiots like him provide a "a vital psycho-social service" for the larger community. Unlike Foucault's assessment of madmen as variously compartmentalized or ostracized by reasonable society, these madmen are socially integrated. Figgis is right that he is serving an important social function. As Porter writes, "All societies judge some people mad . . . it is part of marking out the different, deviant, and perhaps dangerous" (*Madness: A Brief History*, p. 62). Figgis is performing that job in his society.

But, as the sketch continues, we learn that Figgis and the other idiots are perhaps not as different or deviant as Porter implies. "Arthur," our narrator tells us, "takes idioting very seriously. He is up at six o'clock every morning working on special training equipment designed to keep him silly." As we watch Figgis exercise, he finally knocks himself out by ramming his head into a ball apparatus. We also learn that Figgis is quite fastidious about keeping up his appearance. He works carefully on getting his hair just-so, and then jumps into a pond to splash mud on his smock.

Despite the way he looks, the more we get to know Figgis, the more we see that he is not so strange after all. In fact, the narrator compares him to other professionals in the village, such as the doctor, blacksmith, and carpenter. Figgis does things that all villagers must do, like banking. In the sketch, we see Figgis at a teller window depositing things like moss, a dead bird, and wood (which, the bank manager tells us, are deposits involving very complicated rates of interest). The bank manager, moreover, takes Figgis more seriously than others who laugh and point at Figgis as he passes by. The manager explains, "Well, nowadays, a really blithering idiot can make anything up to ten thousand pounds—if he's head of some industrial combine. But, of course, the old-fashioned idiot still refuses money."

Figgis is ordinary in another way, as well. He has colleagues, such as Kevin O'Nassis, whom we meet at the end of the sketch, and Mr. Jenkins. All three wear exactly the same outfit, which we now recognize as nothing less than an idiot uniform. Like many professionals, the idiots also have specializations. For example, Kevin "works largely with walls," and we see him fall off a wall several times.

The more we learn, the more these idiots seem just like other individuals in a given line of work in their community. They are professional idiots, with institutional and educational support. Figgis, in fact, lectures in idiocy at the University of East Anglia. We see him running around, acting loony, leading a group of "third-year students" around a lawn. Later, we see the students receiving their B.A. degrees, along with a kick in the head, and a handful of dirt on their faces.

By this point, the Pythons have turned Foucault's portrayal of the mad on its head. In his role as a professor, Figgis himself has power over individuals, as well as over himself. Not unlike the hermits who created their own social network, these madmen are functionally integrated into society and not dominated or controlled by others, as much of Foucault's analysis suggests.

Urban Idiots: Foucauldian and Pythonesque

Differences between what Foucault and the Pythons say about madness narrow when the sketch gives us a brief glimpse into the lives of four *urban* idiots. A voiceover introduces us to the idiots, all of whom are dressed identically in black business suits. Like the village idiots, they have their uniforms—albeit uniforms that are identical to those of the urban businessman. So, in the urban setting, the Pythons seem to tell us, at least on the surface, it is difficult to differentiate between a "normal" businessman and the urban idiot.

Other differences emerge, however, when these urban idiots speak. Unlike the village idiots, they are not very articulate. Each mumbles about his background before becoming an urban idiot. One says, "Daddy's a banker. He needed a wastepaper basket." And, another mumbles, "Father was Home Secretary, and mother won the Derby." Yet, they too have their professional trappings. The reporter tells us that "The headquarters of these urban idiots is here in St. John's Wood. Inside, they can enjoy the company of other idiots and watch special performances of ritual idioting." We see this posh London neighborhood enclosed by a high brick wall, reminiscent of an asylum, within which these idiots variously act idiotically

The Pythons are thus mixing up our preconceptions about madness and idiocy whenever possible. The visibly idiotic are integrated into society, while those that appear to be everyday professionals are confined within a cricket stadium. Things are not as clear cut as in Foucault's picture of madness, perhaps because the Pythons have turned the question around. Instead of seeking to understand madness by examining how it has been variously excluded, dominated, and medicalized by sane or reasonable society, the Pythons are more interested in the reasonable society and the ways in which madness and idiocy percolate through it. By leading us to see idiocy as something ironic and funny, the Pythons restore that dialogue between reason and unreason that Foucault believes has been lost. Foucault would be happy that, with the Pythons, the mad are accepted as part of society; they speak for themselves; they have agency; and the more we look at them, the more familiar they become.

13

Monty Python and the Search for the Meaning of Life

PATRICK CROSKERY

e all struggle to lead good lives, looking for guidance from a variety of social institutions. For example, many people draw on their religion to help them figure out how to lead an ethical and meaningful life. The members of Monty Python draw humor from the challenges involved in making proper use of the guidance these institutions provide, usually by showing the dismal failure of our efforts. We can explore some of the most influential of these institutions and their relationships to moral theories by taking a tour through the works of Monty Python and examining the themes they discuss.

Markets and Motives: Utilitarianism and *Monty Python's Flying Circus*

One social institution that seems to provide guidance is the marketplace. According to the famous image given by the Scottish Enlightenment philosopher Adam Smith (1723–1790) in his 1776 work *The Wealth of Nations*, the marketplace acts as an "invisible hand" that guides people motivated by their own self-interest to make contributions to the greater good of society. On this view, people work primarily to accumulate wealth for themselves; however, in a market setting the only way to gain this wealth is by providing goods and services that others value, resulting in a happier and more prosperous society overall. This approach suggests that we can lead good lives by vigorously pursuing our own interests in the context of the marketplace. The appeal of this approach can be understood in terms of the moral theory known as *utilitarianism*. As Jeremy Bentham (1748–1832), the eighteenth-century founder of this view explains, the fundamental axiom of utilitarianism is that "it is the greatest happiness of the greatest number that is the measure of right and wrong." The marketplace, if it can lead people to make contributions to overall happiness as they pursue their own interests, ends up being a good utilitarian moral guide. On the other hand, critics have noted a number of limitations to the marketplace, and these limitations are a popular subject of sketches in *Monty Python's Flying Circus.*

A merchant banker is perhaps the ultimate market participant, and the Pythons choose this role to explore the mindset that the market promotes. In the "Merchant Banker" sketch (*Monty Python's Flying Circus*, Episode 30, "Blood, Devastation, Death, War and Horror") a man enters the merchant banker's office to request a pound to help the orphan's home. The merchant banker is quite puzzled—is this a loan? Is he buying a stock? Once the idea of a charitable donation is clarified, he frowns and says, "I don't want to seem stupid, but it looks to me as though I'm a pound down on the whole deal." Here we see the first important limitation of the marketplace—there are important social needs which it simply cannot meet. The marketplace can only work when all the participants have something to exchange. To handle the social problems associated with poverty, a utilitarian who wants to promote overall happiness will have to turn to some other institution, whether it be private charity or the government.

Limitations of the marketplace show up even when we have something to trade. There are some interactions that the market does not seem suitable for. This point is brought out vividly in the "Job Hunter" sketch (Episode 24, "How Not to Be Seen"). A man enters an office to apply for a job as an assistant editor. Before he can even get started, however, the interviewer starts bargaining with him for his briefcase and umbrella. The interviewer says, "take a seat" and then says "I see you chose the canvas chair with the aluminum frame. I'll throw that in. That, and the fiver, for the briefcase and the umbrella." In frustration the job hunter says that his briefcase and umbrella are not for sale. The interviewer replies "'Not for sale', what does that mean?" We laugh at this scene because we recognize that some interactions cannot be understood as market transactions. Unlike charity, which is logically incompatible with market exchange, these interactions are at least compatible with the market. However, to treat every interaction as a negotiation is to lose important dimensions of human relationships. Some parts of our lives, such as family relations, friendship, and even many of the daily interactions we have with fellow members of our community, cannot be treated in market terms without a loss of value.

Important criticisms of the marketplace have come from Marxist thought, and the Pythons show a serious interest in the critical resources Marxism makes available. They draw particular attention to market ideology—the various ways that the capitalistic system shapes the very beliefs and desires that we form. A particularly ironic illustration is provided in the "Communist Quiz" sketch (Episode 25, "Spam"). We see Karl Marx and a collection of famous Marxist leaders (Mao, Lenin, Castro, and Che Guevara) on a talk show. We assume that it is a standard, BBC-style serious discussion. Instead, the various thinkers are asked sports trivia questions about British football. As in many game shows, the contestants are battling for living-room furniture—a traditional object of bourgeois consumer ambition. The skit draws a sharp contrast between the seriousness of the leaders and the triviality of cultural obsessions with sports and consumer goods. This contrast highlights the way that our desires are shaped by market ideology even as it reveals the sometimes troubling conflict between the market ideology and our non-commercial beliefs and values.

The Marxist theme of alienation is another subject that the Pythons frequently explore. A common theme in the sketches is the longing for a job with greater significance. The head of the Careers Advisory Board says, "I wanted to be a doctor, but there we are, I'm Head of the Careers Advisory Board. Or a sculptor, something artistic, or an engineer, with all those dams, but there we are. . . . I'm the Head of this lousy Board" (Episode 5, "Man's Crisis of Identity in the Latter Half of the Twentieth Century"). A chartered accountant takes a series of tests that indicate the job he is perfectly suited for is, naturally, chartered accountancy (Episode 10, untitled). But he really wants to be a lion tamer (and he has the hat). Perhaps the best illustration of this theme is found in the "Homicidal Barber" sketch (Episode 9, "The Ant, an Introduction"). A barber (who is simply pretending to cut his customer's hair), reports that he did not want to be a barber. He wanted to be something more striking—a lumberjack! He breaks into song, joined by the Mounties. The humor of all of these sketches draws on the fact that a modern, highly specialized economy is extremely efficient, but does not necessarily provide employment that feels meaningful and worthwhile. The capitalistic economy can provide the resources we need to survive, but may fall short of providing the requirements of a fulfilling life.

Tradition and Traits: Virtue Theory and *The Holy Grail*

If we are seeking a fulfilling and meaningful life, a natural institution to turn to is our cultural tradition. We draw on this tradition for role models to emulate, such as a hero contributing to a noble cause. Indeed, the barber who wanted to be lumberjack might just as easily have broken into song to express a desire to become one of King Arthur's Knights on a quest for the Holy Grail. What goal could be more worthwhile, what life more worth living?

The appeal of this approach can be understood in terms of an alternative approach to morality known as *virtue theory*. The heroic individual is the person who possesses the virtues, which are admirable character traits such as courage, temperance, and wisdom. The hero is a moral individual who lives up to and indeed exemplifies the moral standards of her community. In *Monty Python and the Holy Grail* much of the humor involves the misapplication of heroic virtues.

Sir Robin shows us precisely how to *lack* a virtue. Despite the fact that he is called "Brave Sir Robin," when faced with danger he runs away. Sir Robin is not brave, but cowardly. A more subtle failure is represented by Sir Lancelot, who, in contrast to Sir Robin, appears to be brave. He charges into situations without fear, swinging his sword. In one particularly dramatic scene, Sir Lancelot dashes into a wedding party, where he hacks and chops away at the guests and guards before storming the tower stairs. Lancelot's case, however, reveals another limitation. While his actions (and background theme music) map more clearly onto our sense of the heroic, Lancelot has not displayed bravery either; he is rash. Aristotle (384–322 B.C.E.), perhaps the most influential thinker on the topic of the virtues, argues that most virtues can be placed between two vices in this way; this view is called the doctrine of the mean. Thus, Sir Robin and Sir Lancelot represent the two extremes that allow us to focus on the Aristotelian mean: Sir Robin runs away when it is not appropriate, and Sir Lancelot attacks in an equally inappropriate fashion. The mean that Aristotle describes is not simply a mathematical average. As Aristotle says in Book II, Section 6 of his *Nicomachean Ethics* (W.D. Ross translation), "both fear and confidence . . . may be felt both too much and too little, and in both cases not well; but to feel them at the right times, with reference to the right objects, towards the right people, with the right motive, and in the right way, is what is both intermediate and best, and this is characteristic of virtue." Sir Lancelot's invasion of the wedding party starkly demonstrates the importance of having the relevant feeling at the right time and towards the right people.

Sir Galahad the Chaste provides another interesting illustration of failed virtue. Galahad appears to be pursuing the right goal as he follows the image of the Grail into Castle Anthrax. However, Castle Anthrax turns out to be perfectly designed to challenge Galahad's virtue, chastity. As Zoot, the mistress of the castle, explains: "We are but eight score young blondes and brunettes, all between sixteen and nineteen-and-a-half, cut off in this castle, with no one to protect us. Oooh. It is a lonely life . . . bathing . . . dressing . . . undressing . . . making exciting underwear. . . ." Galahad is about to yield when Lancelot intervenes and drags him away. Galahad, meanwhile, argues that "it's my duty as a knight to sample as much peril as I can." Galahad's virtue has failed because he has been misled by his desires. Aristotle focuses on the importance of judgment in the application of the mean, and it is precisely this judgment that is distorted in Galahad's case.

It is important, however, that we not confuse judgment with reason or the attempt to reason; good judgment is something more. Sir Bedevere the Wise can help us to understand this point. In a demonstration of unanchored reasoning gone wild, Sir Bedevere assists a group of villagers trying to determine whether a woman is a witch. He gradually helps them to see that since witches burn because they are made of wood, and wood floats, as do ducks, if the woman weighs the same as a duck, then she must be a witch. Throughout the film we are treated to other instances of Sir Bedevere's peculiar reasoning. The large wooden rabbit is his idea. After it is successfully wheeled into the French castle, Bedevere sits outside with the other knights and explains how the plan will be completed: "Well, now, Lancelot, Galahad, and I wait until nightfall and then leap out of the rabbit and take the French by surprise, not only by surprise but totally unarmed!" It slowly dawns on him that although the rabbit is in the castle, he and the others are still outside. Bedevere represents an effective illustration of the difference between unanchored reasoning and genuine good judgment. Judgment requires a grasp of the larger context and significance of a choice.

What about King Arthur himself? Arthur displays numerous virtues throughout the film. In addition, he does not appear to be misguided in the way that Galahad is, and he shows sound judgment in numerous instances. However, Arthur fails to obtain the Grail. In fact, he is arrested and taken into custody as the two timelines of the movie (the medieval and the contemporary) collapse into one another. What went wrong?

The problem, I would suggest, is one of legitimacy. King Arthur's quest for the Grail is only legitimate if his claim to leadership is legitimate. We are given reason to doubt that claim early in the film. A peasant woman asks how he came to be king. Arthur explains: "The Lady of the Lake, her arm clad in the purest shimmering samite, held aloft Excalibur from the bosom of the water signifying by Divine Providence that I, Arthur, was to carry Excalibur. That is why I am your king!" Another peasant argues, reasonably enough, that "strange women lying in ponds handing out swords is no basis for a system of government. Supreme executive power derives from a mandate from the masses, not from some farcical aquatic ceremony."

A hero, in short, can only serve as a model for us to emulate if his cause is justified. While Arthur claims divine support, the basis for his claim is, on reflection, disturbingly mythical in character. Tyrants who do not posses genuine grounds for their power often appeal to such mythic claims to maintain their power. The troublesome character of Arthur's ambitions is starkly demonstrated by his decision to declare war on the French in an effort to take "his" grail from them by force.

Religion and Rules: Deontology and *Monty Python's Life of Brian*

If genuine divine support could serve as the basis for a good life, perhaps we should consider religion as the source of guidelines for this purpose. Religion appears to provide absolute rules that we can follow in our effort to be moral. The appeal to rules rather than overall happiness or virtuous character is associated with yet another basic approach to morality, one called *deontology*. Deontology asserts that what makes an action right or wrong is solely whether it conforms, or fits, to one's duty. One challenging aspect of deontology is determining what duties we have. Religion supplies a possible answer to this question.

Monty Python's Life of Brian has religion as a central topic, so it is not surprising that it can provide us with illustrations of the difficulties involved in drawing on religious rules. It's worth noting that, while this film is certainly critical of religion, several scenes suggest that we are not to understand Brian as Christ—for example, when Brian is born, the three wise men leave his cradle to visit another newly born child. In contrast to Brian's stable, this other child's stable is lit by a holy light. The primary target of the movie is religious dogmatism rather than the figure of Christ.

Early in the film, Brian and his mother are at the back of a crowd listening to a sermon. It is reasonable to assume that this sermon is being given by Christ (another clear case of separation between Christ and Brian). At this great distance, it's difficult to hear, and a member of the crowd reports that the speaker has just said, "blessed are the cheesemakers." This example brings out the fact that before we can apply a moral rule we must have the right rule in mind. Even if a moral rule has a divine source, there is room for error right from the beginning—there are many ways for the text to be corrupted. Moreover, trying to fix a corrupted text can lead to its own problems. One of the crowd members confidently clarifies the rule by saying, "Well, obviously it's not meant to be taken literally; it refers to any manufacturers of dairy products." We cannot simply rely on the words, even if we do not take them literally. We have to develop an interpretation of the words.

Later in the film, Brian needs to escape from the Roman guards and literally drops into a group of prophets. To disguise himself, he needs to pretend to be a prophet. With this goal in mind, Brian attempts to reproduce a parable we assume he has heard from Christ. The crowd does not respond well.

BRIAN: Consider the lilies . . .
WOMAN: Consider the lilies?
BRIAN: Oh, well, the birds, then.
FIRST MAN: What birds?
BRIAN: Any birds.
SECOND MAN: Why?
BRIAN: Well, have they got jobs?
THIRD MAN: Who?
BRIAN: The birds.
SECOND MAN: Have the birds got jobs?!
FOURTH MAN: What's the matter with him?
THIRD MAN: He says the birds are scrounging!
BRIAN: Oh, no, no, the point is: the birds, they do all right, don't they?
FOURTH MAN: Well, and good luck to them!
SECOND MAN: Yeah, they're very pretty.
BRIAN: Okay. And you're much more important than they are, right? So what do you worry about? There you are! See?

Even if we have the right rule and are attempting to interpret it, we can still go awry. Brian's failure to communicate a meaningful message to the crowd reflects his limited understanding of the parable. Interpretation is a challenging process, and simplistic understandings of the rule will not be sufficient to provide us with guidance. It is worth noting that the problem of interpretation is not restricted to parables or metaphors—even the most straightforward rules pose challenges, as the priest supervising the stoning of the blasphemer discovers. The blasphemer chants 'Jehovah' repeatedly, leading the priest to say "If you say 'Jehovah' once more . . ." at which point the priest himself is stoned by the crowd. The priest and the crowd have different interpretations of just what the rule against blasphemy entails, and there is no obvious way to adjudicate between them.

The dangers of blind obedience to authority are illustrated when Brian unintentionally gains a collection of followers. He tries to convince them that he is not the Messiah, but they do not listen. "Only the true Messiah denies his divinity," a woman explains, typifying the way that the crowd reinterprets everything he says to support the conclusion they want to hear. This response reaches its peak when, in frustration, Brian says, "All right. I am the Messiah." The crowd is relieved. "Now, fuck off!" says Brian. The crowd is quiet. Finally, one man asks, "How shall we fuck off, O Lord?" Their desperate desire to have rules to follow prevents them from critically assessing the commands they receive.

Brian highlights this point in a later scene where his followers have grown tremendously in numbers. After accidentally exposing himself (in one of the best uses of male full-frontal nudity in film history), Brian tells the huge crowd "Look, you've got it all wrong! You don't need to follow me! You don't need to follow anybody! You've got to think for yourselves! You're all individuals!" The crowd replies, reverently, "Yes, we're all individuals!" The one rule we cannot follow blindly is the rule that requires us to think for ourselves. The influential eighteenth-century philosopher Immanuel Kant (1724–1804), a devout Christian, made the injunction to think for ourselves—autonomy—the basis of his version of deontology. Even a divinely inspired set of rules must be thought through carefully and critically to serve as an appropriate guideline for living our lives.

Knowledge and Nihilism: Science and *Monty Python's The Meaning of Life*

If we want to think critically, we may be tempted to turn to science to provide answers. However, unlike the other institutions that we have considered, science does not provide any particular advice for living a good life. The great power of science is that it aims simply to describe the world, not to determine what ought to be. Scientific work, unfortunately, often threatens to undermine traditional sources of meaning and value. The result is nihilism,

the destruction of all values. The German philosopher Friedrich
Nietzsche (1844–1900), famous for declaring that "God is dead,"
put it this way in Book 1, Section 1 of his *Will to Power*: "What
does nihilism mean? That the highest values devaluate themselves.
The aim is lacking; 'why?' finds no answer." The challenge that
science poses for value is an important theme in *Monty Python's The
Meaning of Life*. Some of the most powerful points are made, in
typical Python fashion, in song.

Consider our sense that our individual lives are significant, that
the projects we engage in are meaningful. Listen to "The Galaxy
Song," following along in your imagination. We start on earth,
looking down at a revolving planet, then back away and to see our
sun, then our galaxy, the Milky Way (with its "hundred billion
stars"). We aren't even in the center of our own galaxy—"We're
thirty thousand light years from galactic central point." Our entire
galaxy itself is just part of a much larger universe (though "mil-
lions of billions" of galaxies is probably excessive.) Our best
understanding of the universe, in short, is that it is unimaginably
vast in both space and time, and we play a role in it that is beneath
trivial.

In some ways, however, the picture is even worse. The song
that begins the film (also called "The Meaning of Life") poses a
question that has troubled many people since the modern synthe-
sis combined Darwin's evolutionary theory with the understanding
of our genetic code: "[A]re we just simply spiraling coils of self-
replicating DNA?" Our drives and goals and hopes and dreams
may all just be products of evolution. Our very sense of purpo-
siveness—our sense that there is something worth pursuing—may
itself be a product of evolution. An animal that is not driven to
pursue goals will not reproduce, and so will not leave descendents.
But the goals themselves have no greater significance.

The threat of nihilism, then, is quite real, and is perhaps the
most pervasive theme in the work of the Pythons. Part of their
response is to revel in the absurdity—think of the scene in the
middle of *Monty Python's The Meaning of Life*, in which several
bizarre characters try to "Find the Fish," with shouts of encour-
agement from the audience. Throughout all stages of their work,
the Pythons take a gleeful pleasure in the collapse of meaning and
the limitations of human institutions.

But the Pythons have another response to the challenge of nihilism as well. At the end of the film, suddenly and unexpectedly, the meaning of life is revealed: "try and be nice to people, avoid eating fat, read a good book every now and then, get some walking in, and try and live together in peace and harmony with people of all creeds and nations." While this line is presented in a very nonchalant fashion and is immediately buried in a series of jokes about censors and modern audiences, it bears closer scrutiny. This is pretty sound advice for living a good life. Take care of yourself, be sure to continue learning and growing, be decent to other people as individuals and be tolerant of others as members of groups.

A person following this advice could recognize the limitations of the marketplace while also recognizing the contributions it can make for overall happiness. While she might not find a glorious quest to participate in, she would have appropriate grounds for developing a virtuous character in the context of her cultural tradition. Although her religion cannot provide her with simple rules to follow blindly, she can draw on it reflectively to develop a set of rules that she can autonomously endorse. Finally, and above all, by keeping a sense of humor, she can cope with the threat of nihilism and the challenges of the scientific picture of the world while leading a worthwhile and meaningful life.

14

Existentialism in Monty Python: Kafka, Camus, Nietzsche, and Sartre

EDWARD SLOWIK

Unlike any other comedy troupe, Monty Python presents its viewers with a bizarre, unpredictable, and seemingly meaningless world. If one were to try and locate a philosophical message in the shows, recordings, and movies of Monty Python, one might come to the conclusion that the world is incoherent or absurd, such that one can find no meaning or values in it.

In their last movie, *Monty Python's The Meaning of Life*, this possibility is mentioned explicitly in the infamous "Live Organ Transplants" skit: reflecting on Eric Idle's song about the vastness of the universe, Mrs. Bloke (Terry Jones) comments, "Makes you feel so sort of insignificant, doesn't it?"

One might wonder, since this movie is their final group effort, whether Mrs. Bloke's line represents the final judgment of Monty Python concerning the "meaning of life." Do they really believe that life is insignificant? In short, are the Pythons a band of nihilists who believe in nothing, perhaps simply making a joke at the expense of the average, non-philosophical viewer, who believes that life does have a meaning? Are they really, deep-down, a bunch of skeptical, left-leaning, intellectual agitators who enjoy undermining the common beliefs and values of ordinary, law-abiding citizens? Are they just a horde of snooty, namby-pamby, *pinot noir* sipping, Foucault-reading, moral anarchists?! A depraved pack of pseudo-intellectuals who would rather sit on their pampered posteriors while engaging in pretentious, limp-wristed, academically-questionable pursuits, taking time off only to hurl insults at decent hard-working folk?!

Oh, excuse me! I got carried away there for a bit. Actually, though some of these last accusations might be true (at least the wine drinking, in John Cleese's case), Monty Python does, in fact, have a positive message about the meaning of life. Well, sort of: the message is existentialist. And, in order to better understand the existentialist content of Monty Python, we will need to examine some of the major ideas of existentialist philosophy.

Although its origins can be traced to the nineteenth century, existentialism is principally a twentieth-century philosophy. And, like the twentieth century itself, existentialist philosophy is a strange mix of diverse views, trends, and attitudes. One often finds, for instance, a dictionary definition of existentialism that simply groups a host of themes: "the individual, the experience of choice, and the absence of rational understanding of the universe with a consequent dread or sense of absurdity in human life."[1] Given such a broad description, the problem of relating Monty Python to existentialism is not the shortage of analogies or similarities between the two, but the exact opposite; what Monty Python skit does not bring up the individual, our experience of choice, and, in particular, the absurdity of human life?

So, in what follows, we will limit our investigation of existentialism in Monty Python to a few influential representatives of existentialist philosophy and literature. In the work of Friedrich Nietzsche, Franz Kafka, Albert Camus, and Jean-Paul Sartre, there are number of intriguing parallels and similarities with general themes in Monty Python, as well as potential criticisms or comments on the plausibility of their various philosophies. In fact, since existentialism was one of the most influential and important philosophies of the twentieth century, and is still enormously popular in the arts and general culture, it would be surprising if Monty Python did not have something existentialist to say.

---

[1] Simon Blackburn, *Oxford Dictionary of Philosophy* (Oxford: Oxford University Press, 1996), p. 129.

Kafka, Camus, and the "Absurd"

There's a difference between the influence of existentialist *philosophy* in Monty Python and the influence of existentialist *literature*. Since existentialism pervades much of twentieth-century literature, we shouldn't be surprised to find its influence in Monty Python. And, indeed, if one were to look for existentialist literary influences, an obvious source would be the stories and novels of the greatest author of existentialist fiction, the German-Czech, Franz Kafka (1883–1924).

The chaotic and nonsensical world portrayed in Kafka's writings bears an uncanny resemblance to much in Monty Python. Kafka's worlds are often a sort of institutionalized or bureaucratic insanity: worlds that put up impossible, illogical barriers to the lives or progress of the main characters. A well-known parable by Kafka, "Couriers," nicely demonstrates these qualities:

> They were offered the choice between becoming kings or the couriers of kings. The way children would, they all wanted to be couriers. Therefore there are only couriers who hurry about the world, shouting to each other—since there are no kings—messages that have become meaningless. They would like to put an end to this miserable life of theirs but they dare not because of their oaths of service.[2]

Often, the protagonists in Kafka's stories are ordinary people who strive to overcome these irrational barriers by using common sense and reason. But, no matter how hard they try, the walls of their unfathomable maze inevitably close in upon them, leading to gradual frustration and anxiety. And it hardly helps that the bureaucratic members who enforce these insane rules and regulations act as if their crazy systems are the very epitome of rational thought and justice!

Similar situations constantly arise in Monty Python. Many of the famous skits from *Monty Python's Flying Circus* involve an ordi-

---

[2] Franz Kafka, "Couriers," in R.C. Solomon, ed., *Existentialism*, second edition (Oxford: Oxford University Press, 2005), p. 171. Other great works of twentieth-century fiction and drama owe much to Kafka, such as the plays of Samuel Beckett (whose *Waiting for Godot* is subtitled a "tragicomedy") or Joseph Heller's *Catch-22*.

nary, or somewhat silly, customer who cannot overcome the ridiculous barriers set up by a shop owner who doesn't see the insanity in his rules or regulations. For example, the "Cheese Shop" (Episode 33, untitled) depicts a sustained, but ultimately fruitless (or cheeseless), search for cheese in a cheese shop. The "Dead Parrot" sketch (Episode 8, "Full Frontal Nudity") involves a customer's equally futile attempt to convince the shopkeeper of a pet store that his recently purchased parrot is dead.

As with Monty Python, furthermore, one of the strangely entertaining aspects of Kafka's stories is their "black humor." The cruel predicament that the main characters experience is, to some extent, comic. One often finds oneself both laughing and wincing at the same time in both Kafka and Monty Python. In Kafka's "The Metamorphosis," for example, when the anxious salesman, Gregor Samsa, awakes one morning to find himself transformed into a giant insect, he seems more horrified about having missed his train to work! In a genuinely Pythonesque moment, he reasons that he *might* still be able to catch the seven o'clock train, but "to catch that he would need to hurry like mad and his [product] sample weren't even packed up, and he himself wasn't feeling particularly fresh and active."[3]

Among the writers who have been influenced by Kafka, one of the most important is the French existentialist, Albert Camus (1913–1960). Not only did Camus write influential existentialist literature (most notably, the novel, *The Stranger*), but he also wrote a number of essays on the meaning of life that seem directly inspired by Kafka's vision of a meaningless world. Camus famously defined the "absurd" as the confrontation between a rational person and an indifferent universe, and his use of the ancient Greek myth of Sisyphus has become a famous metaphor for this confrontation: "The gods have condemned Sisyphus to ceaselessly rolling a rock to the top of a mountain, whence the stone would fall back of its own weight."[4] The punishment, as Camus goes on to describe, is a "futile and hopeless labor," a pointless task that never can be completed. As soon as the rock

---

[3] Franz Kafka, "The Metamorphosis," in *The Complete Stories* (New York: Schocken, 1971), p. 91.
[4] Albert Camus, "The Myth of Sisyphus," in Solomon, *Existentialism*, p. 197.

reaches the top, it rolls down again, and Sisyphus must start the whole process once more, without any hope of completing his ultimate task of placing the rock on the mountain peak.

For Camus, Sisyphus's fate reveals the long-term or overall meaning of our own lives. Like Sisyphus, we are "condemned" to a life of tasks and projects that seemingly don't amount to any real, lasting worth or value. We go to work each day, raise our families, and eventually die. And the whole process starts over again with the next generation, an endless cycle that apparently has no ultimate goal or point. This is the problem of the meaning of life as understood by the existentialists.

There are no direct references to Camus or the myth of Sisyphus, but the often repetitive triviality of life is nicely captured in several reccurring characters or stereotypes in *Monty Python's Flying Circus*. My favorite examples include the tedium of an office worker's existence, depicted in the aptly named "Dull Life of a City Stockbroker" sketch (Episode 6, untitled), where the joke is that adventure actually occurs all around the stockbroker without his noticing, or the chartered accountant who desires to become a lion-tamer (Episode 10, untitled). These characters share Sisyphus's fate, although without Sisyphus's defiance or heroism. The boring monotony of their occupations mirrors the boring monotony of their lives (which were, apparently, of interest to Michael Palin, who plays nearly all of them). The philosophically-inclined viewer may forever after view chartered accountancy as symbolic of the ultimate lack of significance of a person's life, especially for individuals within our modern, regimented, industrial societies.

The Individual and the Meaning of Life

One might be tempted to counter Camus's interpretation of life by inviting religion, society, or some great philosophical theory to rescue some meaning from our seemingly meaningless lives. For instance, someone might declare that God, or our nation, provides an overall meaning for our day-to-day existence, since our lives gain a meaning by being part of a divine plan or a larger process.

Yet the existentialists were for the most part very skeptical of the use of any higher "being" or universal plan to find meaning. The great German existentialist philosopher Friedrich Nietzsche

(1844–1900) famously declared that "God is dead," by which he meant that the modern scientific world had made belief in God no longer acceptable to the rational person, and so our purpose in life couldn't come from a supernatural source. But the problem can also be stated more generally: What provides the meaning of these larger entities, like God or the State? If the answer is that God or the State provide their own meaning, such that nothing else is required to give them meaning, then why couldn't our individual lives be just as meaningful all by themselves (and thus nothing else, like God or the State, would be required to give our own lives meaning, too)?

All told, one of the most important themes in existentialism is the fate of the individual in acquiring his or her own answer to the meaning to life. Camus called this quest, "living without appeal." It can be understood as a rejection of the quick and easy answers that our societies, religions, and philosophies often use to resolve our existential worries. The celebrated French philosopher and writer Jean-Paul Sartre (1905–1980) made the same point when he declared that our "existence precedes our essence." We are not born with a pre-established essence (a definition, purpose, or goal) provided by some higher power or institution; rather, we must provide our own, freely-chosen purpose to life. We exist first, and we must then determine our meaning or essence.

This individual-centered component of existentialism is strongly endorsed by Monty Python, particularly in a well-known scene from *Monty Python's Life of Brian*. In an attempt to dissuade a horde of would-be disciples, Brian argues:

> Look . . . you've got it all wrong. You don't need to follow me. You don't need to follow anybody. You've got to think for yourselves. You're all individuals.

The importance of this scene cannot be overemphasized in attempting to locate an existential message—or indeed any philosophical message—in Monty Python. It is without a doubt one of their rare moments of open and direct expression of a philosophical idea, although it fits naturally into the plot and scene. The Monty Python members have repeatedly stated that *Monty Python's Life of Brian* is one of their finest achievements *due* to its consistent theme—and the theme, of course, is the (existentialist) plea for a little "critical thinking" on the part of the individual. In various interviews, they have made the following comments on the film's message:

> JOHN CLEESE: One of the themes of the film is, "Do make up your own mind about things and don't do what people tell you." And I find it slightly funny that there are now [1979] religious organizations saying, "Do not go and see this film that tells you *not* to do what you are told."[5]

> MICHAEL PALIN: There's a real feeling that we'd moved up a notch with *Life of Brian*. It was taking on something that could be difficult and controversial, but essentially dealt with all sorts of things that were right at the basis of what Python comedy was all about, which is really resisting people telling you how to behave and how not to behave. It was the freedom of the individual, a very sixties thing, the independence which was part of the way Python had been formed. . . .[6]

Nietzsche too warned of the negative effects of most (if not all) social institutions, traditions, and customs, on the development and freedom of the individual. With respect to morality, he argued:

> The free human being is [judged] immoral because in all things he is *determined* to depend upon himself and not upon a [moral] tradition. . . . [I]f an action is performed not because tradition commands it but for other motives (because of its usefulness to the individual, for example), even indeed for precisely the motives which once founded the tradition, it is called immoral and it is felt to be so by him who performed it.[7]

Nietzsche's analysis of moral traditions even helps to explain why *Monty Python's Life of Brian* aroused so much anger among certain

---

[5] John Cleese *et al.*, *Monty Python Speaks!* (New York: Avon Books, 1999), p. 249.
[6] John Cleese *et al.*, *The Pythons: Autobiography by The Pythons* (New York: Thomas Dunne, 2003), p. 306.
[7] Friedrich Nietzsche, "Daybreak," in *A Nietzsche Reader* (London: Penguin, 1977), p. 87.

religious groups, Christians especially. At some point in the development of the traditions of many religious societies, it became
unacceptable to philosophically investigate (or make a comedy
about) religion—even though one of Jesus's main goals was to get
people to re-think their religious commitments and values.

Moreover, the Pythons have repeatedly claimed that they were
not poking fun at Jesus in *Monty Python's Life of Brian*, but rather at
the social movements that were, and still are, formed to interpret
Jesus's teachings. As Terry Jones put it later:

> [*Monty Python's Life of Brian* is] very critical of the Church, and
> I think that's what the joke of it is, really: to say, here is Christ
> saying all of these wonderful things about people living
> together in peace and love, and then for the next two thousand
> years people are putting each other to death in His name
> because they can't agree on how He said it, or in what order
> He said it. The whole thing about "The sandal" [the follow-
> ers of the Gourd or the Shoe] . . . is like a history of the
> Church in three minutes.[8]

Religious groups and movements, like all social groups, have all
too often become dogmatic and rigid, inhibiting the individual's
exploration of the religion (quite aside from the obvious fact,
mentioned above, that these religious groups constantly inhibit
each other by way of verbal and physical attack). Nietzsche made
many similar criticisms of Christianity. While he admired much of
the teachings of Jesus (since Jesus approached morality in a
thoughtful and individual way), Nietzsche was very critical of the
many followers, most notably Paul, who converted the parables
and sayings of Jesus into a "religion," with all of the "dos" and
"don'ts" common to religions.

And it's not just religion. The existentialists and Monty
Python both refer, frequently, to the negative effects of most (if
not all) other social institutions on the development of the individual. Whether it is politics, the military, science (especially medicine), or the arts and the media, Monty Python has produced a
body of work that is unmatched in its savage, and hilarious, send-

---

[8] *Monty Python Speaks!*, ibid., p. 247.

ups of the illogic and stupidity that underlies so many of our social institutions.

Sartre, Bad Faith, and Freedom

Though the existentialists place the burden of life's meaning on the individual, they are under no illusions. Most individuals are not up to the task. Rather than honestly confront the situation, many people attempt to deny their freedom to make this choice—and the *freedom* of the individual is one of the key concepts of existentialism. Sartre calls this denial of personal freedom or choice "bad faith"; a simple example would be a person who accepts that he is a "sinner," or an "alcoholic," and therefore believes that he is not free to change his actions (for he is determined, and therefore cannot stop being a sinner or alcoholic). A more subtle example is presented when they take on the identity of a stereotype or "role," such as a doctor, policeman, scientist, and so on, and let the stereotypical manners and behavior of the role determine how they should behave and think as individuals. Sartre gives the example of a waiter in a café who displays all the mannerisms of the waiters one sees in movies or reads in books. He has an overly kind or slightly condescending attitude, voice, and use of words ("How are we this evening, sir?"), a stiff, automaton walk and quick bodily movements. On Sartre's view, this person is denying his freedom to be a person who just happens to have the job of a waiter. One can be a waiter without having to follow a stereotyped code of behavior.[9]

Monty Python, of course, loves to present stereotyped characters and, indeed, these characters are some of most recognizable and beloved components of Python. From the aggressive policemen who break into skits intent on arresting anyone and everyone (with their cries of "What's all this then?!"), to the dull office workers obsessed with petty details and paperwork, to the old housewives ("pepperpots") whose lives seem to revolve around complaining (in high-pitched voices) and shopping, Monty Python challenges us to re-think our lives by satirizing or parodying the

---

[9] Jean-Paul Sartre, *Being and Nothingness* (New York: Philosophical Library, 1956), Chapters 4–6.

many ways that people fail to achieve an independence of thought, and thus a freedom to choose. Like Sartre's waiter, these stereo-typed characters seem unable or unwilling to recognize their free-dom to pick a course of action independent of their typecast jobs, social class, or milieux. Perhaps these stereotyped people have allowed some social, religious, or other grand concept to deter-mine their proper conduct and behavior, and thereby to decide their life's meaning for them. Perhaps they are like Brian's follow-ers, who, after Brian tells them that, "You've all got to work it out for yourselves," shout back in unison, "Yes, yes!! We've all got to work it out for ourselves," which is predictably followed by, "Tell us more!" (p. 72).

According to Sartre, another way that people can manifest bad faith is when they fail to acknowledge that their past choices, taken as a whole, represent or define their character. Since there is no pre-established meaning to life, our meaning can only come from our *actual* choices, and so if my choices display a certain pattern (such as heroism, cowardice, dishonesty, and so on), then that is the type of person that I have freely chosen to become. Many people attempt to deny these basic facts about themselves. They might declare, "I am really a hero, but I was never in the right cir-cumstances to display my heroism," an excuse that supposedly explains away their many past flights from any potential danger (this example comes from Sartre's famous play, *No Exit*).[10] But, Sartre tells us, there is no deep-down, internal property (essence) of "heroism" that makes a person heroic. Rather, we are what we do, and our actual choices are the only means of determining our character, and consequently the meaning we have given to our lives. Of course, we are always free to become a *new* person if we so choose to act in the future.

Instances of this type of person (who are, as they say, "in denial") abound in Monty Python. In the "Fish License" sketch, Mr. Praline declares "I am not a loony!," even though he is pester-ing a post office clerk for a (non-existent) fish license for Eric, his pet halibut. "I chose him [Eric the halibut] out of thousands. I didn't like the others. They were all too flat," he tells the clerk (*Monty Python's Flying Circus*, Episode 23, "Scott of the Antarctic").

---

[10] Jean-Paul Sartre, *No Exit and The Flies* (New York: Random House, 1975).

Sartre would accuse Mr. Praline of bad faith: he is definitely a loony!

One of the criticisms commonly raised against Sartre's concept of freedom is that he fails to take into account the influence, or limitations, of our genetics (nature) and up-bringing (nurture). Is the alcoholic really "free" to stop drinking, or the homosexual to "choose" heterosexuality? Most would say they are not. And this limited scope of individual choice plays a role in several *Monty Python's Flying Circus* sketches. The timid, subservient, Arthur Pewtey has decided he won't be "pushed around" anymore, but when he tries to stop his wife's seduction (by the marriage counselor, no less), and is told to "go away," he instinctively backs down with a meek, "Right. Right." (Episode 2, "Sex and Violence"). Is Arthur Pewtey really free to change himself into a confident, aggressive person? Similarly, limitations of a more basic physiological sort persistently thwart Ron Obvious's ambitious stunts, such as jumping the English Channel, or eating Chichester Cathedral (Episode 10, untitled). The point? Monty Python contains much that is existentialist, but it holds the seeds of some powerful objections to existentialism as well.

A Nietzschean Conclusion

I've tried to show that Monty Python has some positive, existentialist advice on life. It's not simply a sarcastic send-up of humanity and the search for meaning. But, Monty Python just wouldn't be Monty Python if it didn't also make fun of philosophers and their theories of life! And, indeed, a sketch from *Monty Python's Flying Circus* involves two pepperpots who go in search of Sartre in order to settle an argument (Episode 27, "Whicker's World"). Along the way, conversation reveals details about Sartre, especially as they talk with his wife (Betty Muriel-Sartre). Sartre can be a bit moody, for example: "'the bourgeoisie this and the bourgeoisie that'—he's like a little child sometimes," his wife tells us. And he isn't much fun on holiday: "He didn't join in the fun much. Just sat there thinking. Still, Mr. Rotter caught him a few times with the whoopee cushion." The satirical target of this skit is the pompous and self-important philosopher, and the moral, possibly, is that philosophers should not take themselves so seriously. Even they can be caught by a whoopee cushion. If this last interpretation of the Sartre sketch is in any way correct, then it once again reveals a latent philosophical message in Monty Python. The ability to step back and take an honest look at ourselves, or to laugh at our own pretensions, is a virtue that Nietzsche emphasized: "I will not deceive, not even myself."[11]

For Nietzsche, the cultivation of personal virtues, such as honesty, is part of the process by which an individual can form a meaningful, authentic life. Nietzsche describes this process on occasion using "artistic" metaphors, as "'giving style' to one's character" (p. 290). This suggests that the creation of a meaningful life is much like the creation of a beautiful, significant art work. The concept of the "will to power" is important in this context: "every living thing does everything it can not to preserve itself but to become *more*."[12] Consequently, by conjoining the striving of individuals to grow or flourish with the creative act of fashioning a unique, virtuous character, we may begin to understand what Nietzsche considered a meaningful life. There is a sense in which Monty Python itself fits Nietzsche's theory. That is, the history or "life" of Monty Python is marked by a continuous internal development and striving to become more, all under the guidance of a well-conceived, if dynamic, artistic plan. As *Monty Python's Flying Circus* progressed, the idea of a fluid, "stream-of-consciousness" method of writing sketches and comedic material gradually evolved. Skits with normal beginnings and endings, and with final punch lines, were replaced by an inventive, constantly developing series of bizarre leaps to new material, and yet the material was often cleverly interconnected on many levels.[13] With the transition to movies, the plots became more unified and presented a more consistent theme, and the content became more daring. Yet the members of the group were not content with simply repeating the same strategy of sketch writing that had succeeded in the past. When the episodes began to merely repeat themselves, such that the show was no longer evolving ("becoming more"), the cast members gradually began to leave the group for new projects.

---

[11] *The Gay Science* (Indianapolis: Hackett, 1995), p. 344.
[12] *The Will to Power* (New York: Random House, 1968), p. 688.
[13] A nice discussion of the development of the show occurs in, G. Perry, *Life of Python* (London: Pavilion, 1983).

Like the ideal Nietzschean individual, Monty Python was not content with just existing. It strove to grow, to "overcome" its present condition and obtain new accomplishments, all under the control of a critical, artistic vision. For many Monty Python fans, it is this unmatched legacy in the annals of comedy writing that continues to resonate over the years.

15

"My Brain Hurts!"

ROSALIND CAREY

magine getting a cramp in your head—a cramp not in your body, but in your *mind*.

That's philosophy!

It's the feeling that you *ought* to be able to answer certain (philosophical) questions but just can't see *how*: a kind of mental cramp—or so says the great, strange, philosopher Ludwig Wittgenstein (1889–1951).

The following sketch from *Monty Python's Flying Circus*, "Spectrum: Talking About Things" (Episode 12, "The Naked Ant"), illustrates his point. The scene opens on the set of a talk show going on air. Cameras roll. To his audience and guests the presenter (Michael Palin) says:

> **PRESENTER**: Good evening. Tonight *Spectrum* looks at one of the major problems in the world today—that old vexed question of *what is going on*. . . . Here to answer this is a professional cricketer. [Cut to cricketer.]
>
> **CRICKETER**: I can say nothing at this point.

Not surprisingly, the cricketer (Eric Idle) is at a loss for words. After all, what kind of a question is "What is going on"? Can *anyone* answer it? Can you? Of course not! But he's got to answer, right? Because it's "one of the major problems in the world

today"—and you don't back down from a challenge just because
of a little cramp in your 'ead.

Welcome to philosophy, Mr. Cricketer.

The presenter's behavior is equally instructive. Since he's
stumped his guest, you'd expect him to back off, rephrase the
question, e-n-u-n-c-i-a-t-e more clearly, that sort of thing. Instead,
he steams ahead:

> So . . . Where do we stand? Where do we sit? Where do we
> come? Where do we go? What do we do? What do we
> say? What do we eat? What do we drink? What do we
> think? What do we do?

The compulsive piling up of questions is another symptom of
philosopher's cramp, according to Wittgenstein. According to
him, the philosophical mind needs to smooth out and relax, and
as a kind of therapeutic mental massage he recommends engaging
in philosophical exercises.

Hair of the Dog

We'll return to "*Spectrum*: Talking About Things" in a moment.
Let's look more closely at what Wittgenstein says. First, why *does*
philosophy give you mental pain? Second, if philosophy is what
put your head in a twist, how can more philosophy unwind it?

To the first question, Wittgenstein has the following response.
Our trouble, he thinks, comes from naively taking philosophical
questions and statements at face value; they appear to be perfectly good questions and statements, and assuming that's what they
in fact *are*, we try to address them as such.

In a sense we're right, says Wittgenstein: from the perspective
of grammar and structure, philosophical sentences *are* exactly like
other perfectly good sentences. However, from a different perspective, philosophical sentences are quite unlike other sentences
and are in fact nonsensical—meaningless. Philosophical
headaches, in short, stem from language.

To the second question, about how philosophy can be both
the cause and the cure of mental distress, Wittgenstein says this.
Properly understood, philosophy is an activity, not a set of Truths.

Properly understood, that activity is an exercise, a therapy, that traces when language makes sense and when it's nonsense. In the end this activity lets us shed the assumptions and habits about philosophy that gave us pain. That is why thinking about philosophy can sooth the distress caused by, well . . . thinking about philosophy.

In his work as a young man and in his later work Wittgenstein views philosophical headaches as a consequence of language, but his reasons for that view and his conception of the remedy evolve throughout his career. The young Wittgenstein's account of philosophy, compared to his later view, is both more ambitious and more, um, *peculiar*. Let's turn to the peculiarity first.

Making Sense

Consider the typical opener to episodes of *Monty Python's Flying Circus*, the sentence "It's . . . *Monty Python's Flying Circus.*" We experience this sentence as a series of sounds. Specifically, the sound of Michael Palin, as "The It's Man," saying the word 'It's', followed by a second voice, saying "Mon-ty Py-thon's . . . " and so on. These sounds form an auditory fact, the sentence 'It's . . . *Monty Python's Flying Circus*', and this fact depicts another fact: that an episode of a *Monty Python's Flying Circus* is about to begin.

This is the position twenty-something Ludwig holds in his first book, *Tractatus Logico-Philosophicus*. According to him, it is *possible* for sentences to mean facts because sentences are facts (relations among sounds, in the case above), and sentences must represent facts to have meaning.

Depicting facts is what sentences do. Period. Thus sentences make no sense when they (attempt to) depict what goes beyond the facts. Period.

So Show Us

This is bad news for philosophy. Sciences like physics, geology, and biology talk about the facts that make up the world, but philosophy talks about what makes *any* world, *any* fact, possible; and it talks about what makes *any* of them possible only by talking about *none* in particular, that is, by transcending the facts of this or any world.

Since on Wittgenstein's view we make sense only when we talk about facts, it follows that philosophy make no sense in talking about what transcends facts and makes them possible. Sure, philosophers can move their lips and utter sounds, but if sentences make sense only when they concern other facts, any use of sentences to go beyond the facts makes no sense. What philosophers say, in short, is nonsensical.

In addition, philosophers typically believe not only that they *can* talk significantly about what makes the world possible but that they *need* to do so: how else to make such issues clear? But Wittgenstein also thinks we don't *need* to use sentences this way. The conditions that make sentences (and facts in general) possible are implicit in their structures.

For example, in using the sentence 'My brain hurts' we exhibit different words ('hurts' and 'brain') having different functions (denoting a property, standing for an object, and so forth) and occurring in a particular kind of structure (a subject-predicate one). What functions and structures occur on any occasion will vary according to the language used, but in any language there are *some* that are constant, and this shows us something very general about what makes facts, and a world of facts, possible.

None of this has to be *said*, because language inevitably *shows* it. Since what philosophy does is talk about what makes any world, or set of facts, possible, it follows that philosophy is unnecessary—its job is already done by language itself.

In short, if philosophers persist in talking philosophically they utter nonsense, but in any event they also aren't needed.

Ouch!

Do You See It?

Looking back at "*Spectrum*: Talking About Things," it seems that our presenter and his guest need to consider whether the (purported) question 'What is going on?' is about any particular fact, or whether it amounts to a philosophical attempt to use language to transcend all the facts. And if the latter, it seems that both characters need to stop what they're doing—they need to stop asking these questions and stop thinking there ought to be answers for them.

Perhaps if Wittgenstein explained to them what I've just relayed to you, they'd sit up and start talking sense. But can Wittgenstein explain this to anyone? Can *I*?

Follow me carefully here.

First, recall that Wittgenstein believes sentences are nonsense if they attempt to talk about what makes facts—of language or the world—possible.

Next, go back to the second line of the second paragraph of the section "Making Sense," which repeats Wittgenstein's view that "it is *possible* for sentences to mean facts because sentences *are* facts."

Now ask yourself: Isn't this assertion a statement about the conditions under which meaning is possible? But what did Wittgenstein say about such statements? He said that they're nonsense.

Do you see it? The problem, I mean?

Through Them, on Them, over Them

That's right: by his own accounting of it, Wittgenstein's theory of sense and nonsense is nonsense—it can't be said. According to his view of sense and the limits on what we can say, he cannot express that very view itself without speaking nonsense.

Now THAT'S a philosophical cramp-and-a-half!

So what's a guy to do? How can Wittgenstein make his point if he can't say what he means?

Imagine yourself in his shoes. You can't just waggle your eyebrows at people, affecting a *mysterioso profundo* expression. Well, you can, but they won't get your point, *and* they'll think you're an ass. Seeing this, Wittgenstein bites the bullet and admits that he cannot say what he means to say without speaking nonsensically. Yet he seems to assume we can learn from his nonsense, or at least he seems to hope *someone* will get behind his mode of speaking to his point. The assumption that we can somehow understand nonsense is evident in the penultimate line of Wittgenstein's *Tractatus*:

> My propositions are elucidatory in this way: he who understands me finally recognizes them as nonsense, when he has

climbed through them, on them, over them. (He must so to speak throw away the ladder, after he has climbed up on it.) (*Tractatus Logico-Philosophicus*, §6.54)

You've just witnessed what's *peculiar* about (the so-called "early") Wittgenstein's view of philosophy. Let's see why his hope to cure philosophy is *ambitious* by contrasting that aim with the more modest one he expresses in mid-life. To do so we need to get into the head of the so-called "later" Wittgenstein by returning to "*Spectrum*: Talking About Things."

An Exercise for the Reader

Consider the presenter's "vexed question." How might we evaluate the query, 'What is going on?'

Is it grossly ungrammatical?

—No. It's fine.

Is it full of obscure words?

—No. It contains just four words, each of which is perfectly commonplace.

Does it make sense?

—It depends! Or so says the mature Wittgenstein, with his eye on the way meaning exists in our *use* of language. Here are two ways to use the words 'What is going on?' and make perfect sense:

Situation A:

The day before your birthday you witness your best friends plotting and whispering. You say: "What is going on?"

Used in this situation, the sentence 'What is going on?' means something like: "You can't fool me, you guys; what are you up to now?" In this context the sentence 'What is going on?' makes perfect sense. It makes equally good sense used in quite different ways, too:

Situation B:

You walk in on your lover in bed with your best friend, and you say: "What is going on?"

The words 'What is going on?' have meaning used in this context too! [What meaning exactly is left as an exercise for the reader.]

Now suppose that instead of asking, you're asked, out of the blue, 'What is going on?' Even then the question makes sense so long as you can guess how the questioner intends it to be understood. Here are two examples:

Situation C:

You hear 'What is going on?' and ask, "Going on *where?*"

By wondering this, you indicate that you take your questioner to be using 'going on' in the sense of happening at a place, as in the question, "What's going on at Jean-Paul Sartre's tonight?"

Situation D:

You hear 'What is going on?' and ask, "Going on *what?*"

This question shows that you've understood your interlocutor to mean *going on* in the sense of *being placed on (to)*, as in: "What's going on (top of) the telly?"

No Ambition

As the four situations illustrate, the meaning of the sentence 'What is going on?' depends on its use, so that its meaning changes as its use changes. Nevertheless, we can make sense of the question used in these ways, whereas we can't make sense of 'What is going on?' as it occurs in "*Spectrum*: Talking About Things." On this both the twenty- and the forty-something Wittgenstein are likely to agree (for different reasons); where they differ is in their conception of and response to nonsense.

Suppose we agree that as the presenter uses it, the sentence 'What is going on?' makes no sense. If it doesn't, and we can figure out *why* it doesn't, can we apply that diagnosis to philosophical statements in general and perhaps *avoid* doing whatever it is that leads to nonsense?

Yes, says the young Wittgenstein. Philosophical nonsense is something distinctive; it is something we can spot and throw away once and for all, after climbing "through it, on it, over it."

Nope, says the older Wittgenstein; sad to say, philosophy isn't like dog-doo. One can't avoid it by stepping over it.

In denying this possibility, Wittgenstein admits that his earlier ambition to wash his hands of philosophy amounts to wishful thinking. Why? Because to be able to avoid nonsense, we'd need to know its characteristics, what it looks like. And as we just saw, the details of context matter to whether the sentence makes sense and what kind of sense it makes. It's easy to see how these contexts might be varied—and so the meaning of sentences occurring in them—in infinitely many ways. Given this, who can describe the contexts that will yield philosophical nonsense. Who can say what nonsense looks like?

From the later Wittgenstein's perspective, the presenter and guests on "*Spectrum*: Talking About Things" can't predict the ways their conversation might lapse into nonsense. Since their (and our) uncertainty in this regard is inevitable, philosophy has no cure.

How to Patent Nonsense

With this in mind, the later Wittgenstein reshapes both his practice of philosophy and his goals. As in the *Tractatus*, he continues to use philosophical language to subvert it, but instead of attempting to solve the problem of philosophical nonsense once and for all, Wittgenstein's later practice is to test particular classes of expressions (color words, for instance) in this and that context in order to reveal the variety of ways sense passes into nonsense. He aims to:

> teach you to pass from a piece of disguised nonsense to something that is patent nonsense. (*Philosophical Investigations*, §464)

Exactly how is this practice—this new way of engaging in philosophy—carried out? Let's use *Monty Python's Flying Circus* to make a preliminary point about the very fine line between making people laugh and liberating them from philosophical headaches.

"Is There Life After Death?"

We have, again, a talk show, but now instead of a guest several corpses are "slumped motionless in their seats." The topic is different as well. The host, Roger Last (John Cleese), asks the question:

> Gentlemen, is there a life after death or not?
> Sir Brian?
> (*Silence*)
> Professor? . . .
> Prebendary? . . .
> Well there we have it, three say no. ("'Is there' . . . Life After Death?," *Monty Python's Flying Circus*, Episode 36, "E. Henry Tripshaw's Disease").

Despite ourselves, we laugh to see corpses dangling off chairs. Why? Perhaps the impiety of laughing at death is a relief, given society's unrelentingly solemn attitude towards death; or perhaps we laugh because the bodies are the remains of an aristocrat, an academic, and a clergyman, and who thinks they have much of a pulse to begin with? Plato himself laughs at this in the *Phaedo*, where he lets fly the quip that you must be dead already if you're a philosopher. If we reflect also on the attempt to interview dead men on the subject of life after death, we may laugh at the idiotic appropriateness: Who could be better to ask? Who could be worse?

Why else do we laugh at the skit? Some of the humor of the sketch comes from using language in ways it normally doesn't get used. For example, we don't expect corpses to speak or people to speak to them, so the concepts of speaking and asking is out of place here, and it's incongruous and funny when the host expects an answer, just as it is would be to talk to a lamppost or a mannequin. Similarly, we know that while *people* use silence meaningfully all the time, in wounded silences, compassionate silences, and so on, *corpses* do not—in this sense, corpses are not *silent*—so it's funny to see someone mistakenly treat the two cases as the same.

"Language Games"

So Monty Python derives some of its funniness from incongruous and absurd uses of language; how is this like or unlike Wittgenstein's philosophy? Certainly, Monty Python's sketches raise (implicitly or explicitly) the kinds of questions about language that the later Wittgenstein poses.

But there is an important difference between the nonsense on which their comedy depends and the nonsense Wittgenstein thinks pervades philosophy. We *know* that comedy misuses language. We know that we are to *laugh* at these misuses. To use Wittgenstein's expression, we understand how the "language game" of comedy is played. In practicing philosophy, however, we're never entirely sure how seriously to take *what* we're doing—indeed, we're often not sure what we're doing!

Remember this difference as we begin to engage in philosophy as Wittgenstein does, that is, by investigating our uses of concepts taken from specific areas within our language.

"I'd Like to Put This Question to You, Please, Lizard"

Let's focus on our language about animals. Monty Python occasionally gives us vicious animals—witness the killer sheep in *Monty Python's Flying Circus*. But the sheep kill only after they become intelligent and human-like, and it's more typical to find animals appearing supremely indifferent to us. This indifference is, moreover, charming. At least, this is the case in "A Duck, a Cat, and a Lizard (Discussion)" (*Monty Python's Flying Circus*, Episode 5, "Man's Crisis of Identity in the Latter Half of the Twentieth Century"). Here a "chairman" (Terry Jones) attempts to engage his animal "experts" in a discussion of police force:

> CHAIRMAN: Now first of all I'd like to put this question to you please, lizard. How effective do you consider the lethal weapons employed by legal customs officers, nowadays?
> (*Shot of lizard; silence*)
> Well while you're thinking about that, I'd like to bring the duck in here, and ask her . . . to clarify the whole question.

(Shot of duck; silence)
Perhaps the cat would rather answer that?
(Shot of cat; silence)
No?
Lizard?
(Shot of lizard again and then back)
No? . . .

What is it that's so absurdly dear about the image of a duck, lizard, and cat sitting in chairs, being queried? And why is it that their absolutely unchanging expressions appear so sweet and goofy in this context?

What is endearing about the duck, cat, and lizard, I think, is that they haven't *got* anything to say. What is utterly lovable about these animals is their muteness and indifference. They are *not* human; they do *not* babble endlessly. Surrounding them with chairs and microphones, placing them before a television camera-crew, the very incongruity of these things, of putting animals in this situation turns what isn't exactly front-page news—animal muteness—into something absurd and laughable. *At the same time*, however, the incongruity and absurdity shows how what we mean by *sitting, talking, thinking*, and even *having a face* shifts from sense to nonsense depending on use.

Does It Sit on a Chair?

Take our concept of *sitting*, for example. We say that people, books, and paper *sit*, that they *sit on* desks or chairs, and that people and not books or papers *sit down*. But what does a lizard do? Does it sit on a chair like a book or like a person or neither?

Similarly, can you really *talk* to a duck? The concept of *expressing*, like the companion ideas *thinking* and *gesturing*, is enmeshed with our knowledge of the human body, especially the human face—its mouth, brows, eyes—and hands. The concept of *expressing* is bound up with the concept of *having a face*, and the concept *having a face* is bound up with having a human mouth and eyes and brows, that is, *the sort that can express*.

Given the interrelationship of concepts about faces and expression, it makes sense to describe a woman's face as expressionless, but what can it mean to use these concepts of a duck? Does it make sense to say a duck is *expressionless*? And if not, can it make sense to say that they have faces?

Notice that we are no longer certain what *having a face* means: do we mean that ducks have faces in the sense that clocks do—as a front or surface—or what *do* we mean?

"But—They Simply Do Not Talk"

Let us consider a conventional philosophical question like "What is thinking?" A philosopher might believe that thinking causes talking, where talking is understood as the emission of meaningful sounds, the hard copy of thought, from our lips. Given the view that thinking causes talking, it might seem to follow that animals can't think, since they evidently can't talk. To this sort of reasoning Wittgenstein responds, in his *Philosophical Investigations*:

> It is sometimes said that animals do not talk because they lack the mental capacity. And this means: "they do not think, and that is why they do not talk." But—they simply do not talk. Or to put it better: they do not use language. . . . (*Philosophical Investigations*, §25)

In a nearby passage Wittgenstein says that if a lion could talk, we wouldn't understand it. His objection in that passage, as well as the one above, is not based on disagreement over the facts: Wittgenstein isn't trying to remind us of dolphins or apes as evidence that animals *do* talk and think. Rather, Wittgenstein is objecting to the tendency to ask questions like "What *is* thinking?" without acknowledging the infinitely many different uses of the concept *thinking* (in thinking aloud, being thoughtless, and so on) in their infinitely varied interrelationships with other concepts in our language. Ignorance of these complexities, he thinks, leads philosophers to generate a hairball of difficulties and puzzles.

"Is There Enough of It About?"

This brings us back to the philosopher's cramp and "*Spectrum*: Talking About Things," our opening sketch. How are we to explain the curious responses of the presenter and the cricketer: the presenter's multiplication of questions, the cricketer's near silence? The cricketer has a mental cramp; he assumes he'd heard a genuine question ('What is going on?') that he feels he should be able to answer, though he can't think how. Though the presenter has also gotten a mental cramp, unlike his guest, he thinks that to meet the challenge he must press further, dig deeper, and soldier on.

Perhaps, like our presenter, philosophers take themselves and their work too seriously. Perhaps they need to get more laughs from the grueling work of philosophizing. But this is not how *"Is There"* ends. There, the presenter treats his work and the topics of the show as eminently serious and worthy of consideration. He closes the show saying:

> On *Is There* next week we'll be discussing the question 'Is there enough of it about?', and until then, goodnight.

Philosophers, no doubt, will tune in.

16

Why Is a Philosopher Like a Python? How Philosophical Examples Work

JAMES TAYLOR

ome people think that all philosophy departments should be closed down faster than a soiled budgie can fly out of a lavatory. It's not hard to see why. After all, not only do philosophers typically dress worse than the Gumbys, but the way that they argue for their views seems exceptionally silly. When discussing practical moral issues such as abortion, euthanasia, or famine relief philosophers frequently come up with fantastic and far-fetched examples that don't seem relevant to the case at hand. To illustrate her view on abortion, for example, the philosopher Judith Jarvis Thomson (born 1929) asks her readers to imagine that they wake up one day to find themselves attached to a famous violinist. Similarly, while arguing that people have a moral duty to aid the starving, the philosopher Peter Singer contends that if you think that a person should be blamed for failing to save a child from drowning in a shallow pond you have committed yourself to thinking that you should give almost all of your income to famine relief.[1]

When faced with such examples normal people (that is, non-philosophers) are often incredulous. How on earth can such bizarre examples be relevant in any way to the moral issues that

---

[1] Peter Singer, "Famine, Affluence, and Morality," *Philosophy and Public Affairs* 1 (1972), pp. 229–243.

the philosophers who use them are discussing? But it's not only the ordinary man on the street who is bemused by the way that philosophers argue about such real-world moral issues as famine, abortion, cloning and the like. People in charge of guiding public policy on such issues are also often completely bemused by (or, worse, contemptuous of) the way that philosophers discuss them. For example, Leon Kass, the Chairman of the President's Council on Bioethics in the United States, has written that the contemporary philosophical discussion of cloning, stem cell research, and markets in human body parts "has grave weaknesses . . . [for] it ignores real moral agents and concrete moral situations . . . [preferring] . . . its own far-out, cleverly contrived dilemmas. . . ."[2] Or, in other words, Kass thinks that the argumentative methods that philosophers use are as relevant to everyday life as a man with a stoat through his head.

Complaints about Complaints and Thinking about Thinking

So, should philosophy be considered just a strange and bizarre hobby, like camel spotting, collecting birdwatchers' eggs, or teaching Scotsmen to play tennis? Not at all! In fact, philosophers' argumentative strategies can be very useful in both clarifying the issues that they address and finding solutions to them. Since this is so, perhaps philosophers should follow the lead of John Cleese in the *Monty Python's Flying Circus* sketch "Complaints" (Episode 16, "Show 5") and complain about people (such as Kass) who make rash complaints about philosophy without making sure that those complaints are justified. But before they do this, philosophers have to show why these complaints are rash and unjustified. And (happily enough!) John Cleese's complaint in this sketch about people who make complaints shows just how philosophers should show this.

When *Monty Python's Flying Circus* was first broadcast many people wrote in to complain about it. Far from being upset by this, the Python team was amused by the fact that many of the people

---

[2] Leon R. Kass, *Life, Liberty, and the Defense of Dignity: The Challenge for Bioethics* (San Francisco: Encounter Books, 2002), p. 65.

who complained about them had clearly missed the point of the sketches they were complaining about. To make fun of such people they started making up complaints of their own to incorporate into their sketches. For example, after a sketch in which a psychiatrist dressed as a milkman made a pat diagnosis of a doctor's depression as being the result of a severe personality disorder, Terry Jones, playing a psychiatrist called Dr. Cream, complained about "the way in which these shows are continually portraying psychiatrists who make pat diagnoses of patients' problems without first obtaining their full medical history" (*Monty Python's Flying Circus*, Episode 16, "Show 5"). The sketch then cut back to the milkman-psychiatrist with the doctor in time to hear the milkman say "Mind you, that's just a pat diagnosis made without first obtaining your full medical history." Given this cut, it turns out that the joke's on Dr. Cream because his complaint fails to be justified once the milkman-psychiatrist issues his caveat to his patient. Moreover, as well as this cut back to the milkman making Dr. Cream the butt of the joke, it also makes fun of certain members of the Python audience, for it highlights how silly it is for the Pythons to be expected to have the characters in their sketches adhere to the professional standards of their occupations. Nobody would believe that a person dressed as a milkman from "Jersey Cream Psychiatrists" who diagnoses people while delivering their morning dairy products is an accurate representation of a real psychiatrist, and so to complain as though someone would believe this is just daft.

Not content with this, though, the Pythons also recognized that people might complain about the inclusion of such complaints into their sketches. To respond to this they had another character in the sketch "Complaints" (the "BALPA Man") complain about "shows that have too many complaints in them as they get very tedious for the average viewer." And, of course, including the BALPA Man's complaint about shows with too many complaints in them itself added to the number of complaints in the show . . . and so Michael Palin then complained about people who hold things up by complaining about people complaining. Such a series of complaints about complaints about complaints could, of course, go on indefinitely, but fortunately a sixteen-ton weight fell on Michael after he'd made his complaint about people who complain about the inclusion of complaints about the Pythons' sketches, and the chain was broken.

So, what does all this have to do with the price of butter? Nothing! But it does have a lot to do with the common complaint that philosophers' examples aren't relevant to the moral issues that they are supposed to illuminate. In "Complaints," the Pythons anticipate complaints about their sketches, and incorporate these complaints into their sketches—and then anticipate complaints about their incorporation of these complaints into their sketches, and so on. We find the Pythons thinking about what their audience are thinking, and including their audiences' thoughts *about* their sketches *into* their sketches humorous. And it is the Pythons' innovative abstraction from *writing* comic sketches to thinking about *why* sketches are comic in order to make them funnier that is the key to explaining the value of the apparently bizarre examples that philosophers use. Like the Pythons' abstraction from complaining about their sketches to complaining about complaining about their sketches (and then complaining about the complaining about the complaining about their sketches!) the examples that philosophers use are supposed to get people to think *about* their thinking about an issue. Through this, such examples can help people clarify what their views are. It can also help them see if their views are well supported by their reasoning. And, if they are not, either to develop support for them or else to revise them. To see how philosophers' examples can help people to think more clearly in this way, consider the following standard philosophical example:

Trolley Case 1: You are working in a coalmine with a Y-shaped shaft. The long part of the shaft leads to the surface. The two arms of the Y are the shafts from which the coal is being mined. The coal is taken out of the mine by a trolley, which is pulled up by a chain. Unfortunately, the chain breaks, and the trolley runs out of control down the main shaft. The points at the junction currently direct the trolley to the right-hand shaft, where it will kill five miners working there. However, you can switch the trolley to the left-hand shaft, where it will only kill one miner. (All miners are equally loved by their families, equally intelligent, and so on.) What is the moral course of action for you to take?

When faced with this example most people would say that they would switch the trolley, justifying their decision by saying that switching the trolley would cause the least amount of suffering. In response to this a philosopher might then offer the following example:

> *Trolley Case 2*: You are working in a coalmine with a single shaft that slopes downward. Trolleys run up and down this shaft taking coal out of the mine. The chain pulling the trolley breaks, and it runs out of control towards five miners working at the bottom of the shaft. You're standing by the side of the trolley track. You're too small to stop it by jumping in front of it, but a coworker standing next to you is very large, and if you push him in front of the trolley he would stop it from killing the five miners. Unfortunately, in doing so he would be killed. What is the moral course of action for you to take?

In this case most people would object to throwing another person in front of the trolley to save the five miners. But at first sight the decision not to throw the coworker in front of the runaway trolley looks odd, since in Trolley Case 1 most people would say that you should sacrifice one person to save five. After all, it seems that the only difference between Trolley Case 1 and Trolley Case 2 is that in the first case one would be throwing a trolley at a person to save five miners, whereas in the second one would be throwing a person at a trolley to save five miners. And it doesn't seem that what is thrown through the air to save the five miners should make so much moral difference, since in both cases your chosen actions would save five persons through sacrificing one.

Now, you might say that you will never be faced with the decision of whether to sacrifice one person to save five, and so rather than being useful in defending philosophers from the charge that their examples are impractical and irrelevant, the above discussion really confirms it. But to argue in this way would be to miss the point of the above two Trolley Cases, which is to help people clarify their thinking about what makes an action morally right. To be sure, you are about as likely to encounter a runaway mine trolley as you are likely to be hit on the head by a rubber chicken wielded by a passing knight. But this doesn't detract from the fact that through using such examples you can assess whether your original view of what makes an action right is correct or not. Like the Pythons' thinking about the thinking of their audiences' thinking when writing the sketch "Complaints," then, your thinking about the Trolley Cases will lead you to think about your own thinking about what makes an action right.

For example, if you started off thinking that an act was right if it minimized pain (a version of the ethical theory known as "utilitarianism") you might have to revise your view when faced with Trolley Case 2. You might need to abandon this view altogether and try to find another principle for determining what makes an act right, or else you might decide to try to revise your original view so that you can accommodate your intuition that you shouldn't push people in front of trolleys, even if doing so will save more lives. In the latter case you might come to endorse a version of "rule utilitarianism," holding that an act is right if it conforms to a general rule that, when followed, would minimize pain. Thus, since the rule "don't push people under trolleys" is likely to minimize pain you could modify your original utilitarian position in this way to accommodate the second trolley case. Like the Pythons finding humor in being both performers and audience to their own performance, in constructing their examples philosophers are encouraging people both to think about a particular issue (such as "What makes an act right?") and also to be the audience to their own thinking, and *think* about their thinking on this issue.

Madmen, Blancmanges, Violinists, and Abortion

The point of the above discussion is not, of course, to show either that people should abandon a utilitarian approach to ethics or that they should become rule utilitarians. Rather, it's to show that just as the Pythons derived humor from their sketches' reflexivity and self-reference, so too do philosophers derive understanding (and help others to derive understanding) though using examples to help people reflexively think about their thinking. So far, however, this discussion of the value of philosophical examples has still been conducted at a pretty abstract level. After all, the question of "What makes an act right?" is a question of ethical *theory*. Given this, even someone suspicious of the worth of bizarre philosophical examples might accept that the type of abstruse reasoning that they seem to encourage would be relevant at this abstract level. After all, such a person might reason, just as the Pythons' sketches have little to do with the real world, so too does ethical theory have little to do with solving practical moral problems. So, although consideration of the Pythons' sketch "Complaints" might help to illuminate the value of bizarre examples for philosophical theorizing, it might not be as useful in combating the worries of people like Leon Kass who don't see what use such examples can be in addressing more immediate, practical issues.

Luckily, another Python sketch can be used to rescue philosophers from the charge that to the extent that their arguments are based on bizarre examples they are irrelevant to discussions of real moral issues. In the "Police Station" sketch (*Monty Python's Flying Circus*, Episode 7, "You're No Fun Anymore") a Scotsman, Angus, reports to the police that a giant blancmange has eaten his wife, and the following exchange ensues:

> **DETECTIVE:** Are you mad?
> **ANGUS:** No, sir.
> **DETECTIVE:** Well that's a relief. 'Cos if you were, your story would be much less plausible.

Like the detective, we usually believe that it's a good thing to tell the truth to the police. So, were Angus mad and his story less plausible as a result, we would normally think that this was regrettable. (This is why the detective was relieved that Angus was sane!) However, since it would be better for there *not* to be carnivorous blancmanges roaming around England eating people's wives it would be better *overall* were Angus's tale to be the product of madness. In this sketch, then, the joke's on everyone who holds the common-sense view (implicitly expressed by the detective when he says that he's relieved that Angus's story is plausible) that it is

always better to report true things to the police, for in this particular situation everyone can see that it would be better were Angus
not to be telling the truth.

   The way in which this sketch works thus has a great deal to
teach us about the usefulness of philosophical examples for
addressing practical, as well as theoretical, issues in ethics. Just as
in the sketch "Complaints" the Pythons derived humor from the
type of thinking about thinking that is the basis for the value of
philosophical examples, here they derive humor from the related
philosophical technique of the "thought experiment." Like scientists, philosophers also test their hypotheses through performing
experiments. However, since philosophers' hypotheses concern
conceptual claims such as "Stealing is always immoral," they are
tested through constructing examples that are designed to discover whether any exceptions could be found that would undermine
the conceptual claim that is at issue. Once we see that this is how
philosophers work, we can see that the Python sketch "Police
Station" is in the form of a philosophical thought experiment that
is designed to show the falsity of the commonsense claim that "It
is always better to tell the truth to the police than to tell them falsehoods." We can test this claim by seeing if there are any coun-
terexamples to it. That is, we can test it by seeing if there might
be any cases where it would be better were someone to be telling
the police falsehoods rather than the truth. And, of course, the
case of Angus is such an example, for it would be better if his tale
of the carnivorous blancmange were to be false.

   Yet philosophical thought experiments don't only enable us to
test individual hypotheses, such as that tested in the sketch "Police
Station." Rather, by developing a *series* of such thought experiments philosophers can help both themselves and their audience
develop a more nuanced view of an issue. To illustrate this, let's
look at how the philosopher Judith Jarvis Thomson uses thought
experiments to address the question of the morality of abortion.
Thomson asks us to imagine that

> You wake up in the morning and find yourself back to back
> with an unconscious violinist . . . . He has been found to have
> a kidney ailment . . . the Society of Music Lovers has kid-
> napped you, and last night the violinist's circulatory system
> was plugged into yours, so that your kidneys can be used to

extract poisons from his blood as well as your own. . . . But never mind, it's only for nine months.[3]

Thomson asks us whether we would consider it morally permissible to unplug the violinist, knowing that if this is done he will die? Thomson expects that most people would say that it is morally permissible to unplug him in these conditions, even if we know that he will die as a result. If she's right, then we know that most people do not believe that a person has a moral obligation to use her body to support the life of another for nine months if she had nothing to do with him coming to be attached to her. But this type of involuntary attachment does not only occur in fictitious cases dreamt up by philosophers after a few pints and choruses of "Bruces' Philosophers Song." It also occurs in the real world. A woman who becomes pregnant through rape will have to decide whether to allow her body to be used by the fetus for nine months, where she came to have it through no action of her own, or whether she should "unplug" it from her. Thus, if you think that it is morally permissible to unplug the violinist, so too should you think it morally permissible to abort in the case of rape. Moreover, if you think that it is morally permissible to unplug the violinist you have to accept that *even if* you think that the fetus has the right to life this does not necessarily mean that it is always morally impermissible to abort it. You believe that the violinist has this right too, and yet even so you do not think that it is morally impermissible to unplug him.

Thomson's thought experiment thus presents a clear-cut case (a violinist is attached to your body without your consent) that allows her to ask a clear-cut question (is it permissible to unplug the violinist?). The answer to this question is then applied back to the real-world issue that Thomson is addressing, and used to show what one would say in that case also. With this in hand we can then turn back to the abortion issue to clarify what our views are about other aspects of it. For example, even though we might think that abortion in the case of rape is permissible we still have to determine whether it is morally permissible to abort a fetus that

---

[3] Judith Jarvis Thomson, "A Defense of Abortion," in Marshall Cohen, Thomas Nagel, and Thomas Scanlon, eds., *The Rights and Wrongs of Abortion* (Princeton: Princeton University Press, 1974), pp. 4–5.

was conceived through voluntary intercourse. Engaging in voluntary sex could be seen as akin to offering a fetus an invitation to "take up residence," and if a person acts as if to invite a fetus in like this then he acquires duties towards it. But how far can we go with this argument?

In the sketch "The Visitors," (*Monty Python's Flying Circus*, Episode 9, "The Ant, an Introduction") Arthur Name takes up Victor's invitation to have a drink sometime and goes to his house to meet him. However, since Victor only casually invited Arthur out for a drink three years ago, no longer remembers him, and is having a romantic evening in with his girlfriend, it's clearly unreasonable of Arthur ("Name by name but not by Nature") to expect Victor to honor the invitation. Thus, simply because one person has issued an invitation to another doesn't mean that he necessarily incurs any obligations as a result. Since this is so, it's not true that if the woman acted in such a way that she could be understood as inviting in the fetus she necessarily acquires duties towards it. Now, we might think that this argument from "The Visitors" moves too fast, since whereas Arthur Name won't die as a result of Victor not honoring his invitation, the fetus will—and this marks a moral difference between the cases. This seems right, but if we say this we're conceding that the fact that a woman acted as if to invite the fetus into her body is *not* enough to establish that she has any moral duty to support it. Instead, what *now* seems to determine whether an abortion is morally permissible is the *relative costs* that would be incurred by both the woman and the fetus were she to abort or not. And once we recognize that this seems to be the question that lies at the heart of the abortion debate we can develop other philosophical thought experiments to see when, if ever, it is morally permissible to abort a fetus conceived through voluntary intercourse.

The Practical Value of Philosophical Examples

Just as the point of the discussion of the two Trolley Cases was not to argue for rule utilitarianism, the point of the above discussion is not to settle the debate over abortion once and for all. Rather, it is to show that the technique that the Pythons used to comic effect in the sketch "Police Station" is relevantly similar to that used by philosophers for a more serious purpose. Just as this sketch showed that we would be wrong to think that it is always better to report the truth to police than to tell them falsehoods, so too can philosophical thought experiments help us to test our beliefs about issues. And this is true even if the subject matter of such thought experiments apparently has nothing to do with the issue at hand. "The Visitors" sketch, for example, doesn't have anything to do with abortion, but it can be used to show that the fact that an invitation was issued doesn't necessarily impose any obligation on the issuer. Moreover, that many philosophical thought experiments don't directly bear on the issues that they have been designed to illuminate is an *advantage*, not a drawback. Many issues of practical ethics (such as that of abortion) are emotionally charged, and so abstracting from them is useful as it enables persons to think without their judgments being clouded by emotion.

By now, it should be clear why the bizarre examples that philosophers use in arguments are not as irrelevant as some people believe. But if philosophers are so useful for their ability to use examples and thought experiments to clarify important issues, why are they commonly perceived as being ineffectual, overly-intellectual buffoons of the sort lampooned by the Pythons in the sketch that features soccer-playing philosophers, "International Philosophy" (originally presented in the "German episodes" of *Monty Python's Flying Circus*, and later presented as part of *Monty Python Live at the Hollywood Bowl*)? Clearly, philosophers' reputation for impracticality has a lot to do with the apparent irrelevance of the bizarre examples and thought experiments that they use. But it also has a lot to do with the irony that although philosophers use these examples to think about how to think about issues, they haven't really taken to heart the lesson to be learned from the Pythons' self-reflexivity in sketches like "Complaints." Much of the Pythons' humor comes from their being aware that they are performing, and playing on their audiences' expectations of them as performers. They often explicitly recognize that they are performing for an audience, and incorporate what they think the audience will be thinking into their sketches. So, for example, one of the recurring characters in *Monty Python's Flying Circus* was a crusty Colonel who stopped sketches when they became too silly. This Colonel stopped the sketch "Hell's Grannies" (*Monty Python's*

Flying Circus, Episode 8, "Full Frontal Nudity"), for example, when the Pythons moved from joking about Hell's Grannies attacking people to having "vicious gangs of keep-left signs" attack a vicar. "Right, right, stop it," he interrupted. "This film's got silly. Started off with a nice little idea about grannies attacking young men, but now it's got silly. . . .")

Unfortunately, philosophers tend not to be as self-aware as Pythons, and so they often fail to think about how their methods of thinking are perceived by others. And given the oddity of their examples and thought experiments, this often leads people to dismiss them as irrelevant and impractical. Since this is so, philosophers should take a leaf out of the Pythons' book, and not just think about thinking but also think about *how* their thinking will be perceived by others—and, after doing so, work to explain to non-philosophers why their examples and thoughts experiments are relevant. And showing how the Pythons use techniques that are very similar to those used by philosophers would be a good place to start.

So, What Have Philosophers Ever Done for Us?

Appearances can be very deceptive, as the milkman-psychiatrist from "Jersey Cream Psychiatrists" might have said to the house-wife who thought that he was just a regular milkman. Although philosophical discussions of runaway trolleys and people being attached to violinists might seem irrelevant to the issues that philosophers use them to address, they're actually extremely useful tools for clarifying thinking about these issues. We can see this by comparing the use of such examples to the humorous techniques used by Monty Python. The Pythons' references to their own show within their show parallels philosophers' aim of thinking about how they (and others) are thinking by means of examples that are designed to identify how to think about such abstract issues as what makes an act morally right. Similarly, the Pythons' use of bizarre examples to undermine humorously our unreflective everyday beliefs parallels philosophers' use of similar examples to address such practical moral issues as, for example, abortion. Once we understand what philosophers are up to when they argue using bizarre examples, then, we can see that criticizing philosophers for their use is a bit like Reg (played by John Cleese in *Monty Python's Life of Brian*) criticizing the Romans for not having done anything for the people of Judea. In that film, Reg, the leader of the militant revolutionary People's Front of Judea, asks what the Romans have ever given the people of Judea. This leads one of his men, Xerxes, to reply "The aqueduct." After Reg admits this, the following dialogue ensues:

> **COMMANDO #3**: And the sanitation.
> **LORETTA**: Oh, yeah, the sanitation, Reg. Remember what the city used to be like?
> **REG**: Yeah. All right. I'll grant you the aqueduct and the sanitation are two things that the Romans have done.
> **MATTHIAS**: And the roads.
> **REG**: Well, yeah. Obviously the roads. I mean, the roads go without saying, don't they? But apart from the sanitation, the aqueduct, and the roads . . .

—and then the other members of the People's Front start listing all the other things that the Romans have given the people of Judea: irrigation, medicine, education, wine, public baths, public order, and peace. Similarly, if we ask "What have philosophers ever done for us?" we get involved in the following dialogue: "Well, their examples help us to decide what we think about issues we haven't thought about before." "Oh, yeah, well, that goes without saying, doesn't it?" "And their examples help us discover whether we really believe what we say we believe, or not." "Yeah, all right. I'll grant you that their examples help us to work out what we think, and to think better. But apart from helping us work out what we think, clarifying our views, and helping us to solve hard problems, what do philosophers ever do for us?!" "Well, their examples are amusing…!"

And now I'll obey Reg's command at the end of this scene from *Monty Python's Life of Brian* and shut up.[4]

---

[4] I thank George Reisch for his excellent comments on an earlier draft of this paper, and Gary Hardcastle for risking accepting a chapter by an Englishman from Gerrards Cross.

Pythonic Aspects of Philosophy

"There's Archimedes, and I
think he's had an idea!"

17
Tractatus Comedo-Philosophicus

ALAN RICHARDSON

> What is the aim of your philosophy?—To shew the fly the way out of the fly bottle.
>
> —Ludwig Wittgenstein, *Philosophical Investigations*, §309

A Senseless Waste of Human Reason

In the late nineteenth century or early twentieth century, philosophers rediscovered an important idea, the idea of nonsense.[1] Throughout the next few decades, philosophy was rife with discussions of nonsense. Indeed, an awful lot of philosophers through the first half of the twentieth century thought that an awful lot of other philosophers were speaking nonsense. (Very few philosophers thought that they themselves were speaking nonsense; nonsense was routinely understood to be what they spoke at the next café over, especially if that café was in Paris or the Black Forest.)

---

[1] Philosophers discover nonsense periodically. David Hume (1711–1776) and Immanuel Kant (1724–1804) did so in the eighteenth century. No one has discussed nonsense philosophically with quite the verve of Thomas Hobbes (1588–1679), however, who devoted a whole chapter of his *Leviathan* (Indianapolis: Hackett, 1994) to "insignificant speech."

Why was nonsense so useful to philosophers at that time? Because those philosophers were coming to understand that much of what passed for philosophy really was, at the end of the day, difficult to understand not because it was deep but because it really did not make any sense at all. Anyone might find occasion to say "Besides the beer, there is nothing in our fridge," but it takes a philosopher to write, with a show of great profundity, something like, "Besides Being, there is Nothing"—and then go on to investigate, as Martin Heidegger (1889–1976) did, the precise nature of that Nothing.[2] The claim about the state of the fridge is either true or false—and if you are interested in making dinner, it matters if it is true or false. It began to dawn on a number of philosophers back in the 1920s that the claim about Being and Nothing, on the other hand, was neither true nor false—and the claim couldn't possibly matter whether you were making dinner, looking to get drunk, or doing anything else. 'Besides Being, there is Nothing' is more like saying "Ni! Ni! Ni!" than like saying there is only beer in the fridge. As you can see, then, the importance of having an account of nonsense for some philosophers was precisely to find good grounds upon which to accuse other philosophers of speaking nonsense. If you have taken philosophy classes, you may well feel the pull of this maneuver; if you teach philosophy classes, you certainly feel the pull.

Where do we meet nonsense in our everyday lives? Most manifestly in certain comedic moments. A man with a thick foreign accent enters a tobacconist's shop, consults a book, and says, "My hovercraft is full of eels." Perhaps it is, perhaps it isn't. Certainly, however, the state of this man's hovercraft is not something a tobacconist is much interested in or can really help with. A blancmange finds itself contesting for the All England Lawn Tennis Championship. Karl Marx finds himself competing for fabulous prizes on a TV game show. Neighborhood women gather round to find out whether the son of one of them—a grown son, who is Minister of Overseas Development—can talk yet. These situa-

---

[2] Note the rhetoric of the upper-case letter in this. No one wants to study nothing; but Nothing, well, that is different. As regards Nothing, there turned out to be a great deal to say, none of it, as one might expect, understood to be nonsense by those who said it. For a whole lot of Nothing, see Martin Heidegger, *Being and Time* (Oxford: Blackwell, 1962).

tions are at best silly and, if taken seriously, would be absurd or nonsensical.[3]

So, on the one hand, there is a certain form of comedy—a form which many of the greatest moments from Monty Python exemplify—that exploits the absurd and the nonsensical for comedic effect. And, on the other hand, we have a clear twenti-eth-century philosophical drive on the part of some philosophers to accuse other philosophers of purveying nonsense. Attention to these two facts can change our attitude toward philosophy entire-ly. Comedy, I shall argue, when viewed as something other than a repository of example, can effect a decisive transformation of a vision of philosophy by which we are possessed.[4]

Let us return to the philosophers. We have a vision, offered by Rudolf Carnap (1891–1970), for example, of Martin Heidegger as engaged in the following sort of activity. Heidegger stands before hundreds of students in a lecture hall and proclaims "I'll have the spam, spam, spam, baked beans, sausage, and spam." To this, the students rise in rapturous applause, as both their existence and their German destiny are revealed to them. Heidegger pub-lishes a book in which he reveals that "the human brain is like an enormous fish; it is flat and slimy and has gills through which it can see." This book is greeted as the profoundest statement of the place of humanity in the world.

Why, according to Carnap, would Heidegger be engaging in this ludicrous behavior? Carnap's view is that when philosophers go on this way they are "expressing an attitude toward life" in somewhat the same way that Beethoven or Mozart is expressing an attitude toward life in his music. But, the Ninth Symphony is not nonsense; even Mozart, the *Requiem* notwithstanding, did not write nonsensical music. Carnap's view was that one got nonsense if one tried to express an attitude toward life in the form of a the-

---

[3] These are all, of course, moments in *Monty Python's Flying Circus*. For the eel-filled hovercraft, see "The Hungarian Phrasebook Sketch," Episode 25, "Spam." Proceed to Episode 7, "You're No Fun Anymore," for the blanc-manges, and then back to Episode 25 for Karl Marx in the sketch titled "Communist Quiz" (aka "World Forum"). Finally, for the fully grown Minister of Overseas Development see "Mrs. Niggerbaiter Explodes," in Episode 28, "Mr. and Mrs. Brian Norris' Ford Popular."

[4] Intertextuality, when viewed as more than plagiarism, can effect a decisive transformation in an image of academic misconduct by which we are pos-sessed, also. This fact has not, however, wholly appeased the editors.

oretical understanding of the world. Thus, Heidegger ought to have offered us music (most likely involving oompah bands and *Lederhosen*, in Heidegger's case, sad to say) and came up with nonsense instead because he thought he was giving an account of the world. This leads Carnap to conclude that "metaphysicians are musicians without musical ability."[5]

We can dig deeper than Carnap does, though. Let us grant that some philosophers, perhaps even Heidegger, unwittingly purvey nonsense. The offering of nonsense in the world is, however, not a mistaken attempt to turn an attitude toward life into a theory—it is an *expression* of a particular attitude toward life. Heidegger does not seek to be Beethoven or Mozart and misfire; he seeks to be Professor I.H. Gumby and misfires. Moreover, he misfires not by making more sense than does Professor Gumby, but by being less funny than Gumby. That is to say, Heidegger, unwittingly to be sure, expresses a comedic attitude toward life in offering nonsense as his contribution to the world, but he is a terrible comic; his nonsense is not amusing. We can alter our lesson from Carnap accordingly and say that we have conjectured that philosophers are comedians without comic ability.

This is a profound conclusion that explains many heretofore inexplicable phenomena. For example, among philosophers, the following is a common, all too common occurrence: scores of philosophers gather for a learned talk by a distinguished philosopher on the topic of, say, philosophy of physics; the speaker expresses a desire to be understood by all in the room, but then gives a talk so technical that only three people in the world could understand it. After the talk, two members of the audience meet in the foyer and this conversation ensues:

DR. A.R.: That was like a Monty Python skit.
DR. G.H.: Yes, a bad Monty Python skit.

---

[5] Carnap offers this diagnosis in his essay "The Elimination of Metaphysics through Logical Analysis of Language," in A.J. Ayer, ed., *Logical Positivism* (New York: The Free Press, 1959), pp. 60–81. I use "overcoming" and not "elimination" in the text since it is both a better translation of the original and more expressive of the Carnap's intent. Some influences on Carnap in this matter are scouted by Gottfried Gabriel in his introduction to Steve Awodey and Carsten Klein, eds., *Carnap Brought Home* (Chicago: Open Court, 2004), pp. 3–23.

Exactly so! On my diagnosis the talk really was bad absurdist humor. The speaker, just like Heidegger, missed the boat right from the start. He didn't even realize he was doing comedy. Lacking such self-awareness, he offered up comedy of the worst sort; comedy that mocks rather than amuses or enlightens his audience.

Another important consequence of my view is that we have an explanation of why many philosophers of the sort who are drawn to Carnap (so-called analytic philosophers) find Monty Python particularly amusing, even to the point (witness this book) of thinking that Monty Python has some secret wisdom about philosophy. These philosophers are, on my view, drawn to the very same thing in philosophy and in Monty Python: a sort of pleasure that derives from "getting the joke." What is it to understand the work of Spinoza or Descartes or Kant, anyway? It is not to learn something about the world, but to learn a style of telling stories about the world. To be sure, these stories are not funny (we are dealing in bad comedy, we must not forget), but this is why we must attend to the peculiarities of absurdist humor. For it is not true that one gets a joke just if one finds it funny. Getting a joke is understanding a joke and understanding why it is, properly speaking, a joke, even if it is not funny. In the case of absurdist humor, we dig down to yet another level, however: sometimes what is most funny about a Monty Python skit is how it resists full comprehension— the way it presupposes wildly bizarre events, often without drawing attention to these presuppositions.[6] Graham Chapman appears as a black African tribesman who is also the son of a white working-class Londoner. Calls to the fire department require that you give your shoe size. The intellectual pleasure here is how very much such things do not reflect or describe the world as we know it; they have their own logic, their own structure. The

---

[6] One of the few great theorists of humor in the history of philosophy was Kant, who expressed clearly that telling stories in which things that happen to be physically impossible happen (a man's hair turning white in one night) is simply boring, whereas telling stories in which wildly bizarre things happen (a man's wig turning white overnight) is often funny. For Kant this was indicative of the need for engagement of the understanding in trying to learn something from the story, an engagement that is frustrated in a unique way in the joke. This is all in his *Critique of the Power of Judgment* (Cambridge: Cambridge University Press, 2002).

world of the joke is not our world, but the joke reveals something about our world precisely by presenting a different world.

The lesson here about philosophy is not that Monty Python has anything in particular to teach about the issues that philosophers find philosophical. Please, do not, despite what anyone else in this book tells you, watch Monty Python to learn about the mind-body problem or the nature of knowledge. There is no particular philosophical content in Monty Python—but the form of the work tells us something about the form of philosophy. Philosophy is formally just like absurd comedy without being funny. The intellectual pleasure in understanding Leibniz's monadology is, thus, just like the intellectual pleasure of watching the Python sketch in which Michael Palin is trying to hijack a plane to Luton (*Monty Python's Flying Circus*, Episode 16, "Show 5")—except in the case of Leibniz, there is no amusement. The intellectual state of doing philosophy (as analytic philosophers do it) is, thus, like comprehending a Monty Python episode minus the amusement. It is like having a keen sense of humor without finding anything actually funny.[7]

On this account, the principal difference between, say, Terry Jones and Martin Heidegger is that Jones is aware that he is a comedian and Heidegger is not aware that he is a comedian. This helps to explain why philosophers come closest to being funny when they are sending up those whom they diagnose as asking silly or meaningless questions or offering meaningless propositions. For, in such instances, the self-awareness that the philosopher in question lacks is provided for us, the readers, by the philosopher who is sending him up. For example, without quite being funny in his remarks on Heidegger, Carnap at least does let us see a glimpse of how hilarious he and his philosophical friends in the Vienna Circle found Heidegger.[8] Another excellent example of this mode of exposing the comedy under the grave facade of the

---

[7] At this point the reader might wish to meditate on the fact that many consider W.V. Quine the greatest analytic philosopher. Moreover, as one of the editors pointed out, when Lenny Bruce started to get serious, he ceased being recognizably a comedian and became a philosopher. I count these as major confirmations of my account.

[8] Peter Heath takes up this very example in a genuinely funny essay on 'Nothing' in the *Encyclopedia of Philosophy* (New York: Macmillan, 1967).

[9] William James, *Pragmatism* (New York: Meridian Books, 1943), p. 163.

philosopher is provided by William James. In one of his essays, James tries to convince his reader that the question "which is more essential to knowledge, the contribution of the mind or of the world?" is silly by comparing it to other questions: "Does the river make its banks, or do the banks make the river? Does a man walk with his right leg or his left leg more essentially?"[9] It is clear that whatever else James is doing in this passage, the argumentative work has already been done through *reductio ad humorum*—once a question has been rendered silly, its possible answers are all silly. James's point is that philosophers should stop asking such questions.[10] (I leave as an exercise for the reader to watch John Cleese as the Minister for Silly Walks as an attempt to answer James's question about walking.)

Indeed, on at least one occasion, a philosopher in a *reductio ad humorum* passage came strangely close to the view that I am here offering. In a well-loved footnote to Chapter 2 of *Our Knowledge of the External World*, Bertrand Russell (1872–1970) becomes dimly aware that G.W.F. Hegel (1770–1831) might be, albeit unconsciously, a comedian. We need not burden ourselves with the particular mistake Russell accuses Hegel of making. Here is, however, the lesson Russell draws: "This is an example of how, from want of care at the start, vast and imposing systems of philosophy are built upon stupid and trivial confusions, which, but for the almost incredible fact that they are unintentional, one would be tempted to characterise as puns."[11]

Hegel is an unintentional punster, led inexorably by the internal logic of punning to an execrable philosophy precisely because he doesn't recognize the humor of his own pun. Accept the original pun, and Hegel's philosophy follows; accept that working class Londoners might beget black African tribesmen, and the rest of the skit follows. Among the many interesting aspects of this passage from Russell is the illumination it offers regarding the errors of philosophers—philosophers do not make factual mistakes at

---

[10] James's sense of humor was observed by Gilbert Ryle, who noted that James "restored to philosophy, what had been missing since Hume, that sense of the ridiculous, which saves one from taking seriously everything that is said solemnly," in A.J. Ayer et al., *The Revolution in Philosophy* (London: MacMillan, 1963), p. 9.

[11] Bertrand Russell, *Our Knowledge of the External World* (Chicago: Open Court, 1929), p. 42.

the start of their work. They are confused and their subsequent mistakes derive from this initial confusion.

On very rare occasions, something of self-consciousness on this matter has dawned in the minds of a few particularly acute philosophers. Friedrich Nietzsche (1844–1900, and note the 's') wrote that philosophers do not feel like friends of wisdom as much as they feel like "disagreeable fools and dangerous question-marks." Nietzsche's "philosophers of the future" were to be free spirits, possessed of a *joie de vivre* that few actual philosophers have shown—they would even know how to laugh.[12] Ludwig Wittgenstein (1889–1951) came to understand that the joke was a potent tool for philosophical clarification, as in this passage from the *Philosophical Investigations*:

> The problems arising through a misinterpretation of our forms of language have the character of *depth*. They are deep disquietudes; their roots are as deep in us as the forms of our language and their significance is as great as the importance of our language.—Let us ask ourselves: why do we feel a grammatical joke [*Witz*] to be *deep*? (And that is what the depth of philosophy is.)[13]

The depth of a grammatical joke is the depth of philosophy. That accords nicely with the view outlined here.

The Overcoming of Philosophy through Comical Paralysis of Language

If we expand a bit upon Wittgenstein's claim and employ it within the framework for thinking about philosophy already given, we will achieve an even more significant conclusion than we have

---

[12] Friedrich Nietzsche, *Beyond Good and Evil: Prelude to a Philosophy of the Future* (New York: Random House, 1966), p. 137. Nietzsche continues the thought by saying that philosophers are the "bad conscience of their time." If we remember that the main and the best political critiques are offered by comedians, we have another startling confirmation of our account.

[13] Ludwig Wittgenstein, *Philosophical Investigations* (Oxford: Blackwell, 1997), p. 47 (§111).

achieved so far. Recall that in claiming Heidegger was speaking nonsense, Carnap was offering an objection to Heidegger. Carnap wished to overcome the nonsense Heidegger offered and philosophize correctly, that is, not nonsensically. Carnap called Heideggerian nonsense "metaphysics" and thus sought to "overcome metaphysics" by looking at the conditions under which language made sense and limiting philosophers to sense-making contexts of language use.

We have disrupted Carnap's picture by claiming that philosophers generally make the sort of nonsense that Monty Python makes, except that philosophical nonsense is typically not funny. Thus, on our view, it would be misguided to try to turn philosophy into a sense-making activity. But, we can continue to ask the sort of question Carnap was asking: If philosophy is what we say it is, is it worth doing? Once we ask this question, we have a way of understanding Monty Python as performing the sort of anti-philosophical service that Wittgenstein was hoping to perform.

Wittgenstein said philosophy has the depth of a grammatical joke. "Grammar" is a word Wittgenstein used often, and he didn't use it to mean the rules of language of the school books. Anything with structure has a philosophical grammar for Wittgenstein. Thus, Wittgenstein is saying that certain jokes reveal the structure of our lives in particularly striking ways and are, thus, deep. Jokes like this are the most significant in the corpus of Monty Python's humor.[14]

Consider Michael Palin in the hijacking sketch again. Palin's character bursts into the cockpit and demands that the pilot and co-pilot not make a move. Immediately, however, this demand becomes qualified in complicated ways: the pilot must move to fly the plane; certain bodily movements are involuntary and cannot be prevented; if the plane is moving then all their bodies are moving with it; and so on. The hijacker tries over and over again to come up with a precisely correct demand to make. Or, to take a different example, John Cleese, as Dennis Moore, endlessly qualifies his

---

[14] No claim about Wittgenstein is small enough to be uncontroversial. I shall simply state dogmatically here that on my reading of Wittgenstein he is really talking about jokes and he thinks grammatical jokes, by revealing grammar that is ordinarily concealed, are genuinely deep. Further elaboration of this thesis awaits the day when there will be a *Wittgenstein and Philosophy* book in this series.

claim that he and his victims know that if they try to resist, one of his victims is dead for sure; Moore seeks the precisely true account, even as the account becomes so long and complicated that he interferes with what he is really trying to do.

Such skits have a genuine poignancy for us analytic philosophers. One can easily imagine a philosopher of action trying to come up with an analysis of "movement" which requires that he reproduce the hijacking sketch—indeed, I rather think I read such essays as a graduate student. One can recognize in Dennis Moore the striving for precision that analytic philosophers accept as their goal and that does, in fact, sometimes prevent them from acting usefully in the world. We now can understand these skits: Michael Palin and John Cleese are comedians. They know that they are putting us on. Their characters are, however, not comedians. Michael Palin's character is a hijacker. But, he is not a hijacker of the sort we meet in the real world. The notion of movement needed for the appropriate understanding of "nobody move!" is taken for granted in the real world and goes without saying. Michael Palin's character is a philosopher as hijacker, inhabiting a world in which philosophers hijack planes. Dennis Moore is philosopher as robber. Similarly for all those peculiar Python characters: the man who gestures during pauses in his speech to indicate that he is pausing and not finished speaking; the man dictating a letter who puts on antlers to indicate when he is dictating and not simply speaking. These are all examples of what philosophy would look like if done in the world of ordinary life.[15] The absurd worlds examined in these sketches are worlds in which people genuinely exhibit the sorts of puzzlement philosophers claim to be clearing up. But these puzzles do not appear in our world.

These skits are strikingly similar to Wittgenstein's writing at its very best. Throughout his *On Certainty*, for example, Wittgenstein places the philosopher G.E. Moore (1873–1958) into various real world scenarios in order to see if there was any sense to be made of Moore's philosophical claims.[16] The book is brilliant comedy

[15] For the first see *Monty Python's Flying Circus*, Episode 30, "Blood, Devastation, Death, War, and Horror," "Gestures to Indicate Pauses in a Televised Talk"; for the antlers it's Episode 33, "Salad Days," "Biggles Dictates a Letter."
[16] Ludwig Wittgenstein, *On Certainty* (Oxford: Blackwell, 1969).

as Wittgenstein imagines conditions under which Moore (or anyone) might significantly say, as Moore did in his "Proof of an External World" that "I know this is my hand." Moore was practicing philosophy. In trying to place this philosophy into the world, Wittgenstein creates a panoply of Pythonesque scenarios. Try it for yourself: Point to your left hand with your right index finger and say with passion that you know that this is your hand. Under what conditions could you imagine doing that with sense?[17]

Wittgenstein remains puzzled throughout *On Certainty*. He keeps trying to imagine scenarios in which someone asserts the things Moore asserts in his philosophy, and he keeps finding these claims to be, in such circumstances, "nonsense." At a moment of illumination in the text (§463), he writes "This is certainly true, that the information 'That is a tree', when no one would doubt it, might be a kind of joke and as such have meaning." This is as close as he comes to recognizing that what he is doing is a sort of comedic imagining: imagine a situation in which someone asserts a claim of a philosopher, and you are *by that very fact* in the realm of jokes.

Wittgenstein does not quite release himself from the hold of the idea that there must be some sense to "I know this is my hand." After all, Moore asserted it in all seriousness when doing philosophy. From our current perspective, we can see this "special scenario" in which the claim makes sense: as a philosopher, Moore is doing something like stand-up comedy. The standard rules of sense-making in the world are altered or suspended because we are in the realm of comedy. Here is the place at which the subversiveness of Monty Python's humor comes to the fore: If philosophy is bad, unconscious comedy, then the philosopher seeks to make the world itself into the setting of his comedy. But, in skits like the hijacking skit, we discover that people who engage in the world in the ways philosophers claim to do not live in our world, and their actions in their worlds render those worlds less comprehensible to us than is our world. The search for clarity and precision that is the stock in trade for philosophers makes the

---

[17] One of the editors reminds me that we, he and I, do this in our pedagogical characters when teaching philosophy. Exactly so. But in those contexts, *I*, at any rate, feel like an actor playing in a comedy skit. It isn't philosophy, really, since the skit is genuinely funny, only no one laughs. Peculiar.

world harder to engage in and more opaque. On this view, Monty Python provides a potent argument by example against (analytic) philosophy. Philosophical engagement with the world makes of the world simply the setting for a joke. It would be better for philosophers to recognize that they are engaged in comedy and to reveal something about the nature of the world through self-conscious construction of comedic scenarios.

Wittgenstein wished in his philosophy to show "the fly the way out of the fly-bottle." Philosophers have puzzled over this Wittgensteinian "philosophical therapy." I suggest the following: One most misunderstands comedy if one believes that one must come to a peculiar and deep understanding of something in order to find it humorous. Rather, finding something humorous might in itself be an expression of the highest understanding you could have of it. (Don't try to find the circumstances in which "I know this is my hand" makes sense; you best understand the specialness of that claim when you see that it makes sense only as a joke.) The peculiar intellectual and affective pleasure of the bizarre is the highest philosophical understanding you can have of the structure of our lives. The paralytic nature of attempting to get to the bottom of things in the world (like the Cardinals of the Spanish Inquisition episode (Episode 15, "The Spanish Inquisition") who try over and over to express precisely the nature of the Inquisition) should be replaced by the pleasure of understanding ourselves outside the world of that skit and in a world in which the hijacker and his striving for precision are nothing more than a joke. A philosophy that reaches self-consciousness is a philosophy that simply becomes humor. In our world, that is philosophy enough.

Coda

A question has been raised as to whether I believe what I have said here. In response I offer this:

> A nun walks into a bar and the bartender says: "So, what is this, a joke?"

Do you believe it? However you answer that question, I answer the first one the same way.[18]

---

[18] I would like to thank this book's editors, who both solicited and inspired this chapter. They also deserve thanks for accepting it despite the fact that, as old Wittgenstein himself used to say, my words have not infrequently missed my thoughts.

18

Monty Python's Utterly Devastating Critique of Ordinary Language Philosophy

GEORGE A. REISCH

I t would have been fascinating to be a fly on a wall (even in a bottle) near those philosophers who had watched *Monty Python's Flying Circus* on November 9th, 1972. In that night's episode, Michael Palin portrayed the host of a television program titled, *The Bols Story: The Story of Holland's Most Famous Aperitif.*

As soon as Palin introduces the program's topic, he becomes mired in precise linguistic analysis:

> Good evening. Tonight we're going to talk about, that is, *I'm* going to talk about, well, actually, I'm talking about it now. [*pauses and laughs nervously*]. Well, I'm not talking about it now, but I *am* talking.[1]

By the time he reaches his fourth word, "we're," Palin is derailed. The problem is that there is no "we" who will be talking. Rather, viewers at home will be listening. He alone will be doing all the talking. And is it true that Palin is *going* to talk about a subject (in a moment or two), or is he in fact already talking about it? No, he decides, he's not talking about it yet, but he is talking.

---

[1] The sketch is titled "Gestures to Indicate Pauses in a Televised Talk" (Episode 30, "Blood, Devastation, Death, War, and Horror").

But what, precisely, does talking consist in? There is room for confusion, here, too:

> I know I'm pausing occasionally and not talking during the pauses but the pauses are part of the whole process of talking. [*pauses and chuckles*] When one talks one has to pause. [*pauses*] Like that. I paused, but I was still talking. [*pauses*] And again there!

So, the initial assertion, now qualified to mean, "Good evening, tonight *I* will *in a moment or two* be talking about . . ." must be further specified as, "Good evening, tonight, *except for when I am pausing*, I will be *in a moment or two* talking about . . . " This qualification is important, after all, for viewers may misinterpret these pauses not as integral parts of the "whole process of talking" but as something else. Palin continues,

> No, the real point of what I'm saying is that when I appear *not* to be talking don't go nipping out to the kitchen, putting the kettle on, buttering scones or getting crumbs and bits of food out of those round, brown straw mats that the teapot goes on, you know. Because in all probability, I'm *still* talking and what you heard was a *pause*. [*pauses*] Like there again!

Now that this ambiguity and its potential dangers have been identified, we need some procedure to distinguish the two cases. Palin knows just the thing:

> Look, to make it absolutely easier so that there's no problem at all, what I'll do is I'll give you some kind of sign, like this [*he uncurls his arm toward the camera, as if he's presenting to us something in his palm*] when I'm still talking and only pausing in between words. And when I've finished altogether I'll do *this*. [*He folds his arms.*] Alright?

No, it's not alright. Any discussion about words or gestures must respect the use-mention distinction, the difference between using a sign or word to communicate and merely mentioning it. When Palin first introduces his two signs, he does not use them—thankfully, for his audience would not know what they are intended to mean. Instead, he first mentions them so that he may explain the meanings they will have later on when he uses them. Yet someone at the BBC supposes that Palin mentions *and* uses this second sign. For just as he folds his arms "The End" appears and Palin lurches into linguistic damage control:

> Oh, no no! Sorry! Just demonstrating! Haven't finished! Haven't started yet. [*pauses, and realizes he's forgotten to use the new pause-gesture*] Oh dear! [*makes pause gesture*] Nearly forgot the gesture! I hope none of you are nipping out into the kitchen getting bits of food out of those round brown mats which the . . .

It doesn't look good. Palin's being sucked into a self-referential whirlpool of qualifications and explanations. But he refuses to be beaten. He takes a deep breath and begins again.

> Good evening [*makes pause gesture*]. Tonight I want to talk about . . .

This time, all goes well until Palin reaches his eighth word, "about." That's when the BBC shuts him down: "We interrupt this program to annoy you and make things generally irritating."

What the Fly Saw

After the episode was over, most philosophers would have returned to their nightly reading. Devotees of ordinary language philosophy, specifically, may well have opened Ludwig Wittgenstein's (1889–1951) *Philosophical Investigations* to read passages like this:

> When I say: "My broom is in the corner,"—is this really a statement about the broomstick and the brush? Well, it could at any rate be replaced by a statement giving the position of the stick and the position of the brush. And this statement is surely a further analyzed form of the first one.—But why do I call it "further analyzed"?—Well, if the broom is there, that

surely means that the stick and the brush must be there, and
in a particular relation to one another. . . .

Or this:

> It is easy to imagine a language consisting only of orders and
> reports in battle. . . . But why should I not on the contrary
> have called the sentence [in such a language] "Bring me a slab"
> a *lengthening* of the sentence "Slab!"?—Because if you shout
> "Slab!" you really mean: "Bring me a slab".—But how do you
> do this: how do you *mean that* while you *say* "Slab!"? Do you
> say the unshortened sentence to yourself? And why should I
> translate the call "Slab!" into a different expression in order to
> say what someone means by it? And if they mean the same
> thing—why should I not say: "When he says 'Slab!' he means
> 'Slab!'"?[2]

With Palin's performance fresh in their memory, at least a few of
these philosophers must have looked up from their books and
thought, "hey, wait a minute!" Palin's joke, at least in part, was on
them. Beneath the silliness of his character and the quality of his
performance there lay the outlines of a pointed critique of
Wittgenstein and his philosophical legacy, ordinary language philosophy.

This critique is first suggested by Palin's strikingly
Wittgensteinian character and style. Both focus like a laser on
words and their use, and both urge us to appreciate the complexities of this "whole process of talking." Like Wittgenstein's prose,
moreover, Palin struggled to contain his rapid fire thoughts in the
form of a dialogue with himself, in which he makes assertions,
interrupts himself, offers objections or corrections, and poses
questions and answers. Second, there is something deeply wrong
with this Wittgensteinian performance precisely because it has no
effect. Consider the Pythons' better known satire about England's
Ministry of Silly Walks. Humor aside, this sketch offers a disarm-
ingly *accurate* interpretation of bureaucratic life as a whirlwind of

---

[2] Ludwig Wittgenstein, *Philosophical Investigations* (New York: Macmillan, 1953), I
§60, I §19.

insignificant techniques and pointless procedures (in this case, involving walking). These silly styles of walking are plainly silly and pointless to us, but to the bureaucrats that cultivate and oversee them, they are serious business indeed. Palin's obsession with linguistic precision, his dedicating all his concentration and intelligence to reducing ambiguity and clarifying meaning, is serious business as well. His skills and acuity make him a model ordinary language philosopher. Yet, like the bureaucrats in the Ministry, he never really achieves anything. For all Palin's tortured efforts and analysis, he tell us exactly *nothing* about Holland's most famous *aperitif*.

The Story of Ordinary Language Philosophy: Britain's Most Influential Philosophical Program

"That's not a critique," ordinary language philosophers might reply. "That's the whole point!" Indeed, Wittgenstein argued persuasively that the proper subject of philosophy was not *aperitifs* or anything else amenable to empirical or scientific study. Rather, the subject of philosophy was language. This is because, Wittgenstein argued, our so-called philosophical problems about nature, ethics, epistemology and so forth are really just tangles or confusions in our language and our linguistic habits. Through proper philosophical analysis they can be untangled and, once they are, they disappear and cease to perplex us. For the philosopher of ordinary language, therefore, philosophy is really a struggle of our own making, "a struggle against the bewitchment of our intelligence by means of language" (§109).[3] Much as flies find it difficult to find their way out fly bottles designed to catch them, we find it difficult to extricate ourselves from our verbal bottles. Wittgenstein asked himself, "What is the aim of your philosophy? And then he answered: "To shew the fly the way out of the fly bottle" (§309).

Wittgenstein was not alone in promoting this linguistic revolution in philosophy in Britain. Others such as Gilbert Ryle

---

[3] Wittgenstein, *Philosophical Investigations*, §109. I substitute "struggle" (*Kampf*) for the traditional translation, "battle."

(1900–1976) and J.L. Austin (1911–1960) took philosophy to be the study of our words and linguistic actions. There were differences and controversies about the proper methods and goals of philosophical analysis. But agreement was at hand that philosophy had found its calling in the analysis of language. A.J. Ayer, for example, who was no champion of ordinary language philosophy, wrote of the perennial problem of truth that "there is no problem of truth as it is ordinarily conceived." He explained in his influential book *Language, Truth, and Logic* that "the traditional conception of truth as a 'real quality' or a 'real relation' is due, like most philosophical mistakes, to a failure to analyze sentences correctly."[4]

One important consequence of this turn to language is that philosophy became increasingly disconnected from other areas of inquiry, both inside and outside of philosophical tradition. History, sociology, and the natural sciences, for example, were taken to contribute nothing to philosophical understanding. In his famous passages exploring the semantics of "seeing" and "seeing as"—made famous by his line drawing of a figure which may be seen *as* a duck or a rabbit—Wittgenstein insists that we keep psychology and physiology out of it: "Above all, don't wonder 'What can be going on in the eyes or brain?'" "Our problem is not a causal one but a conceptual one" (§II, xi).

Ordinary language philosophy became popular on campuses during and after the 1940s (other approaches to philosophy, existentialism most notably, were more popular off-campus). In the wake of a devastating world war, it provided a new, modern, and promising framework for philosophy as a professional activity. University departments in the United States grew dramatically in the 1950s and 1960s and departments of philosophy routinely hired experts in Wittgenstein's philosophy to round out their offerings. Of course, this is not to say that all philosophy departments and philosophers spoke with one voice (like one famous department in Australia) or that the rise of ordinary language philosophy was not without important philosophical critics. Heavyweights such as Bertrand Russell and Karl Popper insisted

---

[4] A.J. Ayer, *Language, Truth, and Logic* (New York: Dover, 1936), p. 89.

that philosophy involved much more than solving linguistic puzzles. Decades after his work with the Pythons, John Cleese made a similar point when paraphrasing the British philosopher P.F. Strawson. These postwar years dominated by ordinary language philosophy were a kind of "backwater," a time when philosophers "weren't dealing with anything important." Besides some overstatement—the study of language is hardly *unimportant*, after all—Cleese recognized the professional rewards that ordinary-language philosophy held for many. It allowed them "to shine" and "to look tremendously bright, and everyone thought 'Aren't they clever! My God, what brilliant minds!'"[5]

The Problem with Brilliance

This kind of brilliance came at a cost, after all. A philosophical program that ignores existentialism, phenomenology, epistemology, ethics, and social philosophy risks becoming disconnected from those areas of life and culture that (arguably) give rise to philosophical problems and curiosity in the first place. We may show, or even shew, the fly out of the bottle, after all, yet remain variously uninformed, perplexed or disturbed by the problems that lead us to philosophy.

So it goes in the sketch, "No Time to Lose." Palin, once again, portrays a man deeply concerned with language and its ordinary use. Seeking some expert advice and training, he finds it at the *No Time to Lose Advice Centre* where Eric Idle sits behind his desk and counsels would-be users of this popular phrase.

Palin's marriage, it appears, is in a semantic rut:

My wife and I have never had a great deal to say to each other. In the old days, we used to find things to say, like, "pass the

---

[5] Cleese's comments are from a lecture of his at Scripps College, 1998. I thank Stephen Erickson for providing a recording of this presentation. Popper and Russell strongly objected to the view that philosophy was entirely constituted by the analysis of ordinary language. Russell sneered at the philosophical "cult of 'common usage'" (in Ray Monk, *Bertrand Russell: The Ghost of Madness, 1921–1970*, [New York: Free Press, 2000], p. 384) and Popper in his autobiography frequently disclaimed "concentration upon *minutiae* (upon 'puzzles')" or "mere puzzles arising out of the misuse of language" (*Unended Quest* [Chicago: Open Court, 1982], pp. 90, 16).

sugar" or "that's *my* flannel." But in the last ten or fifteen years there just doesn't seem to have been anything to say. Anyway I saw your phrase advertised in the paper and I thought, "*that's* the kind of thing I'd like to say to her."

What this sad relationship needs are things to talk *about*. Yet Palin and Idle care only about the phrase and the proper technique for using it. In Idle's first lesson, he pretends to be an alarm clock that wakes Palin up only minutes before he needs to be at work.

IDLE: "Tick tock tick tock. RING! RING! RING! RING!"
PALIN: "No!" "Time to lose!"

Palin is confused by the complexities of pausing and ending and can't get the hang of the expression. As a last resort, Idle turns to phonetics. When used properly, he explains, the words "to lose" sound like the name of the city in France, Toulouse. With Idle and Palin now chanting in unison "No Time Toulouse, No Time Toulouse . . .," the sketch becomes even more detached from the problems that led Palin to seek some help. He may have learned, finally, how to pronounce the phrase. But, just as we learned nothing about Holland's most famous *aperitif,* he learned nothing about how to solve those underlying problems in his marriage. Thus the sketch is free to segue into something similar, but completely different: "No Time Toulouse: The Story of the Wild and Lawless Days of the Post-Impressionists."

Bruces

The analysis of everyday language and our use of it to solve philosophical problems again takes center stage when the Pythons present their famous department of philosophy in a fictional Australian university. These philosophers, however, look more like officers or soldiers. They dress alike (in khaki), they talk alike (loud and ill-mannered) and, as a simple theory of descriptions would have it, they're all the same. Each is named Bruce.

The Bruces are fascinated by language. When one says, "It's hot enough to boil a monkey's bum," another remarks, "That's a strange expression, Bruce."   "Well, Bruce, I heard the Prime

Minister use it." When the department chair makes a joke, most of the other Bruces *use* laughter to express their delight. While they laugh, however, another—Palin (there is a pattern here)—instead *mentions* laughter and bellows, alongside his laughing colleagues, "Howls, howls, of derisive laughter, Bruce!"

Yet when Cleese, the Chairbruce, brings this meeting to order, another aspect of the Pythons' critique of ordinary-language philosophy comes into view. First, he introduces the department's visiting philosopher, Michael Baldwin (played by Terry Jones), whose presence challenges the uniformity and conformity that the Bruces seem to crave. Immediately, they begin to call him "New Bruce" and they impress upon him their departmental rules: They must all drink regularly, Cleese explains, and they must all be heterosexual (No pooftas!). This regimentation and uniformity extends to politics and academic freedom, as well. New Bruce, we learn, will be free to teach "any of the great socialist thinkers provided he makes it clear that they were *wrong*!" The old Bruce's heartily agree as they unleash their nationalistic passion and yell, in unison, "Australia, Australia, We Love You, Amen!" The sketch ends with post-meeting refreshments and a close-up on Cleese, looking increasingly savage and crazed, gnawing a large slab of raw meat.

The joke here is the vast cultural distance between the refined, polite Michael Baldwin and his new fascist-philosopher colleagues. But the sketch is not merely whimsical. It involves kernels of historical truth about the institution of philosophy which, for all its lofty ideals and intellectual refinements, has been affected by these baser social forces and prejudices that animate the Bruces. In the 1970s, for example, many philosophers were scandalized to learn about Martin Heidegger's professional, party-sponsored ascent in Nazi Germany. Others were upset by allegations about Wittgenstein's homosexuality and his mistreatment of persons and colleagues he did not like.[6] Recent studies have focused less on

---

[6] On the controversy about Heidegger, see for example Hans Sluga, *Heidegger's Crisis: Philosophy and Politics in Nazi Germany*. (Cambridge, Massachusetts: Harvard, 1993). Controversy about Wittgenstein's personal life began with Bartley's biography, *Wittgenstein* (second edition, Chicago: Open Court, 1985). For an unflattering portrait of Wittgenstein and his admirers, as well as a sensible appraisal of the Bartley controversy (in the appendix, pp. 581–586), see Ray Monk, *Ludwig Wittgenstein: The Duty of Genius* (New York: Free Press, 1990).

individuals and more on how curricula and pedagogy in philosophy were affected by anticommunism (or McCarthyism) in the
United States and Europe during the cold war. Politically engaged
styles or programs of philosophical activity and research that once
dominated philosophy in the 1920s and 1930s—Marxism, most
prominently—fell into disfavor and survived, at best, as niche spe-
cialties.[7]

The point is not that the Pythons anticipated these historical
claims or investigations. Their sketch simply finds humor in the
idea that philosophers, regardless of how accomplished or
obscure, are nonetheless human and therefore susceptible to
human foibles—be they the allure of nationalism or the joys of
putting whoopee cushions in colleagues' chairs (as Sartre, the
Pythons elsewhere tell us, was fond of doing).

Yet the humor leads us back to our critique. If the Pythons
had in mind a real-world model for the Bruces, who could it have
been but Wittgenstein and his followers at Cambridge and Oxford
(where the Pythons began their careers)? Wittgenstein's personal
magnetism was legendary and helped cement nothing less than a
tribal or cult mentality among his students. Critics may have
described things in extreme terms, but they are surprisingly consistent. Cambridge philosopher C.D. Broad, a contemporary of
Wittgenstein, complained in print about "the philosophical gam-
bols of my younger friends as they dance to the highly syncopat-
ed pipings of Herr Wittgenstein's flute" while Russell disdained
the "cult of 'common usage'" that grew up around Wittgenstein.
Two recent historians note that this "passionately expressed alle-
giance to Wittgenstein" extended beyond philosophy into habits
of lifestyle, dress, and diet. "How religiously the inner circle of
the disciples followed the master has a comical air to it: sleeping in
narrow beds, wearing sneakers, carrying vegetables in string bags

---

[7] For pioneering accounts of anti-communism's effects on intellectual life in the
United States, see Ellen W. Schrecker, *No Ivory Tower: McCarthyism and the
Universities* (New York: Oxford University Press, 1986) and Frances S. Saunders,
The Cultural Cold War: The CIA and the World of Arts and Letters (New York: The
New Press, 1999). Subsequent accounts addressing philosophy in particular
include John McCumber, *Time in the Ditch: American Philosophy and the McCarthy
Era* (Evanston: Northwestern University Press, 2001) and George A. Reisch,
How the Cold War Transformed Philosophy of Science (New York: Cambridge
University Press, 2005). On the fashions of existentialism in cold war America,
see George Crotkin, *Existential America* (Baltimore: Johns Hopkins, 2003).

to let them breathe, and putting celery in water when serving it for dinner. . . ."[8]

None of Wittgenstein's devotees changed his or her name to Bruce, so far as I know. But that is beside the point. The important question this historical research raises is whether social and political circumstances affect philosophers *as thinkers*. Is technical philosophical work—the premises on which dominant theories rest, the subjects philosophers find interesting, the arguments they construct, and the seminar reading lists they create, for example— affected by the forces and politics of professionalism and social life? For the Old Bruces, the answer is clearly 'yes.' They will do nothing without the approval of their colleagues and fellow patriots. New Bruce, on the other hand, presents a challenge. Will he teach socialism and condemn it as "wrong" because he has been ordered to? The sketch does not answer but frames the question effectively: New Bruce must either give in to this departmental pressure or put up a fight.

A Knockout of an Argument

So it goes in the sketch, "The Epilogue: A Question of Belief." Here, Cleese is the host of a high-brow intellectual television program called "The Epilogue" and his two guests are a world-renowned Bishop and a popular professor of philosophy at the University of East Anglia. Their topic is the perennial question, Does God exist? But tonight there is a twist. These two guests, Cleese explains, will employ a special method: they're going to "fight for it—the existence or nonexistence of God is to be determined by two falls, two submissions, or a knockout." Cleese transforms into a sports announcer ("Alright Boys. Let's get to it!") and the monsignor and philosopher begin tossing each other around the ring. As the sketch ends, there is yet no clear winner. Cleese tells the audience, "we'll be bringing you the result of this discussion later on in the program."[9]

---

[8] Broad and Gilbert Ryle are cited in D. Edmonds and J. Eidinow, *Wittgenstein's Poker* (New York: Harper Collins, 2001), pp. 71 and 31. On the mimicry of Wittgenstein's students, see p. 34.

[9] God exists, it later turns out, "by two falls to a submission."

This *discussion*? As with the Bruces, this sketch juxtaposes two very different things not only for the resulting laughs and silliness. Those laughs take some root in the suspicion that these two very different institutions, violent sport and serious intellectual debate, may be fundamentally connected or not so different. Both sketches suggest that philosophical questions and styles are sometimes like prizefights and effectively settled by the power wielded by individuals, departments, or societies and nations.

So understood, these two threads of commentary about philosophy that run throughout *Monty Python's Flying Circus*—the parodies of ordinary language philosophy and the hardball politics involved in the life of the mind—come together in a one-two punch that lands squarely on Wittgenstein's jaw. For if philosophers' beliefs and arguments are *to any extent* influenced by fashions, politics, or overt bullying—whether of nations, professional academic departments, rival intellectuals, and so on—then it cannot be correct to say that philosophy consists exclusively in solving puzzles in everyday language. For in that case, what philosophers say and believe about philosophical subjects is affected by circumstances and pressures that exist outside of language. There is nothing in language or its analysis alone, for example, that makes sense of the Bruces' co-dependencies. Nor do they explain the strong personal and emotional attractions (or aversions) that so many philosophers developed about Wittgenstein or the strategies philosophers adopted to navigate Nazism or McCarthyism. Yet these kinds of extra-linguistic factors (variously historical, sociological, and psychological) most likely contributed to the scope and nature of philosophy as it evolved through the twentieth century.

If philosophy desires to understand and account for its own development and nature, it cannot embrace Wittgenstein's dictum that philosophy consists in solving puzzles in ordinary language. It must instead open itself to perspectives and results offered by history, sociology, and other areas of intellectual life. With more open borders, there should be much more for philosophers to do than belabor the idiosyncrasies of ordinary language or pauses and endings. And for all that, there may be no. Time Toulouse.

19
Word and Objection: How Monty Python Destroyed Modern Philosophy

BRUCE BALDWIN

Some might say that a rather senior philosopher like myself has his creative days behind him.[1] Indeed, some have actually said this. But I am finding, partly because of the circumstances I will discuss here today, that this conventional wisdom has it all backwards: I, even as I near eighty, am behind my most creative days. But then again, as most of you know, I've long been accustomed to being at odds and out of step with most of the "trends" and conventional "wisdoms" in philosophy! [*audience laughter*—Eds.]

In *My* Day . . .

Well, let me begin with a personal reflection of sorts. Many of you know that my heart, along with my intellect, is rooted in Great Britain. On my earlier visits to your department, you may have heard me speak of what went on in the drawing rooms of some of the finer British universities in the middle decades of the last century, in my dear youth. Ah, to be wandering room to room back then! One might spy down one corridor young men furiously debating something called *sense data*—the sight of a red lorry or

---

[1] This chapter was transcribed and edited from audiotape. Sections headings were added for readability—Eds.

the taste of an apple were common examples. You see sense-data
around still, at least occasionally, by the way. And down another
corridor, I recall seeing two rather gawky biologists of indeterminate intellect played giddily with chains of tinker-toys and x-rays
(for some reason) and who, I later learned at High Table, discovered some important result about exactly how to hook-up or
chemically combine two chains of such tinker-toys. And for this
these men became Nobles! Every corner, every drawing room,
contained some fascinating activity or one sort or other. Halcyon
days!

The *philosophical* excitement in those decades swirled dizzying-
ly, of course, around the great Ludwig Wittgenstein (1889–1951),
with whom on several occasions I attempted to talk and dine.
Permit me a bit more in the way of personal anecdote. As you all
know, though we were not on *intimate* terms, I knew Wittgenstein
quite well. And as I made quite clear to the authors of that recent
book, *Wittgenstein: Joker* (though they chose not to respond to, or
even acknowledge, my letters), I myself was even present at that
philosophical *tête-à-tête* many years ago that has lately been attract-
ing so much attention. This is the one, um, you've all heard about
it I'm sure, in which Wittgenstein is rumored to have behaved
poorly. Well, I can tell you that most of what is being said about
this so-called affair has been thoroughly obscured by the interven-
ing years or, as seems more likely, various agendas and postmodern *machinationé* implemented by those endeavoring to revise,
downplay, or trivialize (and presumably popularize!) Wittgenstein's
singularly great and oft-misunderstood contributions. Now let me
be clear that Witt, as I called him, was *not* joking around during
that week's discussion at the Moral Sciences Club. Far from it!
The speaker, however—a nervous, funny-looking Austrian named
'Popper', I recall—I *distinctly* remember him waving around some
stick or something as he talked. When Whitehead asked him to
leave it alone, Popper claimed that the stick had nothing to do with
philosophy, and that he was only gesturing, and I quote, "in philosophical fun"!

Well, I needn't tell you what happened next. Philosophical
fun, indeed! Witt stormed out of that now-fabled *assemblage*, slam-
ming the door in the process. This I remember vividly because I
was sitting at the door, and Witt stepped on *my* foot on the way
out, crushing three of my toes!

And here, gentlemen, is my foot! [*laughter, applause*]

Well, my foot has since healed, but philosophy, I'm afraid, has not. What Wittgenstein taught us that day, as on so many others, was that philosophy is a *most* serious business, and a *most* serious business cannot be interspersed with *anything* else—be it science, literature, or play, even good old-fashioned poker play by the warm hearth. I do believe that I recollect those post-war years so fondly not because *I* was then in my prime (a little logical joke there, eh!), but because *those times* were special. In those days, we *lived* the philosophical homily, imbibed from the writings of Duns Scotus (1265/66–1308), that everything, philosophy especially, has a place and, contrarily, that there is a place for everything. The human mind made great strides then (mostly, but not just, in England), but these strides were premised on the seriousness and intensity of research that comes with keeping intellectual life organized, well-structured, and . . . *in its place*. Everything is, we all agree with Parmenides. But I insist that everything not only *is*, but must *also* be in its right place. [*applause*]

Scotus? Scotus? He is, sadly, a stranger to today's university. He's even more a stranger to today's so-called philosophy. Like the proverbial toothpaste bled from its tube, philosophy has, over the course of my career, spilled out of its proper place to mix, meld, and just generally interlace itself with, well, *everything*—what is called "popular culture." There even appear to be many who nowadays promote, under the rubric of "popular culture," the claim that serious philosophical life should be available for every-one, that every last jot and tittle of movies or plays or comic books or shows *on the telly* even somehow count as philosophically deep or important. There is even, I'm told, a book series dedicated to unearthing philosophical ideas or notions in *movies and television shows!*[2]

Some of you will spot the irony afoot. For it was a certain youthful indiscretion on my part, with certain now-famous ele-ments of popular culture (combined with, I admit, several pints), that first led me to your wonderful department and its uniformly underrated approach to matters *philosophie*. I refer—I can see some of you smirking already—to that BBC excrescence *non*

---

[2] !—Eds.

puerile known as *Monty Python's Flying Grail* [audience: "Circus!
Circus!"]. Right, right, *Circus*. Anyway, as we all know, it was upon
encountering one of these so-called "Pythons" in a Twickenham
Road pub that I learned (and how *he* knew, I haven't the foggiest)
that this very department was at that very time soliciting.
Soliciting applications for a visiting scholar. And again as we all
know, the result has been a long and most fruitful, if sporadic,
intellectual camaraderie.

But let us be clear: if this Monty Python business inadvertently nourished my career, that was a mere accident attendant upon a
substantial *disaster* for twentieth-century philosophy *proper*. The
philosophy I . . . well, we . . . were taught to love, honor, and cher-
ish became, in the course of Monty Python's success, *popularized*—
a circumstance all the more ironic given the fact that, I was once
told, the Pythons themselves were once students at two of the
greatest universities in the history of civilization, Oxford and
Cambridge. Knowing something of the real, true philosophy, they
apparently felt equipped to stun, even kill, it with an *Arbeitkorp*
comprising not just a show on the telly but at least one full-length
movie, the sheer popularity of which surely helped obscure, if not
altogether erase, those crucial disciplinary and cultural borders I
just mentioned. Indeed, Monty Python, I submit, paved the way
for the utterly ridiculous idea that anyone anywhere can not only
pass judgment upon philosophical matters, but do so on national
television. Good Lord, I even witnessed a sketch in which two
washer ladies discuss Sartre! [*laughter*]. Laugh if you must, but all
this mucking about has had dire consequences. It has made it
next-to-impossible to tell who is *really* a philosopher and who is
not; who is a fraud and who has earned a place over Wittgenstein's
knee.

Some of my younger colleagues, back in Slough, dismiss my
worries. They have their standard response about the status of
anything: "Well, it's all negotiable now, isn't it? It's all textual."
[*yelling*] WELL IT'S NOT! [*audience cheers*]. But, I ask you, is their
attitude not the main reason why a walk through the drawing
rooms of today's universities resembles nothing so much as a
muck-about in a postmodern zoo, where the animals have been let
loose from their cages to wander amongst (and, inevitably, mount)
each other, heedless to their heritage as natural kinds? If it is still
a philosophical homily (as I, like so many others, learned from our

graduate advisors) that there can be no distinction without a corresponding instinction, then the present essay can be regarded as a tracing of one triumph of *instinct* over *distinct*.[3] Thus my title.

The Trouble With Dead Parrots, and Sketches About Them

How, precisely, did a comedy troupe with ill-advised access to a television camera create a fissure in the dyke capable of releasing these floodwaters? Well, the reason strikes me as quite plain: they ignored the master. As Wittgenstein says, language *matters*. But to watch these Pythons, you'd think Wittgenstein never even *existed*! It's language on holiday with them, I tell you, and nary a care for the perspicuity, rigors, or quality with language that our profession claims as its very own! All of this is clearest in a sketch I recently chanced upon when preparing my talk to you and which happily remains obscure and, more importantly, largely unknown to my negotiation-intoxicated younger colleagues.   I hesitate to even begin to—ahem!—popularize it here, not only because it tends to agitate me but . . . [*inaudible comment from the audience*]. Right, that's a good idea. Thank you, Bruce. [*sound of bottle opening, pause*]. There. Alright, the sketch goes like this. A Mr. Praline angrily returns to his local pet store to complain about a bird he'd recently purchased. The pet shop owner. . . . Oh, I actually have it transcribed here . . . bugger, I'll just read it.

> **MR. PRALINE**: I wish to complain about this parrot what I purchased not half an hour ago from this very boutique.
> **OWNER**: Oh yes, the, uh, the Norwegian Blue . . . What's, uh . . . What's wrong with it?
> **MR. PRALINE**: I'll tell you what's wrong with it, my lad. 'E's dead, that's what's wrong with it!

---

[3] I have treated this distinction elsewhere, most prominently in my Baldwin, B., "Instinction and Distinction Reconsidered," *Philosophical Gyrations*, 1986, pp. 111–145, an essay which substantially revises and (I admit) corrects the earlier treatment in my *dissertatio*, "Five Aspects of the Instinct-Distinct Problem," a dissertation submitted to the Faculty of Philosophy, Grosvenor Square College, by Michael Baldwin, 1971.

OWNER: No, no, 'e's uh, . . . he's resting.

MR. PRALINE: Look, Matey, I know a dead parrot when I see one, and I'm looking at one right now.

OWNER: No no he's not dead, he's, he's restin'! Remarkable bird, the Norwegian Blue, idn'it, ay? Beautiful plumage!

MR. PRALINE: The plumage don't enter into it. It's stone dead.

OWNER: Nononono, no, no! 'E's resting!

So, here we have in the Owner (who, it should be noted, does *not* own the subject of the sketch, the parrot—see how it's language on holiday already?) a denial of the parrot's very existence; it is, in fact, a bold parrot-denial. The stage is set, therefore, for philosophical debate; if it were in our hands, professional hands, a proper language would be set down, tending to syntax and semantics, and then by means of this language the dispute would be resolved effectively, that is, by way of a method that provides in a finite number of steps the correct answer and no incorrect answers. Such would be the *proper* philosophical resolution of this all-too-philosophical moment.

Yet what these bloody Pythons provide is something quite different—something as disturbing as it is, nowadays at least, familiar. No philosopher enters. *No philosopher is even summoned!* Instead the hapless Mr. Praline takes matters into his own hands and, by an argument that consists, contrary to Occamian precept, in insistences multiplied, he denies the denial of the parrot. Any user of Wittgenstein's slab language, or for that matter any licensed contractor, could predict the outcome. There is no parrot, no refund, and, of course, no resolution. Left to their own untrained amateur language, these reckless non-philosophers simply drift on the open sea to which they have banished themselves. *Bon Voyage.*

Read as a chilling morality play, this Dead Parrot sketch could suffice. But by enacting and promoting this and other philosophical situations into (so-called) popular culture, Monty Python has folded philosophy into the warp and woof of the everyday, the mundane, and the vulgar. This pet shop, of course, reminds us of man's less-than-proud heritage among Thomas Hobbes's "untamed beastes." Need we more of an indication that we are being presented with degeneration incarnate? If so, notice that this scene is presented in a public forum—namely, television—characterized aptly by the eminent Spiro Agnew, the Greek shipping tycoon and later Secretary of State under Jimmy Carter, as a "vast wasteland." To those properly tuned to the message, it can hardly be avoided: philosophical issues should be tossed into this wasteland to be shat upon by, among others, dead parrots. The mocking laughter of the studio audience, recruited no less from the very British citizenry who would go on to invent *punk rock* . . . Well, let me just say that this sketch alone likely damaged real and true philosophy more than *any* event of the twentieth century, and in saying that I include the publication of *Zen and the Art of Motorcycle Maintenance*. [*sustained applause, cheering*]

There is, I admit, a potential terminological puzzle. Wittgenstein showed us that "language games" and "forms of life" were proper foci for philosophical analysis. But his mere usage of those words does not, of course, license entertainers to concoct silly exchanges that run roughshod over the categorical distinctions they put in play. Is this parrot alive or dead? The poor viewer is left with the suggestion—nay, it's not even a suggestion, but just an assertion or implication against which they can have no argument—that it may *or may not* be dead. Every test and analysis of the situation—if the bird is merely sleeping, for instance, then it should be able to be woken up—is deconstructed as some negotiation-rich tug-of-war. When Mr. Praline yells at the bird to see if it can be roused ("'Ello, Mister Polly Parrot! I've got a lovely fresh cuttlefish for you if you show . . . ") the Owner jostles the cage and proclaims, "There, he moved!" Negotiation triumphs again, for now the argument is shifted to whether he jostled the cage:

OWNER: I never!!
MR. PRALINE: Yes, you did!
OWNER: I never, never did anything . . .

As these winds of negotiable ambiguity continue to push these two hapless non-philosophers out to sea, this perverse view of philosophy as some kind of game, some kind of solving of puzzles—a bourgeois pastime, perhaps, like Parcheesi, to be played by philosophers or pet-store owners alike—becomes plain.

Having sailed out of even *potentially* philosophically responsible waters, the sketch goes to its inevitable end—to a shouting match, a noisy string of synonyms and clichés meant to establish, *per impossibile*, some truth of the matter. This parrot, Mr. Praline says (now yelling at the top of his lungs) is

> passed on! This parrot is no more! He has ceased to be! 'E's expired and gone to meet 'is maker! 'E's a stiff! Bereft of life, 'e rests in peace! If you hadn't nailed 'im to the perch 'e'd be pushing up the daisies! 'Is metabolic processes are now 'isto-ry! 'E's off the twig! 'E's kicked the bucket, 'e's shuffled off this mortal coil, run down the curtain and joined the bleedin' choir invisible!! THIS IS AN EX-PARROT!!

What is all this then? What have we got in this sorry excuse for a philosophical discussion? Nothing but a litany of bald assertions, not even an attempt at an argument, and, plainly, the utter absence of real philosophical analysis. And I'll have you know that, after all the shouting, this pair decides to go home together in the fash-ion of pooftas?! [*murmurs and disapproval from the audience*] It's these Monty Pythons who have taken us down this path. So who, I ask, shall grab the wheel and steer things right?

What Is to Be Done?

Some things cannot be shown (Wittgenstein, again, obviously) and must therefore be said, even belabored, because they are so insid-ious and complicated. So forgive me for running on but I want to impress upon you how complicated things have become and what is at stake.

First and foremost, despite Pythonic appearances, philosophy is no game. Careers are at stake! Publishing royalties! These depend upon our ability to responsibly analyze things philosophi-cally and thus to distinguish correctly the *real* philosophers from the frauds and charlatans. Now that the Pythons have so turned poor Witt on his head and let this parrot out of its cage, it's nigh impossible to know who's who and what's what. Your own department, as you well know, is revered as a band of genuine pio-neers in the theory of identity and naming. Yet—I dare say only because some of you mentioned it earlier today—there are some, well many, I've run across who question whether your department remains *in existence* today, or whether it *ever* existed beyond those few moments long ago when it was put in front of Monty Python's cameras. [*laughter from the audience*] Need I say more, then, to illustrate the widespread confusions?

What, then, is to be done? I daresay the answer is obvious. We must *boycott* all these avenues and institutions that have so far promoted this popularization, and we must begin with Monty Python. This means a number of things. First, of course, we must simply assert ourselves. Let us prove that we do indeed exist [*cheers from audience*] and that we must be taken seriously by the philosophical establishment!

That's the easy part. Much harder, I fear—though not impossible, let's hope—is the task of refuting or at least obscuring this notion that Monty Python has anything philosophically interesting or genuine to say. Now, in this case, we can kill two emus with one stone [*cheers and laughter from audience*] simply by organizing ourselves and like-minded (that is, real) philosophers and publishing our own book—say, something like, *Real Philosophy Is Not Popular Philosophy*—in which we can illuminate the pitfalls of the current fashions.

Indeed, that is what I've begun to do in my talk today. Of course, here I am preaching to the converted. So what *I* shall do—and I implore you all to join me—is send round my essays and papers to publishers in hopes that at least one is not yet intoxicated with this blasted *popularization* business. I am quite serious that with the right kind of organization and a publication or two we may inaugurate, really, a *movement* for the *depopularization* of philosophy. [*Cheers and commotion in audience*]

I see that beer and fresh meat are being brought in now, so if you'll all just calm down for yet another minute while I . . . [inaudible above cheering and commotion in audience]. Alright, thank you. I'm almost done here, so . . . just quickly . . . I, I think the most important thing, as each of us plays our role in this anti-popularization movement, is to *downplay* the popularity of Monty Python itself. Really, unless it's absolutely necessary, we must not even *mention* Monty Python in these efforts and obviously not take part in projects or books or conferences that take these mere entertainers seriously as philosophers, popular or unpopular—of any kind *at all*. [*More cheers and calls for food*] Alright, then. Let's have a drink!

20

My Years with Monty Python, or, What's So Funny About Language, Truth, and Analyticity?

GARY L. HARDCASTLE

And though a philosopher may live remote from business, the genius of philosophy, if carefully cultivated by several, must gradually diffuse itself throughout the whole society, and bestow a similar correctness on every art and calling.

—David Hume, *An Enquiry Concerning Human Understanding*, §1

Philosophy [is] on the whole no laughing matter.

—W.V. Quine, *Quiddities*, Preface

Here's a true story. In the early 1990s, as a junior philosophy professor, I was invited to talk to the undergraduate philosophy club at the university where I had recently been hired. I accepted of course, and I even offered a rather promising title: "Themes in Contemporary Analytic Philosophy as Reflected in the Work of Monty Python." That title—inspired by a nervous joke we traded back and forth in graduate school, that the dissertations we were all laboring on, each an example of the painstaking conceptual analysis for which *analytic* philosophy was named, were *in fact* on the philosophy of Monty Python—showed up almost immediately on flyers around campus, above a date, time, place, and—in large letters—my name. One got the distinct impression that *I* would *give* the talk by that name.

Now, I had the title, but not what one might call "the actual talk." If we are going to talk in actualities, I didn't even have an actual idea for the actual talk beyond that suggested by the actual title. It was entirely conceivable (in fact I could conceive it, clearly and distinctly) that I would be introduced and then, at the podium, proceed to repeat that title in various formulations until, somehow, fifty minutes passed. "Well, then [*ponder*] . . . what are the themes of contemporary philosophy, and [*long ponder*] . . . how . . . are they analytic? And what is it to reflect these things I have suggested we call [*extended ponder*] . . . themes [*medium ponder*] . . . in Monty Python? [*extended drink of water*]" That would be a passable Monty Python skit but *terrible* philosophy and, more importantly, an altogether disastrous introduction of me and my work to my new colleagues and students. I had to do something, well, completely different.

As the day approached I staved off panic and thought about it. I needed to show some clips from Monty Python; I had enough sense to know that putting 'Monty Python' in the title and then *not* showing clips from Monty Python would lead the several dozen Python fans in attendance to stone me (though they would don fake beards and unusually low voices for the stoning, a charming but ultimately insufficient consolation). But I also had to say something sensibly philosophical. As we put it in the philosophy biz, I had to *do* some philosophy. It was, after all, a philosophy club, and I a philosopher.

So I sat down a full two days before the talk and . . . well, I don't know how to put this, but . . . it all came together. In fact, it all came together *wonderfully*. I had on the one hand the memory of my favorite Python skits and movies (which at that time included a few dozen episodes of *Monty Python's Flying Circus*, *Monty Python's The Meaning of Life*, *Monty Python Live at the Hollywood Bowl*, and portions of *Monty Python and the Holy Grail*). And, on the other, I had my particular take on the themes of analytic philosophy, which amounted to some very general notions about language, rationality, and philosophy itself. And, lo and behold, many of those skits *really did* reflect, somehow, many of those themes.[1]

---

[1] For your convenience, the talk itself is reproduced in the chapter following this one. Yes, in this very book.

In "International Philosophy," for example, a football team of German philosophers ("led by their skipper 'Nobby' Hegel," the announcer tells us) play their Greek counterparts ("there's Plato, always the man in form!"). The members of both teams quietly pace the field in thought until it occurs to one of them, near the end of the match, to actually *kick the ball* (this is, remember, the game Americans call 'soccer'). This I used to comment on philosophers' frustration with philosophy itself, which seems to involve, to put it plainly, excessive pondering. "Nudge Nudge," in which the randy Norman pelts his fellow pub-goer, a staid Englishman, with innuendoes ("your wife . . . she likes *sport*, does she? Nudge nudge, wink wink, say no more?") I presented as an embodiment of the notion that people could have very different ways of looking at the world—different conceptual schemes, we might say—and that this could go *undetected* in everyday interactions, like, well, having a drink in a pub. And everyone's favorite, the Dead Parrot sketch, in which a Mr. Praline attempts to return a clearly dead Norwegian Blue parrot to the pet shop where he "bought it not 'alf an hour ago" only to be confronted by a shop-owner who insists, by means of successive mental contortions, that the parrot is alive ("It's sleeping! It's stunned! It's . . . pining for the fjords!"), struck me as a dead-on enactment of *holism*, the notion that *any* belief can be held in the face of any experience *whatsoever* so long as one is willing to make adjustments in one's *other* beliefs. I used "The Argument Clinic," the "Cheese Shop," and "Burn the Witch" (from *Monty Python and The Holy Grail*) to similar purposes, and planned to close the whole affair with a sing-along of the "Bruce's Philosophers Song" ("Aristotle, Aristotle was a bugger for the bottle, Hobbes was fond of his dram . . . "); I offered that as Monty Python's non-trivial contribution to the *history* of philosophy. Excited as much by the fact that it was *done* as by the fact that I *had* managed to weave analytic philosophy together with Monty Python, I gave the talk. Just as the flyer had promised.

But that's just the start. That talk not only went well; people loved it. In fact, the club requested the talk for the following semester, and each year after that. And word traveled. I sent a videotape of its inaugural delivery to my Ph.D. advisor (who, having braved uncountably many dry-as-dust dissertations, himself pined for the fabled Monty Python tome), and he showed it to

others. Soon I was giving the talk at other universities, sometimes
to their philosophy department and sometimes to their philosophy
club. Its text showed up on the internet (Python fans, truth be
told, are a bit geekish) and I began receiving email from Pythonites
and fellow philosophers. A few years later, when I found myself
in the great American Midwest (aka Wisconsin) I asked the
Wisconsin Humanities Council if ordinary Wisconsinites might
enjoy this sort of thing, and soon I was showing Monty Python
clips and talking about holism, rationality, and philosophy in
libraries, schools, and the occasional church basement across the
Dairy State. It continues; as I write, I'm scheduled to talk about
philosophy and Monty Python in Harrisburg, Pennsylvania, next
week, as part of an Honors Lecture Series. This sixtieth or so
delivery will be as much fun as the others. I may do this well into
retirement.

So here's a question: what has made this talk such a hit? It's
not, I think, merely that it offers a way to see some Monty Python
clips; these are readily available without the trouble or expense of
having me show them. Nor do I think it's anything to do with *me*,
since nearly all the people that come to see the talk don't know me
from Professor Gumby. What is it, then, about this talk's juxtapo-
sition of philosophy and Monty Python that makes it appealing to
so many? Here's a successful mix of popular culture and something quite definitely *detached* from popular culture, analytic philosophy. What's behind the success? And what might that tell us
about philosophy, or about Monty Python?

Hume's Gap

That gap that I just mentioned between popular culture and philosophy has been around, it appears, for some time. It's the starting point the Scottish philosopher David Hume chose for his 1748
essay, *An Enquiry Concerning Human Understanding*, although Hume
described it as a gap as between two "manners" of philosophy.
The first of these, the "easy and obvious philosophy," Hume said,
devotes itself to getting people to feel and, thus, to act. Such philosophy, according to Hume (feel free to read this in a rich Scottish
brogue), "make[s] us *feel* the difference between vice and virtue; [it]
excite[s] and regulate[s] our sentiments" (p. 1). Now this sort of

thing is still with us; indeed, attempts to excite and regulate our sentiments are nearly *everywhere*, from TV to radio to books and magazines to advertising to greeting cards. Make no mistake; it is thoroughly entertaining stuff, gripping, even, and (in moving us to act—to laugh, cry, applaud, protest, vote, or spend money) stunningly successful. We love it. Of course, we don't call it 'philosophy' anymore; we call it *popular culture*. And it includes Monty Python.

Hume's *other* manner of philosophy *is* the sort of thing that today goes by the name 'philosophy'. This "accurate and abstruse philosophy," as Hume called it, "regard[s] human nature as a subject of speculation; and . . . examine[s] it, in order to find those principles, which regulate our understanding, excite our sentiments, and make us approve or blame any particular object" (p. 1). In a nutshell, then, the "accurate and abstruse" philosophy is about figuring out *why* people get excited and move, while the "easy and obvious" philosophy is about *actually* exciting and moving them.

Given that description, it's no surprise when Hume goes on to note that all the excitement (not to mention the fame and wealth) attaches itself to the easy and obvious philosophy. After all, that's the sort of thing that, as Hume put it, "enters more into common life; molds the heart and affections; and by touching those principles which actuate men, reforms their conduct, and brings them nearer to the model of perfection which it describes" (p. 2). And the hard and abstruse philosophy? It, by contrast, is "found on a turn of mind, which cannot enter into business and action, [and] vanishes when the philosopher leaves the shade, and comes into open day; nor can its principles easily retain any influence over our conduct and behavior" (p. 2).

That description may sound a bit extreme—harsh, even—but I think we have that very same gap today, right now. In the role of the easy philosophy witness the avalanche of popular culture and its unvarying sentimental assault. The hard and abstruse philosophy, what came to be called simply "analytic philosophy," lives in the offices and classrooms of our colleges and universities. And never the twain do meet.

For me, this gap is *very* familiar, and not just because I'm a philosopher. Imagine a comedian on stage in a packed house, doing really well. The audience is roaring. And offstage, next on in fact, is an analytic philosopher with a few comments on, oh, the relation of indexicals to Goodman's new riddle of induction (if you have *no* idea what that means, well, then, that's the point). Maybe the philosopher has an overhead transparency or two, each displaying a full page of quotations from *other philosophers* in a flashy nine-point font. Here there is a gap, literally, between popular culture and philosophy. Closing it—which the philosopher must do, or try to do, when it's time to head out on stage—is no small feat. In giving my talk, I've been in that same position. That is, I've all but *been* that philosopher at stage right, waiting to say something about empirical research on human rationality or the existentialist predicament, while the audience loses itself in the looniness of the "Burn the Witch!" scene or the impeccable absurdity of the Cheese Shop sketch. The fact that it all turned out okay—that I was able to go out on stage and close that gap— is good news not just for me but, I think, for philosophy itself.

In light of this gap between popular culture and philosophy, then, let's pose the obvious questions. Chief among them, perhaps, is the question that passes through the head (if not over the tongue) of every student not sleeping through *Introduction to Philosophy*: why do we have philosophy at all? And given that we do have it, what should we *do* about the huge gap between it and, well, nearly everything else, including popular culture?

Hume's Incomplete Advice

Hume offered one and a half answers to these two questions. For the first one, the one about why we have philosophy at all, he gave a psychological answer: he claimed that it was simply part of our psychological make-up that we aim not only to excite and move the people and things around us but to *understand* the true principles that govern our own excitement and movement. He writes that "man is a reasonable being; and as such, receives from science his proper food and nourishment" (p. 3). But hold on; Hume adds, right away, that human understanding is so very limited that we are inevitably *unsatisfied* by science alone. Actually, it's worse than that. Man, Hume writes, "is a sociable, no less than a reasonable being: But neither can he always enjoy company agreeable and amusing, or preserve the proper relish for them. Man is also an active being; but the mind requires some relaxation, and cannot always support its bent to care and industry" (p. 3). Apparently, we can't win. We are driven to seemingly incompatible ways of living—the active, the social, the philosophical, maybe there are more—but none *by itself* satisfies us.

In fact we've just managed to pose the second of our questions, in slightly different terms. Having cast the first question—the question of why we have philosophy at all—in terms of our psychological make-up, it's hardly surprising when he casts the *second* question in psychological terms as well. The gap between philosophy and popular culture is, for Hume, the difference between the philosophical and the active disposition in all of us. Notice that this makes the gap between philosophy and popular culture a *personal* problem—for you, for me, and for everyone else. Having managed to make the question so, well, *personal*, a good answer to it might be all the more pressing, no? How are we to manage these competing tendencies? Hume's advice is to seek them all, *in a suitable balance*. Cue the brogue . . .

> nature has pointed out a mixed kind of life as most suitable to human race. . . . Indulge your passion for science, says she, but let your science be human, and such as may have a direct reference to action and society. Abstruse thought and profound researches I . . . will severely punish, by the pensive melancholy which they introduce, by the endless uncertainly in which they involve you, and by the cold reception which your pretended discoveries shall meet with, when communicated. Be a philosopher; but, amidst all your philosophy, be still a man. (pp. 3–4)

Eloquent prose. But rather incomplete advice, isn't it? Seek a balance. Of course! But . . . what is the balance? And how do we find it?

Some, confronted by the gap between popular culture and philosophy, will shrug their shoulders and offer the Nirvanian mantra, "Whatever." Maybe conflicting tendencies and a fragmented culture—philosophy in this corner, popular culture everywhere else—is just the way it is. But I think we don't need to settle for that. We can fill in what Hume left incomplete. Remember what I said earlier about my talk on Monty Python and philosophy. It offers a way to think about philosophy and popular culture so that they fit together. To see how it does this, though, we need to learn something about *conceptual schemes.*

The Complete Two-Minute Introduction to Conceptual Schemes

All of us see the world (metaphorically, but not just metaphorically) in different ways, if only because of the rather trivial fact that none of us are ever in exactly the same place at exactly the same time. But two people who see the world differently might nevertheless use similar *categories or concepts* in their seeing. You believe that Californians are the secret controllers of the world and read the news accordingly, spotting the devilish Californian hand in every market fluctuation and weather report. I think you're nuts, because I know its the *Texans* who *really* run things, calling all the shots. For all our differences we have much in common, insofar as we both see the world by means of the same categories—*secret oppressor, oppressed, news report,* and so on. Conceptually-speaking, we are pretty much a match; we use the same concepts and have the same conceptual scheme. And for our purposes, this is all we need to understand by 'conceptual scheme'.

I invite you to venture beyond the safety of this book and read more about conceptual schemes. (Though you should do so with care; much of the discussion is hard going and some of it is not just confusing, but confused. It's also a bit dull, but more about that later.) You'll find much more to read, because conceptual schemes—and they go by many names, among them 'linguistic frameworks' and the overused 'paradigm'—have been all the rage, inside as well as outside the world of college professors. In fact, it's become popular to regard philosophy as a sort of manufacturing and testing facility for conceptual schemes. This is actually a rather radical idea, since it departs from the notion of philosophy that Hume, for example, had in mind. Hume thought philosophy was after various *truths* about, for example, how humans work. If we think of philosophy as the manufacturing facility for conceptual schemes, though, *truth* itself shows up as a part of one conceptual scheme among others, indeed, among many. So if philosophy is the construction and examination of conceptual schemes—ways for us to think about the world—then it's *not* a search for truth, whether it's truth about us, the Holy Grail, or anything else.

And Therefore . . .

I once believed that philosophy was the search for truth. In fact, I went on and on about it in my Ph. D. dissertation, and I remember around the same time that when non-philosophers sidled up to me and said "Hey, Gary, what is philosophy?" I'd say back, "Well, it's the search for truth." But now I think philosophy is the presentation and elaboration of conceptual schemes, *not* a search for truth. This *doesn't* mean I have anything *against* truth; I don't. I just see it as part of a conceptual scheme that we can adopt or not, as we choose.

One reason I like the conceptual schemes idea, and not the only one, is that it explains why that particular mix of Monty Python and philosophy worked, and still works. Believe for the moment the notion that philosophy consists in the construction and elaboration of, and reflection upon, conceptual schemes. Think if you will of philosophy as a remarkably elaborate and often ridiculously precise exercise of describing how, in general, we can look at things, in general. And though it *presents* this or that conceptual scheme, it is not the *adoption* of this or that conceptual scheme. Philosophers build the conceptual glasses, but they don't actually wear them or even, perhaps, put them on. They look *at* them, not *through* them.

Even people who love to do this recognize it is rather dry and removed from everyday life. All of us, though, are driven to do this sort of thing to some degree; we are inclined not just to see the world but to reflect upon how we see the world. Hume didn't know anything about conceptual schemes, but I think he would have appreciated that constructing and examining conceptual schemes is in this respect akin to the search for truth he imagined philosophy to be.

And Hume would have appreciated what a difference there is between such reflection and *actually seeing*, or at least being shown, the world in some new way—that is, actually taking on, or being shown, some new conceptual scheme. *The latter* is far more exciting, for one. So we can cast Hume's philosophy-popular culture divide in terms of conceptual schemes. It is just the difference between, say, *skiing* and *talking about* skiing, between *eating* great Indian food and *discussing* Indian food, between *visiting* a cheese shop uncontaminated by cheese and *talking about* visiting such a cheese shop.

And *that's it*. *That's* the connection between Monty Python and philosophy. What we have in philosophy is the discussion of conceptual schemes. What we have, so often and so well, in Monty Python is a glimpse of what some new conceptual schema *would be like* if we, or those around us, actually lived in it. In philosophy you *talk* the aesthetics of skiing, the nature of the taste of Indian food, and the meaning of life in a world of disappointment. What Monty Python gives you is the conceptual scheme *in action*, as it were, animated, brought to life. You're on skis headed toward the cheese shop, Indian food in mouth. Well, not really of course; but at least you're not *just talking* anymore.

From the philosophy-as-examining-conceptual-schema point of view, my talk on philosophy and Monty Python looks something like this: Philosopher talks about philosophy and how philosophy has been understood by philosophers. Philosopher shows Monty Python clip of philosophers playing football. Philosopher talks about the notion that any belief could be held in the face of any evidence at all *if* one is willing to make adjustments in one's *other* beliefs. Philosopher shows clip of "Dead Parrot" sketch. . . .

This works because the philosophy and the popular culture are in the right balance; as you have had enough of one, the other takes its place (not always precisely when everyone would like though; a few complain that there's not enough Monty Python in the talk, and fewer complain that there's not enough philosophy). But what is in balance involves conceptual schemes—we have the construction and examination of some conceptual scheme, be it holism or existentialism or whatever, and then the nearest thing we might expect to the world with that scheme in force. We have a shopkeeper insisting a dead parrot isn't dead, for example, and a man determined to find cheese in a plainly empty, albeit very clean, cheese shop. I don't think we can make sense of this talk without reference to conceptual schemes. We certainly, at any rate, can't make sense of it as Hume would have wanted, as an alternation between laughter, say, and a search for truths about what makes us laugh.

No Shoes for Muskrats: How the 1956 Olympic Games Destroyed Indonesian Art

Of course I'm still a philosopher, so my inclination is to keep on writing about what I suggested in the previous section. But you are probably eager to stop reading about all this and start actually visiting some of these conceptual schemes, that is, actually participate in some Monty Python . . . you know, laugh at it. Me too, actually. But hang on; I have one last thing to draw your attention to. Why is it that we *laugh* at these alternative conceptual schemes? Why are they funny?

This is not as deep a question as it sounds, or at least it isn't if we regard Monty Python as being in the business of enacting different conceptual schema. We laugh for many reasons, but one reason is because we encounter something unexpected, that is, unfamiliar or surprising. And one thing that a new conceptual scheme is, by definition, is unfamiliar or surprising. So we laugh when we are shown a way the world *isn't*, but *could be*. And that's what Monty Python does; they present genuinely new conceptual schemas for us to participate in vicariously. And we laugh because, well . . . imagine a world that includes an *All-England Summarize Proust Competition*. See, you laughed.

Now I'm not so interested in this fact as part of a theory of humor, or laughter, as I am in what it suggests about laughter's connection to the intellect or, as we might say, to being smart. Laughter has been treated like an emotional reaction just like the other sentiments (disgust, envy, attraction and so on) for centuries. But laughter is more than that. Laughter and humor have a connection to intelligence, to intellect, that disgust, for example, doesn't have. Being witty isn't just a *sign* of intelligence, moreover; being witty *is* being smart. Laughter's connection to the intellect is rather puzzling *unless* we think of laughter in the way I've suggested, as the natural byproduct of partaking in new conceptual schemes, something which itself comes on the heels of inventing those conceptual schemes. I quoted W.V. Quine at the very start of this essay, and Quine was right; philosophy itself is no laughing matter. But Hume, who I also quoted at the start of this chapter, was right as well. Philosophy, done well, is surrounded by our culture, and by laughter particularly: the laughter of contemplating the things philosophy suggests. And either one of these things *by itself* is not much fun at all.

If I'm right about this, you're probably more than ready to stop reading and put some Monty Python in the DVD player. Do it. And while you're at it, invite a philosopher over to join you. I'm, uh, probably able to make it . . . especially if you're showing *Life of Brian.*

21
Themes in Contemporary Analytic Philosophy as Reflected in the Work of Monty Python

GARY L. HARDCASTLE

My aim in this talk[1] is to present a comprehensive overview of each and every one of the main themes endured by analytic philosophy in the last sixty years or so, and to argue the bold historical claim that the whole lot is well represented—indeed, often best represented—in the work of Graham Chapman, John Cleese, Terry Gilliam, Eric Idle, Terry Jones, and Michael Palin, collectively and henceforth referred to as "Monty Python." Since I have all of fifty minutes to make my case, I expect we'll have time for a song at the end. So let's get to it.

Analytic philosophy has spent the last seventy years engaged in two successive revolts. If you didn't know this, don't feel bad—philosophers engaged in revolt look pretty much exactly like philosophers not engaged in revolt. They go to the office, teach introduction to philosophy, make a few phone calls, have office hours, work on a rough draft, and head home. There's no storm-

---

[1] This chapter is the text of a presentation I have given many times at many places, including prestigious universities and even more prestigious pubs. It's also the topic of Chapter 20 of this volume, which is another reason to include it here. When I present this talk I read a bit and then show a clip (there are eight altogether). For the purposes of this book, though, except for The Bruces' Philosophers Song (from *Monty Python Live at the Hollywood Bowl*), I've replaced the clips themselves with their sources. So, to get the full experience, secure the clips beforehand and play them as you read. Some of you, however, will be able to play the clips in your head, such is your fandom. Try to get out more, okay?

ing of the parliament building, ripping up of city streets, or lob-
bing of Molotov cocktails for your revolting philosopher, or, I
should say, the philosopher in revolt. To see philosophical revolt
you have to go to the philosophical journals, and indeed that's
where you find the first revolt, the famous revolt against metaphysics. This occurred in the 1920s and 1930s and was carried out
by the logical positivists, who are now regarded in analytic circles
as something like folk heroes. If you have been conditioned by
college life to feel guilty if you have not yet written something
down, then write down the names of the leading logical positivists:
'Moritz Schlick', 'Rudolf Carnap', 'Hans Hahn', 'Otto Neurath',
'Herbert Feigl', 'Philipp Frank', and 'A.J. Ayer'.

The positivists' revolt against metaphysics was really successful. Really, really, successful. It was so successful that even now,
when everyone agrees that (a) logical positivism is dead, and that
(2) even if it isn't dead, its arguments against metaphysics, to use
the technical phrase, suck pond water, upper-level courses in metaphysics taught in universities throughout the analytic world—
indeed, in this very university—typically begin with self-conscious,
multi-week, probing reflections on whether or not it's really okay
to now do metaphysics.

There's a wonderful irony behind this revolt against metaphysics. It's that the logical positivists, whose basic complaint
against metaphysics was that it was all irretrievably confused and
fuzzy, themselves had a notion of metaphysics that was, you
guessed it, somewhat confused and fuzzy. The fuzziness was
manifested in a couple of now-famous technical glitches in the
positivist program. Whenever anyone came up with a means of
sorting out the good philosophy from the metaphysical, some
young upstart logic whiz always pointed out that the proposed
means either ruled out some clearly good philosophy or ruled in
some ghastly bit of metaphysics. Even worse, nobody could ever
find an acceptable way to defend the main sail on the positivist's
ship, the verifiability criterion. The verifiability criterion said that
the meaning of a meaningful statement was conveyed completely
by the means by which it is verified. The criterion was enormously useful in accomplishing sort of an end-run around metaphysics;
since metaphysical statements couldn't be verified, the criterion
told you they were meaningless. The positivists were pretty happy

about all this until it sank in that the verifiability criterion itself couldn't be verified. Think about it—to verify the verifiability criterion, you'd have to sort out all the meaningful statements beforehand, and that you couldn't do without first assuming the verifiability criterion! So the verifiability criterion is not verifiable. If it's not verifiable, then, according to itself, it's meaningless. So the verifiability criterion might as well be a bit of metaphysics. In the possible world in which Homer Simpson is not only a real person but a logical positivist living in Vienna in the 1930s, Homer just said "D'oh!"

Now, I'm sure you're wondering when I'm going to stop rambling on about logical positivism and show something from Monty Python. Hang on, I've got one more thing to say. It's now pretty clear that the positivists weren't revolting against metaphysics *per se*, but against philosophy itself. Really, they were quite upset that philosophy had not made much progress. Other sciences had, of course; consider, for example, physics, chemistry, astronomy, biology, metallurgy, geology, geography, archeology, agriculture, mathematics, genetics, political science, poultry science, economics, anthropology, horticulture, nutrition, medicine, psychology, sociology, forestry . . . well, you get the idea. It seemed like philosophy had even had a head start over all the other intellectual enterprises, but had somehow forgotten to keep in touch with the real world. Instead it spiraled off into bizarro metaphysics, where you could say anything at all and get away with it because there was no way to determine the truth of what you said or indeed if you even really said anything at all in the first place. This is really the first, and the biggest theme, of contemporary analytic philosophy—the contempt for innumerable philosophers of yore, who managed to get nothing done while everyone else was off figuring out neat things like natural selection and the heliocentricity of the solar system. Now let's look at our first clip.

"International Philosophy," from Monty Python Live at the Hollywood Bowl

Notice a few things. First, not one of the players is a logical positivist. That's because all the logical positivists are in the stands (if they've come to the game at all), screaming something like "Kick

the ball already, you silly nits!!" Okay, there is Wittgenstein, playing for Deutschland, but you can tell by the tweed that it's the later
Wittgenstein, the Wittgenstein who wrote *Philosophical Investigations*,
and who was reviled by Russell, for example, for having abandoned good (in other words, analytic) philosophy. Notice also that
it's not even a philosopher who starts the ball rolling, so to speak,
but Archimedes, an engineer. You saw all the others wandering
around—isn't it annoying? Well, the positivists were annoyed too,
and that's why they revolted.

The positivists' version of the Molotov Cocktail, you'll recall,
was the verifiability criterion. I have a good clip for that, too, but
I have a thing or two to say first. Despite its troubling aspects, the
verifiability criterion became the cornerstone of verificationism,
which is roughly the position that the only way to say something
meaningful about the world is to say something that can, in principle, be determined to be either true or false in light of experience. Central to verificationism is the notion that for each statement about the world there is a definite set of experiences that by
itself determines whether the statement in question is true or
false. This is sometimes called "semantic reductionism" at the
level of statements, as in: any meaningful statement can be
reduced to a set of experiences (more correctly, statements about
experience, if you favor the brand of philosophy I call "annoying
particularism"). If you're out to verify the statement 'The cat is on
the mat', for example, then presumably you're in search of certain
experiences—like seeing the cat on the mat. Having the experience guaranteed the truth of the statement, or at least that is what
verificationism told you. A really important spear that felled the
mastodon of positivism—more important, perhaps, than the
embarrassing bit about the verifiability criterion not itself being
verifiable—was the discovery that reductionism simply wasn't
true. It couldn't be true! To determine the truth or falsity of a
statement you not only need a set of special experiences, but you
need to know the truth or falsity of a host of other different statements as well. That is, verifying that the cat is on the mat is not a
matter of experience alone, but of accepting all sorts of other different statements, all the way from 'Light rays travel in straight
lines' to 'I am not having another one of those darn flashbacks.'

Now, in response to this you might be inclined to say, as are
my friends on occasion, something along the lines of "So what?

Big deal." Well, hang on. We've just shown that if you admit that language gets its meaning by being hooked up with the world, so to speak, then you have to deny that, strictly speaking, sentences have meanings all by themselves. Instead, they have meanings only when they hang out with other sentences. Willard Van Orman Quine, a philosopher who has the distinction of being one of the best logicians of the twentieth century (and having a pretty cool name, to boot), put it best in 1951, in a now-massively famous paper titled "Two Dogmas of Empiricism" (in his *From a Logical Point of View* [Cambridge, Massachusetts: Harvard University Press, 1951]). He said, "statements about the external world face the tribunal of experience not individually but only as a corporate body." Quine's remark is an expression of semantic holism—the view which opposes semantic reductionism. The key idea of semantic holism is that meaning is had by the whole language, but not by any of its parts alone.

Semantic holism has some absolutely marvelous consequences. One is that you can't really assert a meaningful statement without sort of implicitly asserting a bunch of other statements—indeed, perhaps the entire language—at the same time. Another is that it seems possible to hold any arbitrarily chosen statement as true no matter what empirical evidence is presented against it, and to do so rationally, by rejecting and accepting the right related statements. So if you want to maintain that the cat is on the mat when everybody else denies it, you can do so by deciding that certain atmospheric phenomena are making it look like there's no cat, or that the cat on the mat is a special kind of transparent cat, and so on. And you can maintain these claims by making still further adjustments in other claims. This sounds like silliness, but the point is that it is just the kind of silliness that verificationism had hoped to do away with.

I know, it's been a long time since a clip. So let's have two. First, watch how Monty Python conveys this conflict between verificationism and semantic holism, by means of parrot.

"Dead Parrot," Episode 8 of Monty Python's Flying Circus, "Full Frontal Nudity"

Mr. Praline, the man attempting to return the parrot, is our verificationist, as is evidenced by his attempt to verify the death of the parrot by reference to experience, such as seeing that it's motion-less, its falling to the ground when sent aloft, its being nailed to its perch, and so on. The shopkeeper is our philosophically more sophisticated holist. He knows that maintaining the truth of other statements, concerning for example the bird's strength and its affection for the fjords, will allow him to maintain that the parrot is alive. Notice who wins: the shopkeeper is never brought to accept that the parrot is dead. Indeed, the sketch could go on indefinitely without *that* ever happening.

Here's a rather more graphic depiction of holism.

Arthur Meets the Black Knight, Monty Python and the Holy Grail

Despite the successive loss of limbs, it is the Black Knight who is our holist. That's because he maintains as true that he shall pre-vent the bridge from being crossed, and he knows how to main-tain it come what may. If King Arthur ultimately triumphs over the Black Knight to cross the bridge, it is for contingent and empirical reasons, I would argue, and not for any weakness in the Knight's arguments. And you realize that I could even argue that Arthur didn't cross the bridge at all; now *that's* semantic holism.

I bet you've guessed by now what the second of the two revolts in contemporary analytic philosophy is. It's the revolt against logical positivism, of course! If you're starting to feel guilty again for not having written anything down, then write down the names 'Carl Hempel', 'Thomas Kuhn', 'Norwood Russell Hanson,' 'Nelson Goodman,' 'Hilary Putnam', and, of course, 'W.V. Quine'. These are just a few of the prominent post-positivists. There are lots more. Indeed, it's much easier to list all the living positivists, and barring a change in the philosophical winds it's going to get easier and easier with the passing of every year.

At any rate, unlike most revolts, the revolt against positivism was either sufficiently sensitive or sufficiently indiscriminate—it's hard to tell which—to retain the essentially correct aspects of what it was revolting against. Specifically, it retained positivism's love affair with language. Post-positivists, like the positivists, believed that understanding anything really important, like how we know, what there is, or what's right and wrong, meant first understanding our language, which after all is pretty much the best and only means by which we express what we know, what there is, and what's right and wrong. Throw in semantic holism, and it should come as no surprise that the story of analytic philosophy since the downfall of logical positivism is essentially the story of successive, multi-pronged and somewhat uncoordinated attempts to sort out the consequences of the fact that the unit of meaning in a language is not the sentence but the language itself.

One consequence of semantic holism, believe it or not, comes in the form of a threat to the very foundation of society. Let me explain. Holism seems to warrant bad reasoning, for it allows one to rationally maintain any statement come what may. That's bad enough. But it took about half a second for analytic philosophers to realize that things were, potentially, much worse. You see, philosophers from way, way, back in the analytic tradition believed deeply that, one way or another, reason was the proper foundation for society; it was both the mechanism that runs society and the grease on which the mechanism turned. Ever eager to be of use, philosophers have worked hard at coming up with a theory of argument to describe how reason ought to work in daily life. This is why you, as undergraduates, are subjected to classes like Symbolic Logic; your philosophy department sincerely believes that this class will make you a better citizen. But, as some of you might have noticed in Symbolic Logic, the theory of argument asks that you grant certain crucial statements beforehand, without argument. Statements like, for example, that something can't both be true and false at the same time. Well, if holism is true, then we can't count on our fellow citizens accepting such statements. Nor can we count on being able to convince them that they ought to accept such statements, if they don't! We shouldn't even call them crazy if they don't accept such statements, though we do it anyway! In short, if holism is true then the whole notion of argument, and of reason, is up for grabs. Would you like to see what that looks like?

"Argument Clinic," Monty Python's Flying Circus, Episode 29, "The Money Programme"

Ah, you laugh, you laugh. But be aware, on some philosophical accounts, you've just witnessed a small piece of the end of civilization.

Of course, not all the post-positivists were as deeply imbued with this apocalyptic vision. Indeed, some were decidedly unimpressed by the news that rationality could not be the foundation of society, they having already decided that rationality was overrated. After all, we'd been managing marginally well as a species so far without much of it, so there was no reason now to worry about everything falling apart. What grabbed these folk about semantic holism was that it suggested that it took only a very small difference in the linguistic behavior of two individuals to warrant the conclusion that they were speaking altogether different languages. For example, if you and I mean very different things when we make the noise "My brain hurts," and if this difference reverberates throughout the rest of our linguistic utterances, then maybe it makes sense to say that we are speaking different languages, despite the fact that each sounds like English and even despite the fact that we think we understand each other perfectly well. Now, if you also suspect that a speaker's language plays a big role in determining the nature of the world in which the speaker lives, then you can put these two together and conclude that each of us has our own world, perhaps wildly different than our neighbors'. This line of reasoning has been tossed around in the philosophical literature quite a bit in the last forty years; you could run off and read all about it in the library, or you could get the basic idea from Monty Python.

"Nudge Nudge," Monty Python's Flying Circus, Episode 3, "How To Recognise Different Types of Trees from Quite a Long Way Away"

Different worlds, indeed, and perhaps different languages too. They eventually do "connect," of course, though not quite in the manner desired by Norman, the man on our left.

I spoke about the project of founding society on reason, and about the blow that that project was dealt by semantic holism. Very recently, things have gotten even worse for that particular project. Imagine that holism could somehow be circumvented, so that we could all be assured that we shared the same language and the same world. It now looks, in light of empirical evidence about human reasoning, as if even these rosy conditions shouldn't make for optimism about rationality in society. What the empirical evidence has suggested—and, to be fair, this is the topic of heated debate—is that, from the point of view of logic, human reasoning is very bad indeed, and that there's little hope of improving it. We're wired up, psychologically speaking, to reason badly. How badly, exactly? About as badly as the individuals in the following clip.

Burn The Witch, Monty Python and the Holy Grail

The folks who fail to see what's so funny about this, by the way, are exactly the folks who at one time or another have taught Introduction to Logic; they don't need psychologists or their empirical studies to tell them about the reasoning abilities of the average citizen. To the rest of the analytic world, however, it's been something of a shock, although, as I said, there's quite a bit of debate over the whole matter.

I know what some of you are thinking. It's something like, "Okay, I'm convinced. The best expositor of contemporary analytic philosophy is Monty Python. But let's not get carried away. There's a lot more to philosophy than analytic philosophy, and what do these Monty Python people have to say about all of that? Not much, I imagine!" Those of you saying this have in mind Continental philosophy, named I believe after the continental breakfast. I could go on at length in thorough refutation of this complaint, but as my area of specialty, not to mention my topic today, is analytic philosophy, I'll refute it with a single counterexample. Here it is.

"The Cheese Shop," Episode 33, Monty Python's Flying Circus, "Salad Days"

Now I hope you see that Mr. Mousebender's attempt to get a little cheese resembles various other life experiences, most obviously, perhaps, a typical attempt to register for classes at a university. But I'd like to suggest something more grand. I'd like to suggest that the cheese shop is life itself, as described to us by existentialism. Mr. Mousebender is our existentialist hero, creating himself through choices of cheese in an uncooperative, nay, unfeeling world. Mr. Wensleydale, the keeper of the cheese shop, is the burden of life incarnate, who, in the fashion of Sisyphus's rock, unfailingly returns a negative answer only to be queried again by our hero. Did Nietzsche, Sartre, or Camus, those all-stars of Continental philosophy, ever put it any better, in any of their often abstruse and sometimes impenetrable scribblings? Say no more, say no more.

I know there are some folks out there who are still unconvinced of the philosophical stature of Monty Python. This is not because they worry that Monty Python has ignored continental philosophy, but because they think Monty Python is insensitive to THE HISTORY OF PHILOSOPHY, where every letter in that expression is capitalized. Philosophy is a conversation going back to Thales, they will say, and if you don't know what's been said then you're simply not doing philosophy, let alone good philosophy. This is a criticism leveled not infrequently at contemporary analytic philosophy, and though I agree with the sentiment, I do not agree that it works against Monty Python. As before, I rest my response on a single counter-example, prefaced with a comment or two. Good history of philosophy doesn't just tell you what past philosophers said. It reveals connections between what they said, and connections between the philosophers themselves. And even better history discovers connections which are novel, surprising, and provocative. And the absolute best history of philosophy ties all this together and presents it in a manner so striking and harmonious that it just must be true. And since song is that thing which is striking and harmonious, the absolute most spectacularly best history of philosophy must be done in song. With this in mind, I present Monty Python's "Bruces' Philosophers Song." It speaks for itself, and so, out of respect for Monty Python, whose brilliant explications of the central themes of contemporary analytic philosophy have gone unnoticed until today, and out of respect for the glorious history of philosophy, let us rise and sing the "Bruces' Philosophers Song" with the members of Monty Python.

Immanuel Kant was a real piss-ant who was very rarely stable.
Heidegger, Heidegger was a boozy beggar who could think
     you under the table.
David Hume could out-consume Schopenhauer and Hegel.
And Wittgenstein was a beery swine who was
     just as sloshed as Schlegel.
There's nothing Nietzsche couldn't teach ya 'bout the raising of the wrist.
Socrates himself was permanently pissed.

John Stuart Mill, of his own free will, on half a pint of shandy
  was particularly ill.
Plato, they say, could stick it away, half a crate of whisky every day!
Aristotle, Aristotle was a bugger for the bottle, And Hobbes was
  fond of his Dram.
And René Descartes was a drunken fart: "I drink, therefore I am."
Yes, Socrates himself is particularly missed;
A lovely little thinker, but a bugger when he's pissed.

Thank you very much.[2]

---

[2] This presentation was first given to the Undergraduate Philosophy Club at Virginia Tech, who solicited it in 1993. Undergraduate philosophy majors generally don't get enough credit for the good they bring to the world, so let me note here that this presentation, and in a way this book, started with them.

Everyone Remembers Their First Time: About the authors, nearly all of whom have an 's' in their name.

STEPHEN ASMA holds a Ph.D. in Philosophy from Southern Illinois University, Carbondale and he is currently a professor at Columbia College, Chicago. He is the author of several books, including *The Gods Drink Whiskey: Stumbling Toward Enlightenment in the Land of the Tattered Buddha* and *Stuffed Animals and Pickled Heads: The Culture and Evolution of Natural History Museums*. He was corrupted by *Monty Python's Flying Circus* reruns at a young age, and credits this as the origin of his lifelong pursuit of profound absurdity. His website is www.stephenasma.com.

RANDALL E. AUXIER first learned of Monty Python at the tender age of sixteen in 1977, attending the FM-100 Midnight Flicks at the Plaza Theatre in Memphis, Tennessee, where *Monty Python and the Holy Grail* was showing. Whether it was on account of the drugs or the movie (he cannot be certain), this was the one and only time he ever physically rolled into the aisle laughing at a movie (during King Arthur's battle with the Black Knight), which was especially noteworthy since he did not have an aisle seat. He teaches philosophy at Southern Illinois University, Carbondale, and knows the air-speed velocity of an unladen swallow.

BRUCE BALDWIN hails presently from the University of Free Slough, where he teaches courses on Ludwig Wittgenstein, political science, and the theory of opaque names. He is the author of several articles as well as *Getting Perfectly Clear: An Introduction to Political Theory* (Camford University Press). He met the members of Monty Python in England in the early 1970s, a meeting that, as his contribution to this volume recounts, set off a chain of events that affected him professionally and personally.

HARRY BRIGHOUSE is Professor of Philosophy and Affiliate Professor of Educational Policy Studies at the University of Wisconsin, Madison, and author of numerous papers on political philosophy, philosophy of education, and educational policy. He has unnerving expertise on the history of British comedy, especially the prehistory of Monty Python, having spent his formative years doing very little other than listening to *Round The Horne, Hancock's Half Hour, Men from the Ministry* and *I'm Sorry I'll Read That Again.* Although a broadly liberal egalitarian he strongly believes that there should be a law forbidding anyone from watching *Monty Python's Life of Brian* without first having seen *Spartacus*.

An assistant professor of philosophy at Lehman College of the City University of New York, ROSALIND CAREY received the M.A. in Religious Studies and the Ph.D. in Philosophy from Boston University. Co-editor of the *Bertrand Russell Society Quarterly,* her publications include several articles and two books (both forthcoming) on Bertrand Russell's exchanges with Ludwig Wittgenstein on the nature of philosophy, logic and belief. Rosalind Carey was inducted into a Monty Python fan club as an adolescent, where she has remained ever since.

NOËL CARROLL, in this life, is Andrew Mellon Professor of the Humanities at Temple University, and the author, most recently, of *Beyond Aesthetics* (2001) and *Engaging the Moving Image* (2003). In ultimate reality, on the other hand, he is a perpetual stand-up comic, eternally auditioning for Monty Python (with no success). Such is the meaning of life.

PATRICK CROSKERY was a double major in Philosophy and English at the University of Virginia, and received his Ph.D. in Philosophy from the University of Chicago. He first started thinking seriously about the philosophical dimensions of Monty Python while teaching with Gary Hardcastle at Virginia Tech;

Gary's annual Monty Python talk was a highlight of the Philosophy Club speaker series Patrick organized. He is now associate professor of philosophy and director of the Honors Program at Ohio Northern University. His research interests include the philosophical foundations of professional ethics and the implications of intellectual property for political philosophy.

STEPHEN A. ERICKSON is Professor of Philosophy and the E. Wilson Lyon Professor of Humanities at Pomona College. He received his PhD at Yale (1964) and is author of *Language and Being, Human Presence: At the Boundaries of Meaning*, and *The (Coming) Age of Thresholding*, as well as numerous articles in journals such as *The Review of Metaphysics, Man and World, Philosophy Today, The Harvard Review of Philosophy*, and *International Philosophical Quarterly*. He lectures worldwide and, having been contacted by John Cleese in the nineties, has done public performances regarding "the meaning of life" with Cleese at several California colleges.

STEVE FAISON was introduced to Monty Python indirectly when he happened upon *Fawlty Towers* reruns on American Public Television and went in search of more John Cleese. Steve earned his B.A. in philosophy at the University of Colorado at Denver. He is on schedule to receive his Ph.D. in philosophy from Vanderbilt University later this year. Steve recently had his essay on Santayana published in the *Santayana Society Bulletin*. In the near future you can catch Steve teaching at a college or university near you.

GARY HARDCASTLE first encountered Monty Python by way of the American Corporation for Public Broadcasting and philosophy by way of the University of Pittsburgh, where he received his B.S. in psychology and the history and philosophy of science. He subsequently received his Ph.D. in Philosophy from the University of California—San Diego and has taught philosophy at Virginia Tech, the University of Wisconsin—Stevens Point, Bucknell University, and (currently) Bloomsburg University of Pennsylvania. He is the editor, with Alan Richardson, of *Logical Empiricism in North America* (2003) and the author of several articles in the philosophy of science and over a thousand emails.

REBECCA HOUSEL teaches writing and literature in upstate New York where Ecuadorian llamas first introduced her to Monty Python and Spam. She has contributed to *Superheroes and Philosophy* (2005) and *Poker and Philosophy* (2006). Rebecca has also published a series of five children's novels and writes book reviews and articles for publications like *Redbook* and the *Journal of Popular Culture*. After receiving her B.A. and M.A. in English from the University of Rochester, she traveled to Sydney to complete her doctoral studies at the University of New South Wales, as well as continue her search for the elusive, yet deadly, killer rabbit.

JOHN HUSS converted to Pythonism on his twelfth birthday at a screening of *Monty Python and the Holy Grail* at the Colonial Twin in Pompton Lakes, New Jersey. He received his B.S. in geology from Beloit College, an M.S. in geophysical sciences and a Ph.D. in the history and philosophy of science from the University of Chicago, while rocking out with The John Huss Moderate Combo. He is currently Director of the Quantitative Skills Center at Reed College and Adjunct Assistant Professor of Philosophy at Portland State University.

GEORGE REISCH first glimpsed the life of the mind when, in 1977, he encountered *Monty Python's Flying Circus* playing on a suburban television set that was not far from Pompton Lakes, New Jersey. His career path thus determined, he studied physics and history and philosophy of science at Bowdoin College and the University of Chicago, and then wrote *How the Cold War Transformed Philosophy of Science* (2005) in a single afternoon. He likes strong coffee, occasionally teaches philosophy at Northwestern University, and edits books at Open Court Publishing Company.

ALAN RICHARDSON is Professor of Philosophy and Distinguished University Scholar at the University of British Columbia. (No, really.) He is author or editor of many, many things that have 'logical empiricism' in the title. When he first started watching *Monty Python's Flying Circus*, the PBS station in Philadelphia showed it just before Jacob Bronowski's *The Ascent of Man*. Ever since then he has felt that a properly cultured life requires a combination of comedy and history and philosophy of science. Currently, he is working with the internationally known cultural critic Lars Adrian Cohn on *elimiDATE and Philosophy*, which will include a special section offering advice for those on the philosophy job market.

KEVIN SCHILBRACK earned his Ph.D. at the University of Chicago Divinity School. A philosopher of religions, he is the editor of *Thinking through Myths: Philosophical Perspectives* (2002) and *Thinking through Rituals: Philosophical Perspectives* (2004). He teaches at Wesleyan College in Macon, Georgia, the first college in the world chartered to grant degrees to women and where the students are quite unlike "wicked, bad, naughty Zoot." His quest is to rehabilitate metaphysics as a form of rational inquiry, and his favorite color is blue. No—black!

EDWARD SLOWIK became an avid Monty Python fan in his early teens, viewing the original series on public television in Chicago during the mid-1970s. The cumulative effect of watching the show at such a tender age (he did not heed the warnings about "young or more sensitive viewers") left him incapacitated, such that only an academic career remained open to him. He received his Ph.D. in Philosophy from Ohio State University, specializing in the history and philosophy of science, especially space and time, and Early Modern philosophy. He has many publications in these areas, including *Cartesian Spacetime* (2002). He is Associate Professor in Philosophy at Winona State University in Winona, Minnesota.

KURT SMITH is an Assistant Professor of philosophy at Bloomsburg University of Pennsylvania. He earned his Ph.D. in philosophy at Claremont Graduate University. His area of specialization is early modern philosophy, which focuses on theories of perception and representation. He caught a moment of *Monty Python's Flying Circus* once when he was a kid flipping through channels (very likely racing to ABC in order to get his weekly fix of *The Six Million Dollar Man*). He thinks he saw part of an episode once while stoned as an undergraduate as UC Irvine, but this may have been an episode of *Fawlty Towers*. His contribution here is pretty much the result of an online postmodern random essay generator. His "turn-ons" are world peace and long walks on the beach. He hopes that this book will sell so that he can score a quick couple of hundred bucks.

MICHELLE SPINELLI has been an avid fan of British television and movies for the last fifteen years. With a B.A. in English from Oberlin College and an M.A. in Women's History from Sarah Lawrence College, Michelle has published in the area of women writers and reformers in the United States. She has a strong interest in the history of "madness" and is currently studying how the treatment of individuals with mental illness has changed over time in New York City, where she lives.

JAMES STACEY TAYLOR first encountered philosophy when growing up in England through watching Monty Python. As a result he came to believe that were he to move to Scotland he would secure instant fame as a great tennis player, and so decided to study for his first degree (an MA.) at St. Andrews University. He went on to complete an M.Litt. at St. Andrews, and then an M.A. and a Ph.D. at Bowling Green State University, Ohio. His most recent books are *Personal Autonomy: New Essays* (2005) and *Stakes and Kidneys: Why Markets in Human Body Parts are Morally Imperative* (2005). He likes bad puns.

What Was All That, Then?

theistic, 18
Hume, David, 6, 15, 49, 261, 263, 274
  on Argument from Design, 146–48
  Dialogues Concerning Natural Religion, 144, 148
  An Enquiry Concerning Human Understanding, 256
  on gossip, 14
  Natural History of Religion, 141–42, 150
  "Of Miracles," 150
  on philosophy, 258, 259, 260
    types of, 256–57
  on religious belief, 150
humor
  and absurdity, 48
  truth in, 83
  versus horror, 28–29

Idle, Eric, 1, 2, 84, 265
  in *Monty Python's Flying Circus*, 37, 157, 187, 237
  in *Monty Python and The Holy Grail*, 90, 130, 135
  in *Monty Python's The Meaning of Life*, 105, 109, 128, 133, 145, 173
In Living Color (TV show), 2

James, William, 223
Jaspers, Karl, 112
Jaws (movie), 26
Jefferson, Thomas, 41
Jenkins, Mr. (Monty Python character), 158, 159
Jesus, 16, 126, 180
  humanism of, 18
  miracles of, 149
  Monty Python references to, 14, 15
Job (Biblical), 139
Jones, Terry, 1, 3, 15, 75, 180, 222, 267

  in *Monty Python and The Holy Grail*, 90, 135
  in *Monty Python's Flying Circus*, 37, 196, 203
  in *Monty Python's The Meaning of Life*, 105, 127, 133, 173
    as Mr. Creosote, 105
    as New Bruce, 239
Judith (in *Monty Python's Life of Brian*), 18, 23

Kafka, Franz, 34, 174, 175
  "The Metamorphosis," 176
Kant, Immanuel, 17, 119, 169, 276
Kass, Leon, 202, 207
Kaufman, Andy, 2
Kids in the Hall (TV show), 2
Kierkegaard, Søren, 17
King, Stephen, 68
Knights of the Round Table, 84
Krishna, 97–98
Kuhn, Thomas, 270

Lane, Bob, 19
language, and world, 271
laughter
  and intelligence, 263
  as liberating, 118–19
  retributive/vindictive, 33
Launcelot, Sir (in *Monty Python and The Holy Grail*), 88–89, 90–91, 164–65
Law of Excluded Middle, 80
Lazarus (Biblical), 149
life, as journey, 112, 114
logical positivism, 266, 267, 271
  revolt against, 270
Lucky, Princess (in *Monty Python and The Holy Grail*), 90
Luther, Martin, 128

madness, history of, 155–56
Magritte, René, 51
Malory, Sir Thomas, 84